Stitchery
and
Needle
Lace

Stitchery and Needle Lace

from

Threads MAGAZINE

The Taunton Press

Cover photo by John Bagley

First printing: July 1991
Printed in the United States of America

A THREADS Book

THREADS magazine® is a trademark of The Taunton Press, Inc.
registered in the U.S. Patent and Trademark Office.

The Taunton Press
63 South Main Street
Box 5506
Newtown, CT 06470-5506

Library of Congress Cataloging-in-Publication Data

Stitchery and needle lace from Threads.
    p.   cm.
    Includes index.
    ISBN 1-56158-010-4
    1. Embroidery.   2. Lace and lace making.   I. Threads magazine
TT770.S77   1991   91-13242
746—dc20   CIP

Contents

Introduction

a needle and thread and a piece of fabric serve many of us as a primary means of expression. The simple act of taking a stitch, having chosen among the multitude of colors and textures, begins the process of creating an image on cloth. And the possibilities are limitless, as this glimpse of the needleworker's art, drawn from issues of *Threads* magazine, shows.

There's something for everyone — inspiration, ideas, tips, and stories — in this medley of techniques and traditions, from the Hmong *pa ndau* and Indian shisha, or mirror, embroidery by machine to Eastern European cross stitch and contemporary needle lace.

— Betsy Levine, editor

A Flourishing Art: China
Guizhou women continue to embroider their legends

by Gail Rossi

first met nine-year-old Ah-ji on my way to her parents' two-story home high on a remote mountainside. I turned the bend of a precariously narrow path, and there she sat, in the shade of a huge cypress tree, immersed in her embroidery. Under her dexterous fingers, a continuous row of geometric figures emerged to populate her handwoven cloth. When the embroidery is 15m long, her work will be complete. After it is sewn onto the edge of a skirt and folded into hundreds of tiny pleats, she will wear the skirt to the weekly market, during festivals, and when special guests come to visit.

In China's Huangping County in the Province of Guizhou (where Ah-ji, of Miao nationality, is from) there's little difference between present-day costumes and those over 100 years old. Ah-au, her elder cousin, showed me a gold-colored jacket, its back of solid embroidery. The intricate geometric designs were copied exactly from her mother's jacket, which in turn were copied from her grandmother's garment. It took

Ah-au two years to complete the embroidery for the jacket, yet she will wear it only a few times: to several commemorative and courting festivals before marriage, on her wedding day, and when she dies.

Since the early 1900s, foreigners working or studying in southwest China have lamented the demise of traditional fine embroidery among various national minority groups. David Crockett Graham, who lived many years in Sichuan Province among the Miao during the 1920s, wrote at the time:

> The Ch'uan Miao men no longer wear embroidered garments and the women are imitating, to save time, the styles of the Chinese embroideries.... The change is taking place so fast that the difference between the clothing worn now and even two years ago is quite noticeable.... Within 20 years there will probably be no such embroideries among the Ch'uan Miao.

But some 60 years later, textiles of exceptional design and meticulous workmanship can still be found in many parts of

China. Though some Miao groups seem to be following the course of Graham's Ch'uan Miao, many Miao in China's southwest continue to carry on their time-honored embroidery traditions.

The Miao, also known as the Hmong, have a long history of forced migrations. As the Han population gradually outgrew the Miao and instituted government policies at odds with traditional tribal customs, the Miao retreated south into the rugged mountain areas. From the fertile northern plains of both the Yellow and Yangtze rivers, where they are thought to have lived between 2700 B.C. and 2300 B.C., they came to the southern provinces of Yunnan, Sichuan, Guangxi, Hunan, and especially to Guizhou, their heartland, where I have observed their diverse costumes and textile techniques. Other Miao groups have spilled over the borders into Thailand, Laos, Vietnam, and Burma, and more recently to the United States (see pages 11-15).

Over five million Miao in China, composed of many subgroups, wear at least 100

Above, a young woman in Huangping pleats a skirt made from cypress-smoked cloth and yards of red embroidered edging. Liquid from hyacinth tubers will be brushed on the cloth. After seven or eight months, the skirt will be beaten with a mallet, and the stitching removed.

At left, nine-year-old Ah-ji from Huangping County embroiders her first band of edging for a skirt. The pattern is a row of girls holding hands.

At right, the Heroes Festival in Guiyang City in southern China. Miao women interpret the creation legends through the characters and stories they choose for the sleeves and backs of their garments. This one is from Ashun County.

From *Threads* magazine (February 1987) 29:30-32

The Huaxi man's halter (top) is modern, fine counted cross-stitch. (Photo by Tony Rossi.) Below it is a 100-year-old counted cross-stitch from a Huaxi jacket. Only a few Miao groups continue the tradition of men's festive clothes.

distinct costume variations. A few groups have adopted the Han Chinese clothes, but the majority of Miao groups have retained their traditional clothing to varying degrees.

Embroidered costume in Huangping—The Huangping Miao's costume decoration consists of fine, silk-embroidered bands. A few basic stitches are employed: cross-stitch, counted satin stitch, chain stitch, outline stitch, and running stitch. Though each stitch is uncomplicated, the skillful combining of colors, the well-integrated geometric designs, and the women's proficiency with a needle render the simple stitches works of art.

Their counted embroidery stitches are often minute (cross-stitches are less than ¹⁄₃₂ in. long), especially on pieces worn by middle-aged and older women. All embroidery, except the chain stitch, is worked from the wrong side of the cloth.

Silk threads are handspun from silkworms raised at home. Chemical dyes are bought at weekly markets to dye the silk. Girls and young women clothe themselves in bright red embroideries interspersed with smaller amounts of blue and green, yellow, orange and white; middle-aged women prefer blue, wine, purple, and brown; old women are content with black and blue embroideries decorating their wide sleeves.

The cotton fabric to be embroidered is either a plain-weave cloth that has been dyed black or a chemically dyed special gold-color cloth cherished by the Huangping Miao. This cloth is also smoked with the leaves of fragrant cypress and then beaten to enhance the golden sheen.

It will take nine-year-old Ah-ji many months to complete her lengthy skirt edging. Already her work is skillfully done, even though this piece is among one of her first attempts at duplicating the embroidery carried down from her ancestors.

Changing traditions—Changes in traditional designs and techniques, for good or bad, are inevitable over time; some groups are more vulnerable to change than others. Miao living in Taijiang County 100 years ago embroidered tight, abstract motifs symbolizing aspects of ancient folk tales. They may have done abstractions because they had never seen the creatures mentioned in the legends. Today, young girls have ready access to books with pictures of elephants

Satin and chain stitches tell the legends in modern Tiajiang, as they did there 100 years ago (third photo). The creatures of today (bottom photo) are less abstract, and the stitches that compose them are larger, but the artistry of the tradition has not diminished.

and other animals, which now appear in characterized form on their embroidered festive garments. The stitches on the older costumes were fine, and the small, abstract motifs were packed tightly together; the creatures depicted on today's young women's clothes are larger and quicker to make. These contemporary motifs present the same aspects of ancient legends in a lively and often humorous manner.

The Taijiang Miao use satin stitch, tight chain stitch to outline satin-stitched motifs (on sleeves), fine counted stitches of geometric design (on sleeves of older costumes), and a miniature patchwork of folded silk fabrics (on collar and front pieces). They design larger motifs by scissoring floral or animal motifs out of paper. Then they satin-stitch over the paper cuts.

In the Huaxi area near Guiyang City, the capital of Guizhou Province, costumes of the late 1800s were detailed in tiny geometric batik and cross-stitch patterns of blues, purples, and reds. Today, batik is no longer used, and the color preferences have changed to bright pinks, reds, and yellows. Hastily made cross-stitch, bands of store-bought braid, printed cloth resembling handwoven patterns, and nylon fringe of bright yellow, red, or lime complete the costume. Though it resembles the basic form of older Huaxi garments, the level of workmanship is noticeably diminishing.

In other areas, color alone has changed. In Anshun County, one particular Miao group wears a beautiful costume composed of many layers of embroidered cloth. Harmonious shades of pink abstract designs embellish the black cloth (see photo on page 9). Such color was absent in their grandmothers' outfits, yet the skill and the eye for creating a pleasing design remain true.

Two years ago I visited a yearly festival in Guiyang City. Over 16 groups of Miao, in exquisite costumes, arrived at the site, where, for hundreds of years, their ancestors have celebrated the Heroes Festival. The distinctive, fine detail of each group's embroidery, weaving, and batik was spellbinding. This spring I saw the same festival and discovered (to quote Graham again) that "the difference between the clothing worn now and even two years ago is quite noticeable." Store-bought braids, printed fabric replacing embroidery, nylon fringes in fluorescent colors, plastic sequins, and carelessly made embroidery decorated most garments.

Nonetheless, the Miao's resplendent textile art is not in danger of being completely lost. As the workmanship of Ah-ji (and countless other young Miao) so clearly indicates, the beauty, history, and group individuality of this diverse nationality's costumes will endure for many more years. □

Gail Rossi is a weaver and an embroiderer who has been teaching English in Beijing and studying the textiles of Guizhou Province for the past seven years. All photos by author, except where noted.

A Flourishing Art: USA

Hmong women show how to stitch *pa ndau,* their flowery cloth

by Wendy Porter-Francis

Without embroidery hoops, transfer pencils, patterns, rulers, or pins, the Hmong women from Laos design and stitch *pa ndau,* their "flowery cloth." In their freehand needlework, they combine techniques that include reverse appliqué, appliqué, and embroidery—mainly chain and counted cross-stitch.

The Hmong women I've come to know in San Diego are from Laos. Their ancestors came from China, where they were also called Miao, which has been interpreted as "seedling," "sons of the soil," and "wild, uncultivated tribe." As early as age six, Hmong girls began learning to make the ornate clothing embellished with religious symbolism and group identification that set them apart from other Chinese.

The Hmong fled China in the early 1800s for the rugged mountains of northern Thailand, Vietnam, and Laos. Before the Vietnam War, there were about 300,000 Hmong in Laos. Under the leadership of General Vang Pao, many of them aided the American CIA in its secret war in Laos in the '70s. They became refugees after the war and victims of chemical-warfare attacks by the Communists. About 60,000 Hmong, who call themselves "free men," have been resettled in the United States, bringing with them some exquisite folk art.

The designs—Traditional *pa ndau* designs, closely tied to Hmong concepts of life, death, and religion, can be found on Hmong clothing. Many Hmong patterns resemble ancient Chinese symbols of fortune and long life: the swastika, shou, and panchang.

Since few of the isolated mountain dwellers were literate, the Hmong recorded significant information on cloth. (Their ancient script was lost, and a written Hmong language—probably created by French missionaries—is only 40 years old.) Some people believe that the ancient symbols on cloth were cryptic messages containing the

Appliquéd triangles, reverse-appliquéd channels, and cross-stitches are worked into protective symbols on this Hmong baby carrier to ward off evil spirits approaching from behind.

Cutting a reverse-appliqué design

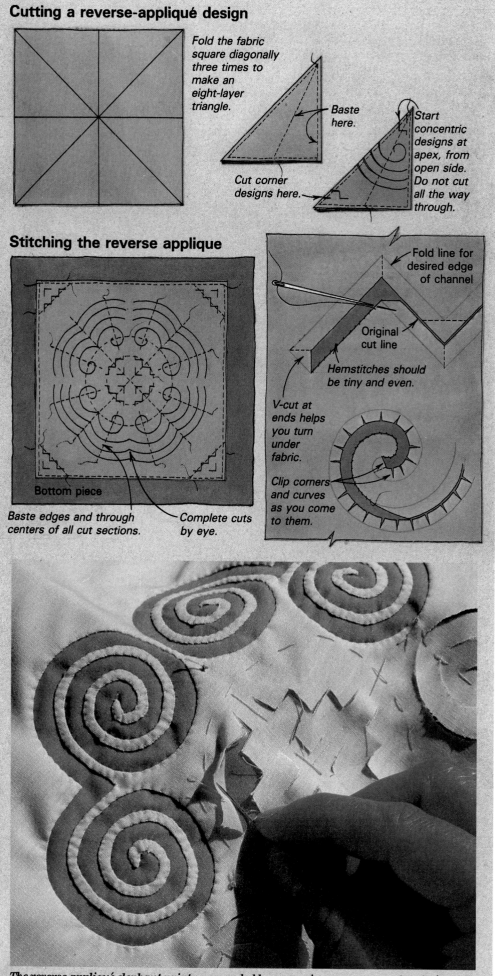

Fold the fabric square diagonally three times to make an eight-layer triangle.

Baste here.

Cut corner designs here.

Start concentric designs at apex, from open side. Do not cut all the way through.

Stitching the reverse applique

Fold line for desired edge of channel

Original cut line

Hemstitches should be tiny and even.

V-cut at ends helps you turn under fabric.

Clip corners and curves as you come to them.

Bottom piece

Baste edges and through centers of all cut sections.

Complete cuts by eye.

The reverse-appliqué elephant print surrounded by a maze is a common pa ndau design. The design is scissored from a folded square of fabric, as shown in the drawing above. A small piece of contrasting colored fabric can be basted between the top and bottom layers before it is stitched, which introduces a third color, as shown above.

knowledge required for one's soul to reach the "place of the ancestors," the afterworld.

Folk art often preserves ancient motifs, adding color and spirit by incorporating imagery from local surroundings: plants, animals, insects, fish, and birds; and that of the Hmong is no exception. These patterns exist today in the folk art of the Miao and other ethnic minority peoples in the Guizhou and Yunnan provinces of southern China (see Maio embroidery, page 8). One can isolate and identify symbols (see *"Pa ndau* designs and their meanings," page 14), but they take on new meaning when integrated into a structured composition and used for a particular purpose.

The Hmong feel especially vulnerable to a bad spirit approaching from behind. The back sides of their clothing—the collars of women's jackets and their baby carriers—are decorated with protective symbols.

Reverse-appliqué technique—Reverse appliqué, at its most intriguing in designs like the elephant paw and dream maze, is probably the most difficult form of *pa ndau* to master. Like the Mola folk art of the Cuna Indians from the San Blas Islands in Panama, the process is begun with the cutting of a pattern of slits in one piece of fabric, which is basted on top of a contrasting colored piece. The cut edges are turned under and stitched, revealing the color underneath and producing exquisite positive-negative symmetrical designs.

The Hmong make reverse-appliqué squares with borders, which they sew on a garment back or sleeve. The squares can also be made into pillows or quilts. One square takes approximately ½ yd. each of two or three colors of fabric. A cotton/poly blend is acceptable, but 100% evenly woven fine-count cotton is best. If the fabric frays too easily, it will be difficult to work with, since the pieces are torn as well as cut.

Other materials needed are sewing shears—the smaller the better—sharp size 10 needles, and sewing thread. For fine hand stitching, silk is strong and smooth. Cotton or cotton/poly thread is acceptable, but 100% polyester tends to kink up and separate. Thread color should match the top fabric color. For embellishments, 100% cotton embroidery floss works well, although the Hmong women prefer silk floss. Choose three or four colors of floss to contrast brightly with the fabric.

Preparing a design for stitching—After choosing the top and bottom colors for your design, tear the pieces into squares. A 10-in. square is a good size. However, for a built-in border, the bottom piece of fabric should be larger, perhaps 14 in. square. A third color may be worked into the design; I'll explain that later.

Select a design by copying one of the *pa ndau* pieces or experimenting with your own. The method for creating the reverse-appliqué design is to fold and cut, as you would do to make the paper snowflakes of childhood. The key to success is to fold and cut precisely. Practice on paper first. To demonstrate, I will use the "elephant-footprint" or eight-spiral design with a central-cross motif, surrounded by a maze of concentric lines, and with some corner centipede motif, shown in the photo at right.

Fold the top square in half diagonally. Then fold it in half two more times, as shown in the drawing at top left on the facing page. The number of folds determines the number of repeating designs in the pattern. Holding the folds firmly, baste along all edges and down the center of the triangle. A brightly colored basting thread will be easy to remove later.

Cuts for the spiral, the center cross, and the concentric lines for this design begin on the long side of the triangle, near its apex. Do not cut all the way through, or the piece will separate. Keep the cuts at least ⅜ in. apart to allow sufficient space for hemming each side of the cut. Hems ⅛ in. deep will leave a finished relief strip of ⅛ in. Cut the corner designs from the base of the folded triangle. After you've cut the design, pull out the basting stitches.

Basting and stitching—Basting top and bottom pieces together keeps all sections of the cut pattern in place for stitching. Center the cut piece on the bottom piece. If you want a third color, cut a shape to fit between the layers where needed, as shown in the photo on the facing page. Baste all edges across the piece in two directions and through the center of all cut sections. Baste around the third-color shape to keep it from moving. Now the sections won't pucker or shift while you work, and you need not use an embroidery hoop. At this point, eyeball and cut all incomplete cuts for the concentric lines, or wait until you are working on a section to cut it.

Begin at the center and work outward, hemming the edges of all cuts with small, even stitches. Use the needle point to grab the fabric, turning it under as you go. Hold the hem with your thumb while stitching. Keep the width of the bottom channel even, and likewise the top relief strip.

At the end of a straight cut, make a tiny V-cut ⅛ in. deep to make it easier to turn the fabric under. Clip curves and outer corners. The stitching is time-consuming, yet watching the finished design take shape seems not too far short of miraculous.

You can add more cuts to the opened piece after you have done some of the hemming. This is a fine method for an asymmetrical design, but it's not as precise for symmetrical designs. When you have completed the reverse-appliqué stitching, pull out all basting stitches.

Borders—Determine the approximate finished size of your piece, including its borders. To give more body to the finished piece, cut a piece of fabric to be used as

When the appliqué stitching is complete, small running stitches are worked in embroidery floss into the channels, and tiny triangles are satin-stitched. Borders are applied to the squares, as shown in the drawing below.

Applying a border to *pa ndau*

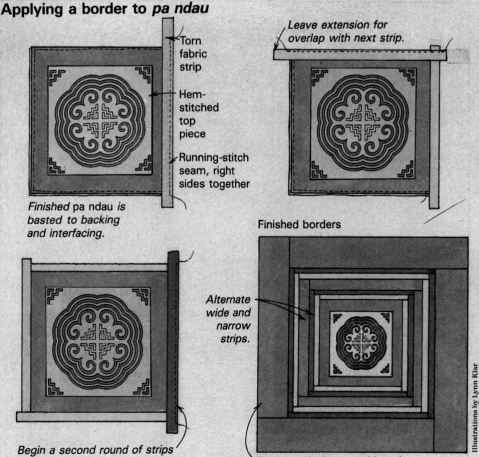

Torn fabric strip

Hem-stitched top piece

Running-stitch seam, right sides together

Finished pa ndau *is basted to backing and interfacing.*

Leave extension for overlap with next strip.

Finished borders

Alternate wide and narrow strips.

Begin a second round of strips in the same manner as the first.

Final round of extra-wide strips

Illustrations by Lynn Klar

Pa ndau designs and their meanings

Pa ndau designs have been handed down for generations. They are arrangements of symbols that are drawn from Hmong folklore, spirit beliefs and rituals, and ceremonies commemorating the milestones of life. Some symbols are derived from tales of origin and folk heroes, repeated in praise of the spirits and ancestors who established the inherited social order. Others relate to rituals of exorcism, where sharp objects are employed. Their destructive qualities are sometimes used protectively to ward off danger and evil spirits. Recovery rites and the transport devices needed by the priest to travel after a lost soul and bring it back where it belongs are other image sources.

Symbols have many meanings, and their meanings change with time and circumstance. The interpretations below are compiled from interviews with members of the San Diego Hmong community and with anthropologists and volunteers working with the Hmong in other parts of the country. —*W.P.-F.*

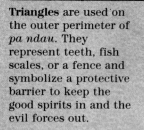

Triangles are used on the outer perimeter of *pa ndau*. They represent teeth, fish scales, or a fence and symbolize a protective barrier to keep the good spirits in and the evil forces out.

Mouse tracks are also used on the perimeter. Tracks are considered the spirit imprint of the person or animal who has passed by.

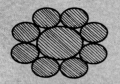

Tiger paw prints are spirit imprints of tigers, the greatest threat to a small village. Paws of sacrificed animals would be hung across a sick person's threshold as protection from harmful spirits.

Elephant footprints are used on the collars and cuffs of Miao clothing. The design, also known to the Miao as *Wotuo*, is surrounded by a closed maze. One folktale tells of a Miao woman who adapted the pattern from the spiral formation atop an ox's head to show reverence to the ancestors.

Centipedes, some of which are poisonous and some of which are known for their medicinal qualities, are all highly respected.

The dream maze is a complex, repeating pattern of right-angled appliqués. Legend has it that a Hmong woman awoke from a dream to cut out a new and different pattern.

A diamond in a square most often appears as a tiny, scattered appliqué. It has several interpretations: the altar maintained in the home, the floor plan of a Buddhist pagoda, and the spirit imprint of the most powerful good spirit.

The snail-and-pumpkin-seed pattern is found on children's hats. Their young souls tend to wander, and this pattern bonds their souls to their heads until they are used to their environment.

The fish hook symbolizes a young girl's hope to find a suitor.

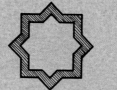

The eight-pointed star is sometimes referred to by the Hmong as the "left star." It indicates good luck and is also known to the Yao (another highland tribe) as the "Umbrella of Faam Ts'ing." As such, it commemorates protective action by the "Three Pure Ones," who ruled the spiritual world during a legendary flood on earth.

The snail shell represents the extended family. The center of the coil symbolizes the ancestors; the outer spirals, successive generations. The double snail shell represents the union of two families. It symbolizes the spinning motion used in many spiritual chants.

The protective armor of the dragon represents the mythical dragon that lives forever, knows nothing of sickness, and is respected by all.

backing and interfacing. Center the finished *pa ndau* on this larger backing and baste. You now have a base for the border strips. If you left the bottom piece of fabric on the reverse appliqué larger, you already have a 2-in.-wide border (see drawing on page 13). Finish the edges of the top piece by turning them under and hemstitching.

Usually a wide border is followed by two ¼-in. borders. For these, tear fabric strips about ¾ in. wide. Use your third color; or, if you're introducing the third color here, choose a contrasting color that can be repeated with designs to be added later.

Place the border strips along the edges of the main piece, right sides together. Make sure each strip is long enough to line up with the outside edge of the adjacent strip. Sew with a running stitch close to the outside edge. Continue adding rounds of strips in either a clockwise or counterclockwise direction—just be consistent. Make the last, wide round of strips wider than needed to accommodate a seam allowance for finishing. You can appliqué triangular pieces of cloth inside one of the wide borders, or you can use long cross-stitches (mouse tracks).

Adding surface-embroidery designs—The finishing touch on a reverse-appliqué design is the addition of embroidery stitches in contrasting colors: running stitches in the reverse-appliqué bottom color channels, tiny triangles made of three stitches placed symmetrically throughout the design, and mouse tracks around the wide borders, with tiny crosses at each intersecting thread. The pearly quality of silk embroidery floss adds highlights to the pieces.

Backing and finishing—To finish off your work, cut a backing the same size as the original interfacing fabric. The outer border was left larger for hemming. Work from the back, folding one edge of the border fabric at a time over the centered new backing. Stitch and miter corners as you go. This new, separate backing can be eliminated if you don't mind the exposed stitches on the back of the interfacing. The *pa ndau* is now ready to be framed or applied to a purse, tote bag, dress, jacket, or apron.

Changing traditions in embroidery—The embroidery patterns of the Hmong, learned from childhood, are counted and usually worked from the center outward. Border designs are stitched last because, as it was explained to me, "It is easier to cover a mistake by altering the border than to have to alter the inside design." The cross-stitch is done on 18-count Aida cloth, with a No. 26 tapestry needle and silk or cotton floss.

A variation of counted cross-stitch, actually a counted backstitch or an outline stitch, is done on 22-count hardanger. These stitches form outlined shapes, which are then filled in with appliquéd strips of cloth (see center photo, facing page), much as appliquéd fabric is integrated into batik designs.

The story quilt has become a popular form of modern embroidery expression. It is the only form of embroidery in which pictures are drawn, usually by a male artist, before stitching begins. The story quilt depicts typical Hmong village life, celebrations, religious ceremonies, war, and other aspects of the Hmong experience.

The pictures are drawn on either cotton cloth or cotton/poly cloth and are embroidered with running stitches, outline stitch, chain stitch, and long and short fill stitches in vibrant colors. They often include minute details of traditional dress and ceremonial elements. While for the Westernized Hmong, who spend increasing amounts of time pursuing education and jobs, *pa ndau* is a dying art form, the tradition of recording history on textiles is still very much alive with the first generation of Hmong immigrants to the United States, many of whom have only recently acquired reading and writing skills. □

Wendy Porter-Francis is a San Diego-based photographer, graphic artist, and writer, who has worked with Hmong refugees for the past five years. For a list of places to buy pa ndau, *write to her at Threads magazine. Photos by the author.*

Further reading

Adams, Monni. "Dress and Design in Highland Southeast Asia: The Hmong (Miao) and the Yao." *Textile Museum Journal,* Dec. 1974, Vol. 4, No. 1, pp.51-66.

Garret, W.E. "No Place to Run: The Hmong of Laos." *National Geographic,* Vol. 145, No. 1, January 1974, pp. 78-111.

"Hang it, Wear it, Pillow it . . . the vibrant and adaptable needlework of the Hmong." *Sunset Magazine,* Vol. 175, Oct. 1985, p. 54.

Knox, Gerald, ed. *Better Homes and Gardens Embroidery.* Des Moines, IA: Meredith Corporation, 1978.

Lu, Pu. *Designs of Chinese Indigo Batik.* New York: Lee Publishers Group, 1981.

Lutheran Immigration & Refugee Service. *An Introduction to Various Ethnic Groups from Laos.* New York: LIRS, 1978.

Lutheran Immigration and Refugee Service. *The Hmong, Their History and Culture.* New York: LIRS, 1979.

Nye, Thelma, ed. Cross Stitch Patterns. New York: Van Nostrand Reinhold, 1969 (out of print).

Schuster, Carl. "A Comparison of Aboriginal Textile Designs from Southwestern China with Peasant Designs from Eastern Europe." *Man, A Monthly Record of Anthropological Science,* Vol. XXXVII, July 1937, pp 105-107.

Smith, Don. "The Hmong." *San Diego Magazine,* Vol. 33, July 1981, pp. 110-113.

Winninghof, Ellie. "The Textile Art of the Hmong." *Minnesota Monthly,* May 1981, pp. 40-41.

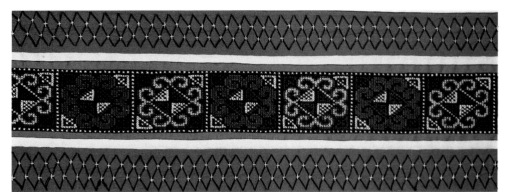

Border motifs are significant for protection as well as decoration. The tiny cross stitches in the center are done on 18-count Aida cloth with a No. 26 tapestry needle and 100% cotton or silk embroidery floss. The mouse-track borders are large cross-stitches on cotton.

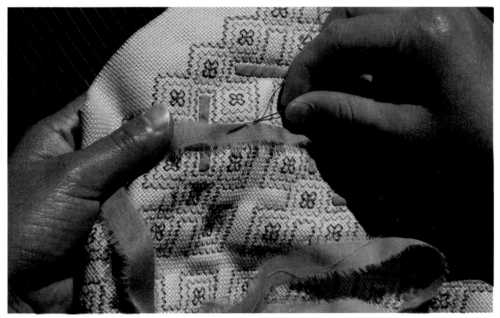

A counted cross-stitch variation on 22-count hardanger. Torn strips of cloth are appliquéd over areas of the embroidered cloth. The vegetable-seed motif ensures against starvation.

The story quilt is a new development in a changing tradition. Chain and satin stitches are the basis of this scene depicting village life.

Battenberg Lace

Making lace with woven tape and a needle

by Jules and Kaethe Kliot

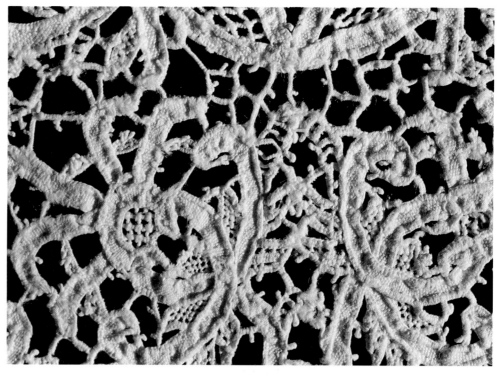

*f*rom the time man donned his first garment, he has consistently endeavored through decoration to distinguish his own garment from that of others. From shaped animal skins to man-made woven, dyed, and decorated fabric took thousands of years. In the 15th century, the concept of openwork—the cutting of openings in fabrics for the sole purpose of decoration—was conceived. The holes themselves shortly became the framework for elaborate decoration made with needle and thread. Eventually, the base woven fabric was dispensed with, and a simple outline thread defined the holes within which the openwork needle designs were executed. For the first time, "true" lace—decorative openwork without any base or foundation—was created. This needle lace is called *punto in aria* (point lace), which literally means "points in the air." The basic stitch for this needle lace was the buttonhole stitch (*punto a festone*), used in unlimited variations.

The development of tape lace—Tape lace, which in the United States is most often called Battenberg lace, originated in the 16th century, the earliest period of lace-making. In tape lace, a tape or braid is used in place of the single outlining thread of the true point laces. This tape outlines the main design elements, much like the lead work in a stained-glass design. The tape expedited the lace work because it filled in more of the design area than the single outlining thread and because it required no further finishing. In true point laces the outlining thread was always worked over with tight buttonhole stitches—a tedious, expensive process.

In the making of tape lace, a narrow, premade tape is basted over the design lines of a pattern. The needle-made stitches are worked across the openings between the tape. When all the spaces between the tapes have been worked with lace stitches, the basting stitches are cut, and the lace is separated from the pattern.

The first form of this lace, *mezzo punto*, dates from about 1550. It used the techniques of both bobbin and needle laces: The tape was premade by bobbin-lace technique, and the infillings were made by bobbin or needle. The infilling stitches joined the tape edges, resulting in an integral and self-supporting piece of lace. These laces clearly mimicked the precious Venetian laces of the same period. After the 16th century, the popularity of tape lace declined until the latter part of the 19th century.

(continued on page 20)

The decorative infilling stitches impart richness and variety to this tape-lace collar (left) from the late 19th century. This is Renaissance lace, which is characterized by bars of twisted threads, spider wheels, and other flat stitches. Photo by John Kane.

Early forms of tape lace, like this mezzo punto from the 17th century, above, imitated the more expensive Venetian laces. Heavy buttonholing on both edges of the braid gives the lace a raised effect.

In the handkerchief at right, from the late 19th century, the elaborate design created by the tape is more important than the relatively simple lace stitches, which include twisted threads and various wheel stitches.

The insert below, which would be used in clothing, pillows, or linens, is a fine example of true Battenberg lace from the 20th century. The solidly buttonholed bars are typical of this heavy style of lace.

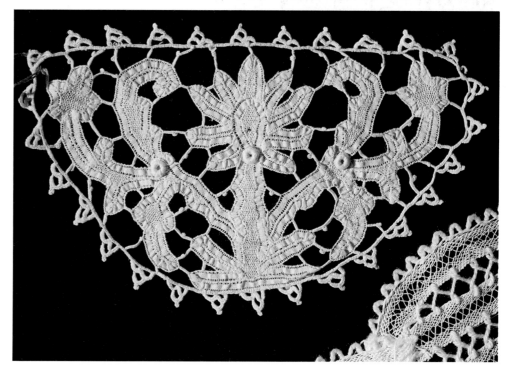

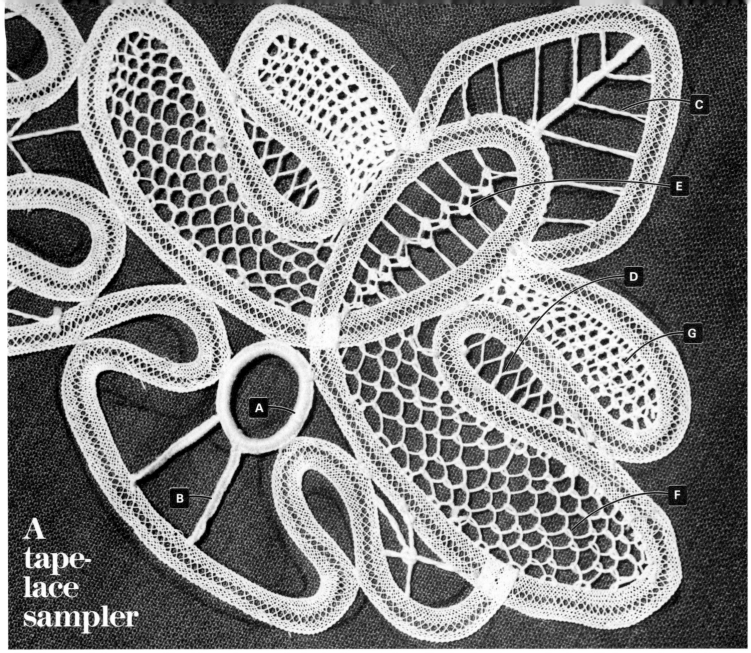

The following stitches are used in this tape-lace sampler in the shape of a butterfly: (A) Ring; (B) Venetian bar; (C) Sorrento bar; (D) Russian stitch; (E) Russian-stitch variation; (F) Single net stitch; (G) Point d'Alençon stitch.

This butterfly-design sampler contains a variety of needle-lace stitches, including buttonhole and twisted stitches. The completed sampler could be used at the corner of a handkerchief or collar or appliquéd to, or inserted in, a curtain or dress.

A. The ring—Used for the butterfly's head, the ring is a common Battenberg-lace technique. To make a ring, wind the thread loosely several times around a ring gauge or your finger. Without removing the coil, work buttonhole stitches completely around it (photo at top left, facing page). Secure the thread by weaving the needle back through several stitches. Sew the finished ring to the tape edges with overcast stitches.

B. Venetian bar—The Venetian Bar is the basic bar, or "bride," of traditional needle laces. Work buttonhole stitches closely over two or more straight threads (photo at top right, facing page).

C. Sorrento bar—The Sorrento bar is a quickly made twisted bar. Carry the working thread across the space to be filled,

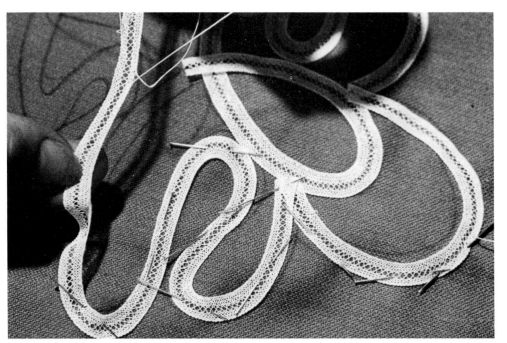

Shaping the tape around corners is easy with bias-woven pull tape. After pinning the tape in position, pull the heavy thread on the inner edge of the curve.

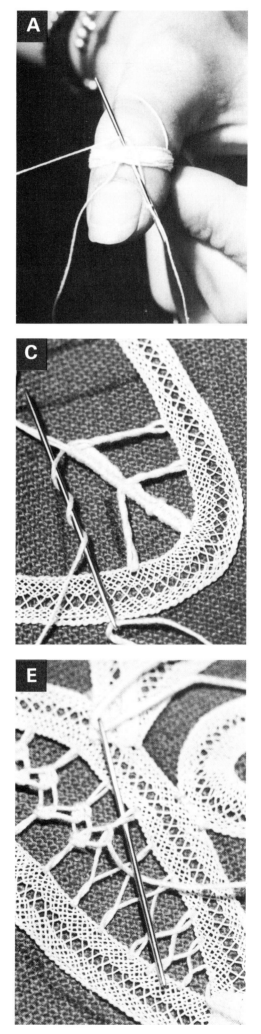

and secure it with one or two stitches (photo at center left). Then return to the starting point, winding the needle around the first thread.

D. Russian stitch—The basic stitch of all contemporary tape laces, this is also the basis from which many more elaborate stitches are formed. It is ideally suited to long, narrow spaces. Make a series of buttonhole stitches on alternate sides of the space to be filled (photo at center right).

E. Russian-stitch variation—This stitch is built from the basic Russian stitch. After the area is filled with Russian stitches, turn the work 180°. Work two or three buttonhole stitches over each pair of crossing threads (photo at bottom left). Make the first buttonhole stitch for each pair near the edge of the tape, where it is easy to see the crossing, and then pull the buttonhole stitch toward the center of the space. Work another buttonhole stitch or two, and then proceed to the next crossing on the opposite side.

F. Single net stitch—This is the basic ground stitch of all needle lace. It is a series of interlocking, loosely made buttonhole stitches. Maintaining the regularity of the stitches takes practice, however. The stitch can be worked back and forth in rows or in a spiral, from the outer edge of the area to be filled to the center (photo at bottom center). Worked closely and tightly, this same stitch creates a solid fabric.

G. Point d'Alençon stitch—This is a variation of the single net stitch. Work net stitches left to right over the opening. Attach the last stitch to the right tape edge. Return the thread to the left tape edge and attach it (photo at bottom right). Work buttonhole stitches around this thread and through the loops of the previous row. All buttonhole stitches are thus worked in the same direction. —*J.K. and K.K.*

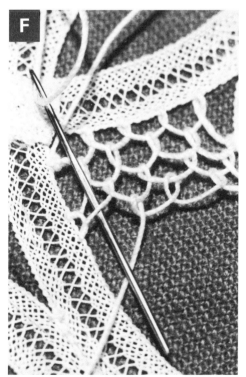

The tape laces of the 19th century utilized one of the earliest products of the machine age—machine-woven tape. This tape was inexpensive and available in many widths and designs and thus gave new impetus to the tape-lace revival. The infilling stitches initially varied little from those of the true point laces, and the laces were simply referred to as modern point. Before the end of the 19th century, hundreds of tape designs were available, permitting the simulation of most of the popular handmade laces. Tapes and patterns could be ordered from mail-order houses, such as Priscilla, Butterick, Sears, and Montgomery Ward. Simpler versions of the stitches were developed, and heavier infilling threads were used. Even threads with premade picots or loops were available. New stitches, including knotted stitches (*point turque* and *point de filet*), woven stitches (rosette, spinning stitch, and *point d'Angleterre*), and twisted threads (*point d'Alençon* and Sorrento bar) supplemented the traditional buttonhole stitches. They not only expedited the creation of a piece of lace but gave this lace a new grace and delicacy.

Lace names derived from the various tape styles, as well as from the lace designs and infilling stitches. The name Battenberg, which first appeared in pattern books after 1892, has become the generic term for all tape lace in the United States. It originally referred to a particular heavy style of lace that had bars of solid buttonhole stitches and picots and that usually included cords, rings, and buttons.

Other names for tape lace include Renaissance lace, Honiton lace, Milanese lace, Branscombe point, Belgium lace, real lace, princess lace, and Dichtl lace. Some refer to particular design styles, but others only add to the confusion of lace terminology.

As a result of the current popularity of the lace craft, premade tapes, as well as patterns and kits, are again becoming available through specialty shops. Tape can also be crocheted or made by bobbin-lace technique. For more decorative work, fancy soutache cords or braids found at fabric shops can be used.

Technique—Battenberg-lace patterns are full-size and show the outline of the tape and usually the major lines of the needle-made stitches. The preferred pattern is of a stiff cloth, such as cotton or muslin, tinted so that the white working threads are easy to see. Traditionally the cloth pattern was basted to a stiff paper to give it body. You can transfer a paper pattern to cloth with a pencil or dressmaker's carbon. With care, you can use a paper pattern as is for one-time use. You should crush it first and then smooth it out to make it pliable.

To make Battenberg lace, first pin the tape to the pattern directly over the pattern lines. Work as long lengths of tape as possible to avoid unnecessary ends. The wrong side of the work will be facing you.

Join tape sections only where the tapes overlap or intersect. Fold under all ends to prevent fraying. At curves, pin only the outer edge of the curve. This will cause the inner edge to buckle and raise from the pattern. Using a colored sewing thread and sharp needle, baste the tape directly to the pattern, along the line of the pins.

After you have basted the outer edges of the tape to the pattern, you must also contour the loose inner edge to the curves. The tapes available today are of two general types: the traditional woven tape and the modern bias-woven pull tape. If you're using the woven tape, you must gather the inner edge until the tape lies smooth on the pattern. If you're using the pull tape, however, simply pull the draw thread on the inner edge from a cut end of tape or from any point where tapes overlap, until the inner edge lies flat and smooth. To conceal the pulled loop, twist it and tuck it between the layers of tape. When working the infilling stitches, stitch the overlapping tape edges together with running or overcast stitches.

With both tapes, make sharp bends by folding the tape. Secure the fold later, when working the infilling stitches, with a few overcast stitches. Whipstitch tangent tape edges together and all cut ends as well.

Starting in the smallest areas, work the infilling stitches until you have perfected your techniques. Use a blunt needle, such as a No. 24 or No. 26 tapestry needle, and a fine white thread, such as DMC Cordonnet No. 40 or No. 50. When beginning a length of thread, tie it to the edge of the tape with a square knot; don't rely on a knot at the end of your working thread. The infilling stitches, which join only to the edges of the tape and thus float free of the pattern, can be any of the stitches developed for needle lace, some of which are shown in the sample on page 18. After completing the infillings, cut the basting threads from the back of the pattern, freeing the lace from the pattern.

Fillings can also be made of fabrics, such as satin, velvet, or lace netting. Fabric fillings can be combined with needle-lace infillings or used alone. When making a fabric filling, sew the fabric to the inner edge of the tape with closely spaced buttonhole stitches. Cut the fabric to shape after the stitching is complete.

Premade hand- or machine-made lace inserts can be used as fillings, in which case the filling should be basted to the pattern first and the tape then basted around it. Woven or Tenerife lace fillings can also be used. These can fill a small area or can be the central focus of a piece.

Traditional patterns often used rings as design elements, many in the form of grape clusters, which are characteristic of Victorian designs. Premade rings can no longer be purchased, but you can make them with a ring or hedebo gauge made specifically for the purpose. A hedebo gauge is a stepped or tapered stick onto which a thread is wrapped several times. The wrapped threads are then solidly buttonholed around the ring. Alternatively, plastic rings can be used as the core and buttonholed over. Rings can be crocheted, or they can be tatted with picots for joining them to the tape.

The thread used for infilling stitches can be as varied as the fillings. Traditional pieces used thread in a weight comparable to that of the tape itself. Contemporary pieces often use a heavier thread to simplify the work and contrast with the tape. In the 1920s decorative threads incorporating premade picots were made specifically for tape lace. Threads can also be used in color to accent either the filling or the tape.

In the most recent interpretation of tape lace, the sewing machine creates the various infilling stitches. The tape is sewn to a dissolving fabric, and the fabric is cut away in the openings. The infilling stitches are straight stitches worked by free-machine embroidery techniques, beginning and ending at the tape edges. The fabric is dissolved by water, leaving the lace free. This is a relatively quick technique and is ideally suited for garments. □

Jules and Kaethe Kliot own and run Lacis, a shop that carries lace and lacemaking supplies, including tapes, patterns, kits, and books for all lace techniques. For a catalog, send $1 to Lacis, 2982 Adeline St., Berkeley, CA 94703.

References

Brown, Nellie Clarke. *Battenberg and Point Lace Book*, eds. Jules and Kaethe Kliot. Berkeley, CA: Lacis Publications, 1986.
Explains many infilling stitches and gives 120 patterns.

Katalin, Kardos. *Kalocsai Gephimzes.* Kalossa, Hungary, 1984.
Machine-made infilling designs for openwork. Stitch patterns clearly diagrammed.

Kibiger, Gail. *How to Make Needle Lace on Your Sewing Machine.* Self-published, 1810 N. Robb Rd., Warsaw, IN 46580, 1986.
A good introduction to machine openwork techniques.

Kliot, Jules and Kaethe, eds. *Needle Laces: Battenberg, Point and Reticella.* Berkeley: Lacis Publications, 1981.
Instructions and illustrations for Battenberg and related needle-lace techniques from 19th-century instruction books.

McNeil, Moyra. *Machine Embroidery Lace and See-through Techniques.* London: Batsford, 1985.
Explains openwork techniques possible on the sewing machine.

Pizzo Rinascimento. Milan, Italy: Mani di Fata Publications, 1982.
Contemporary designs and full-size pull-out patterns.

Stitches for Silk-and-Metal Embroidery

Unusual threads, used alone or together, to create a special effect

by Lynn Payette

Silk was cultivated in China as early as 2000 B.C. for weaving and for embroidering exquisite motifs on clothing. To enhance the beauty of the embroidery, metallic threads were added. Silk and gold threads were used on Byzantine church hangings and vestments, as they are today, and eventually decorated clothing worn in the glittering courts of Europe—vests, coats, and gloves for men, dresses and dainty slippers for women. Undergarments, and even jewelry chests, were stitched with silk threads and shiny metallics. What an exciting prospect that today we can work fine embroideries with the same fibers. In this article, I'll discuss several of the stitches shown in the sampler on page 22 to illustrate the techniques of working with silk and metallic threads, and the ways in which they can enhance your embroidery work.

Materials

Silk and metallic threads are usually available at fine needlework and craft shops, especially sewing metallics and DMC twisted cord. However, many of the threads can be bought by mail only (see list, page 25).

Silks—There are several brands of silk floss on the market, each one with its own special qualities. Ping Ling silk is especially nice to work with. It is a lustrous six-strand floss that I separate into single strands before using. Zwicky silk is also very lustrous and separates easily into single strands. Au Ver à Soie, while easier to work with because of its tight twist, is much flatter in luster than Ping Ling or Zwicky. All these silks have a beautiful color range.

Silk is a delicate fiber, so some extra care must be taken when you stitch with it. Rough hands are silk's enemy—they catch and snag it as you work. Coat your hands with Acid Mantle or a similar cream about 20 minutes before you begin.

Silk threads are about three or four times as expensive as embroidery floss and are sometimes difficult to find. Instead of silk, you may use a single strand of six-strand embroidery floss. I prefer DMC Mouline because of its semiluster.

I use silk sewing thread for tying down, or couching, the metallics. It comes on spools from Belding in a variety of shades that blend with the metallics. Since it's thin, I coat it with beeswax to make it stronger and less likely to tangle.

Metallics—There's a variety of metallic threads available, and most come in silver as well as gold. Twisted cords and sewing metallics are also available in colors.

One of the most commonly used metallic threads is Japanese gold, which consists of a thin sheet of gold wrapped around a foundation of silk threads. Sewing gold is a thin, synthetic gold wrapped on a thread core. It is sold on spools in various colors in most notions stores. This versatile metallic is an excellent addition to silk-and-metal work. Its uses are virtually endless. Be sure your needle is large enough so the thread can pass through the hole in the fabric without peeling off its core. Never use more than an 18-in. length of metallic sewing thread, as it will begin to wear thin and fray.

DMC twisted gold thread is a twisted synthetic, and each strand consists of a thin metallic wrapped on a thread core. These twisted cords also come in a variety of sizes and colors. Lurex twist is a heavier cord made up of several separate twisted strands, each one on a thread core. Twisted golds are good to use as stems or to outline shapes; I often use them in combination with other golds.

Purls, or bullions, are tightly twisted metal threads coiled into a tube. They're available with a smooth finish, known as smooth purl, with a rough crinkled finish (check purl), or as a stiff, tight coil (pearl purl). Purls are the most intriguing metal threads to use. I cut smooth and check purls into various lengths, string them on thread, and stitch them down like beads. They can be used in rows and in combination with other stitches. Don't stretch smooth or check purls, as they don't spring back. Once they are uncoiled, they're ruined. Pearl purl is a very stiff coil and should be stretched slightly before use to make it more cooperative and easier to shape and sew down.

Needles—The needles for silk and metal work vary from very fine (for silk work) to

1. *Open fly stitch in silk, outlined with couched Japanese gold tied down with silk.*

2. *Solid couched gold tied down with silk.*

3. *Open buttonhole stitch with couched Japanese gold.*

4. *Open buttonhole with smooth purls.*

5. *Satin stitch.*

6. *Battlemented couching, outlined with couched Japanese gold.*

7. *Open fly stitch with check purls.*

8. *Squared filling with silk and gold.*

9. *Squared filling with sewing gold over silk satin stitch, outlined with pearl purl.*

10. *Bricking.*

11. *Shaded laid work.*

12. *Shaded laid work with open fly stitch in sewing gold.*

13. *Solid French knots.*

14. *Fishbone stitch.*

15. *Scattered check purls, threaded onto needle and stitched down with a single stitch.*

16. *Squared filling with French knots.*

17. *Battlemented couching, outlined with chain stitch.*

18. *Closed fly stitch.*

19. *Lurex twist tied down with silk sewing thread.*

20. *Long-and-short stitch.*

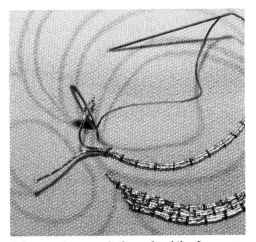

After you have sunk the ends of the Japanese gold with a second needle, place tie-down stitches at equal intervals across the strands.

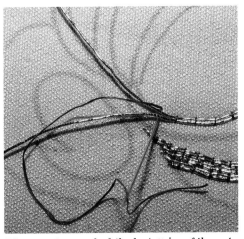

When you've reached the last ½ in. of the outline, cut the gold, leaving an extra 1 in. free, sink the end, and finish tying down.

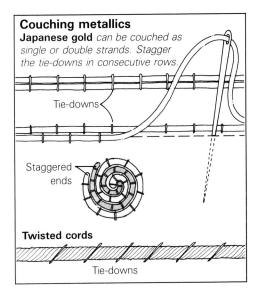

Couching metallics
Japanese gold can be couched as single or double strands. Stagger the tie-downs in consecutive rows.

Tie-downs

Staggered ends

Twisted cords

Tie-downs

very large (for couching gold threads), but all have sharp points. I use No. 10, No. 9, or No. 8 crewel needles for silk work; a No. 22 chenille needle for the sewing gold; and a No. 18 chenille needle for sinking metallic threads, such as cords and Japanese gold.

Fabrics—The ground fabric is mounted and therefore won't have to be wet and blocked when the stitching is completed, so your fabric choices are endless. Depending on your design, you may choose a smooth, shiny fabric; a smooth, flat fabric; a rough fabric; or a fabric that has slubs or another interesting texture. Finely woven fabrics, silk or silklike fabrics, and antique satins are all possibilities. The color again depends on the design—silk and metal threads are very attractive on light or dark fabrics; you can even use a monochromatic color scheme, with the ground fabric and silks all various shades of one color and offset by the metal threads.

Transferring designs
Silk and metallic threads do not cover an area very quickly, so I keep the designs small and workable. They can, however, be quite intricate, because the threads are fine and the stitches somewhat delicate. Oriental and floral motifs especially lend themselves to silk-and-metal embroidery. The design on the facing page is my own.

You can transfer a design to fabric with a transfer pencil (available in notions stores) and tracing paper without a waxy finish. Trace the design on the paper backward, flip the design over onto the fabric, and iron on the transfer. The iron must be quite warm; be sure to test this method on a scrap of fabric first.

You can also place dressmaker's carbon (carbon side down) between the design and fabric, and with a sharp, hard pencil or an out-of-ink ballpoint pen, trace over the design, pressing hard. Again, test first.

A third method involves tracing the design onto a piece of sheer fabric, then basting the fabric onto the ground fabric and through the design areas. Before stitching,

the sheer fabric is cut and pulled away. This is the most unsatisfactory and time-consuming method of transferring, but if you are working on a dark ground fabric, it may be the only way to apply the design.

Stitching silk and metal
Before you can begin stitching, you must decide which stitches and areas will be silk and which will be metallic. You also need to decide which areas will be filled in completely, which will be partially filled in, and which will be open. In general, solid areas of metallics should be used sparingly and offset by solid areas of silk, done in a satin stitch, for example. Here and there, open, lacy stitches, such as the open fly and couching, should be used to give the piece some airiness.

To start stitching, don't knot the end of the thread; instead, run a few stitches on a line that will be covered; splitting one of the stitches will anchor it securely. All the stitches I describe here, unless otherwise noted, are worked with a single strand of silk or metal. They're not sewn, that is, worked in and out of the fabric in one motion, but stitched with a punch-and-pull method. When working with double threads, place two separate threads in the needle rather than doubling up one thread; and if you must take out work that is unsatisfactory, cut it out rather than picking back.

Silk and metallic threads catch the light; therefore, care should be taken to use that quality to its best advantage. Satin stitch done in silk will look like two different shades of color when stitched in two different directions. All of the metallics work well by themselves or with stitches worked in silk. You can't, however, work all of these stitches in both materials—for example, you can't work satin or fishbone stitches with gold.

Couching—Many of the metallic threads, such as Japanese gold, are far too delicate to be stitched back and forth through the fabric, so they are laid on the outline or within the shape to be filled and tied, or

couched, down. The ends of the gold are "sunk" through to the back of the fabric with a large needle. This needle makes a temporary hole in the fabric large enough to allow the gold to pass through without damage. (Once the gold is through the fabric, however, it is not wise to bring it back out; it cannot take that much abuse.)

A single strand of Japanese gold can be couched down to outline a satin stitch. Two pieces of Japanese gold can also be laid side by side and couched or tied down as one with gold-colored sewing thread or a colored silk, as shown in the photos and drawing above. The tie-down stitches are placed at right angles to the gold and spaced an equal distance apart. When the couching comes to within about ½ in. of the spot at which you want to end, cut the Japanese gold at least 1 in. longer than it needs to be, and sink the end to the back. Each piece of Japanese gold should be sunk separately. For successive rows of Japanese gold, stagger the tie-down stitches.

Japanese gold can also be worked in a circle. Start at the outer edge of the circle and work in toward the center. Stagger the beginnings of the two strands of Japanese gold slightly so that they do not begin right next to each other; one should be in front of the other, as shown in the drawing, to give the circle a smoother beginning. The staggered tie-down stitches will get closer together toward the center.

Twisted cords are sunk in the same manner as Japanese gold, but the tie-downs differ in that they are always stitched with the twist of the cord. The idea is to have the tie-downs virtually disappear. Use a thread that closely resembles the cord to be tied down: either sewing gold or gold-colored sewing silk for gold cords; invisible thread or a colored metallic sewing thread for colored cords.

Smooth, check, and pearl purls are not sunk to the back of the fabric. Instead, they are cut to fit exactly the line or shape desired and tied down with gold-colored silk thread or sewing gold. Remember to stretch pearl purls slightly before sewing them down and then secure them at every other crimp.

Buttonhole stitch—This is a most versatile stitch. It can be used either closed (with the stitches close together) or open (with the stitches equally spaced) in silk or sewing gold. The buttonhole stitch can also be used with Japanese gold and purls. For a closed buttonhole stitch, keep the stitches as close together as for a satin stitch; no ground fabric should show through. For an open buttonhole stitch, keep the stitches equally spaced, no more than ¾₆ in. Japanese gold may be couched down under and inside the ridge of open buttonhole for an interesting effect (see sampler, page 22). Couch the Japanese gold first with silk

sewing thread, and then work the buttonhole stitch over it.

Smooth or check purls may also be worked into an open buttonhole stitch, as shown in the drawing below. Before putting the needle in at *b* to create the L-shape in the stitch, place a purl (cut to the length of the buttonhole stitch) on the thread. Then go in at *b* and come up at *c* and push the purl down to *b* before pulling the thread up snugly. This is a little tricky, but it's well worth the effort.

Squared filling—This technique may be done with either silk or sewing gold, or with a combination of both. The stitch consists of a series of parallel lines that cross each other at right angles and are tied

down at the intersections in a variety of methods. The most important thing is to keep all of the lines parallel and equidistant from each other. (Sometimes I use a Lucite ruler so that I can better see where I should place the stitches.)

Squared filling is nice over a satin stitch, especially when it's done with sewing gold. The parallel lines do not, however, need to be tied down, because the gold clings to the satin stitch and stays where it's been put. There is also a danger of distorting the satin stitch if you stitch gold through it to make tie-downs.

Battlemented couching is a form of squared filling in which several shades of a color are laid next to each other. The vertical and horizontal stitches of one color are completed before another shade begins. When the desired number of shades has been used (usually three to five), only the last two threads in each grouping are tied down, with a tiny stitch at their intersection.

Split stitch—This simple stitch, shown in the drawing at left, is used alone for lines or in rows for a textured filling. Before I make a satin stitch, I split-stitch around the outline to give the satin a finer edge. Bring the needle out at *a*, in at *b*, out at *c*, and then in again to pierce the *a-b* stitch.

Satin stitch—The satin stitch is a filling stitch and the backbone of much silk-and-metal work. Take care to place the stitches side by side to get maximum coverage with the minimum number of stitches. There should be no stitches piling atop each other, in other words, coverage but no bulkiness. Work the stitch by coming up outside the split stitch, across the shape, and again to the outside of the split stitch, as shown in the drawing. (The split stitch will be covered completely when the shape is filled in.)

Cutting a shape in half or cutting it at its widest point with the first stitch helps to establish a direction for the satin stitch. I also find that leaves filled in "on the slant" fill better and look smoother. Hint: Keep

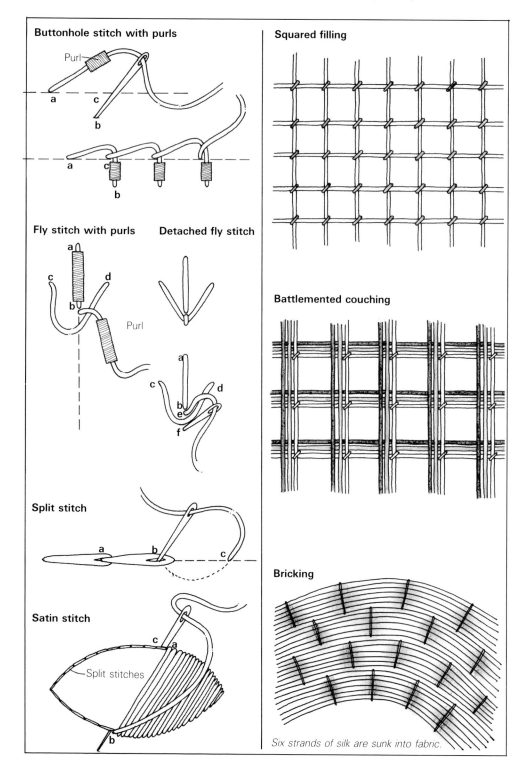

Six strands of silk are sunk into fabric.

Lynn Payette.

your needle perpendicular to the fabric as you go in and out, and the edge of the satin stitch will be much smoother. A satin stitch that is well done sets off metallic threads exquisitely.

Fly stitch—Like the buttonhole stitch, the fly stitch can also be done closed or open. Closed, it makes a superb leaf stitch (the stitches must be placed as close together as satin stitches). Open fly is lovely and lacy by itself, either in silk or sewing gold; it is also effective when worked over satin stitch with sewing gold.

Smooth or check purls can be placed on the center stitch of the open fly as it is worked (see drawing, facing page). When making the *a-b* stitch, place a purl on the thread. The fly stitch may also be done detached. The center stitches only tie down each loop—they don't connect with the next center stitch—but a purl can be placed on each of the tie-downs.

Bricking—Bricking is an attractive textured stitch, done with silk, and I often use it either for filling or in rows next to metallic. It is similar to couching metallics. Before working this stitch, separate four to six strands and put them back together; this adds fullness to the stitch. The strands are sunk, then they are tied down at equal intervals so the threads are flattened—take care not to pinch the strands with the tie-downs. Successive rows are laid close to each other, and the tie-down stitches are placed in between the tie-down stitches of the previous row. Tie-downs can be worked with the same color thread as the couched threads, with a contrasting color, or with sewing gold. When working a pointed leaf or shape, stagger the ends of the rows of couching threads to prevent a lumpy, rounded ending.

Lynn Payette, of Wethersfield, CT, teaches silk-and-metal embroidery, crewel, stumpwork, and mixed media stitchery. Photos by Judy Monigetti.

Sources of supply
The companies that are listed below have silk-and-metal embroidery supplies available. Ask for their catalog and their price lists for silk and metallic threads.

American Crewel and Canvas Studio
P.O. Box 453
Canastota, NY 13031

Craft Gallery Ltd.
P.O. Box 541
New City, NY 10956

The Needlecraft Shop
P.O. Box 1406
Canoga Park, CA 91304

The World in Stitches
P.O. Box 198, Osgood Rd.
Milford, NH 03055

Framing up
Before you can begin to stitch, you must stabilize the ground fabric by attaching it to a taut backing fabric on a working frame. You'll need firm muslin or broadcloth, four artist's wooden stretcher strips, four thumbtacks, strong lacing thread, and a staple gun or more thumbtacks. Figure on stretcher strips at least 6 in. longer than the design on all sides for ample working area.

Put the stretcher strips together. Then cut the muslin to the exact width of the frame opening and 2 in. longer at each end than the length of the strips. Turn under the long edges 1 in. and machine-stitch. Place the short edges over the short stretcher strips, and staple or tack them in place. Pull the muslin tightly and staple the second side. Next, lace the sides, using a strong thread and sharp needle. After lacing, pull the thread tightly, and wrap the ends in a figure-eight motion around the thumbtacks. The backing fabric should now be very taut.

Place the ground fabric with the design applied to it on the backing, and position it carefully so that the grain lines of both are in the same direction. Place four pins on the outside four corners to stabilize the fabric. Then fold a tissue-paper strip several times for thickness. Stitch the paper around the design area with white sewing thread and two rows of running stitches or a herringbone stitch. This will keep the backing and ground fabrics together while you are working.

You can also use a strong wooden hoop for silk-and-metal embroidery, but only for small projects, as the image area cannot be kept uniformly firm and taut if it is too large. The backing fabric is placed in the hoop as tightly as possible, and the ground fabric is basted to it. (The ground fabric does not go into the hoop.) Make sure the grain lines of the backing fabric and ground fabric are all in the same direction.

There are three types of frames available for holding your working frame stable while you stitch: floor models, table models, and folding frames. All of them free both your hands for stitching. The folding, or portable, frame I use is called a Needle Easel. It has a hinged slat that you sit on to stabilize the frame while you are working. The table model I use, made by Gripit Company, attaches to the edge of a table, and the same company also makes a floor stand, which is what I prefer to use. All of these are available from American Crewel and Canvas Studio, listed in the sources of supply on this page.

A C-clamp, which you can find in any hardware store, can be used in place of any of these frames. Lay one edge of the working frame on the edge of the table, and clamp the frame and the table together.

Finishing and mounting
After your silk-and-metal embroidery is completed, and before it can be mounted and framed, the back of the piece must be cleaned up. With silk sewing thread, simply overcast-stitch any loose gold or silk threads to the stitchery on the back. The piece is now ready to be mounted.

I have found that double-weight illustration board makes the best mounting board. It can be purchased in any arts-and-crafts store in a sheet large enough to provide mounting boards for all your silk-and-metal projects. I also occasionally pad a silk-and-metal piece with a nonwoven felt-type batting to absorb any lumps on the back. The padding is laced over the illustration board, and the piece is laced over that.

To lace, first lay the board on the back of the piece, and secure it with four T-pins. With unwaxed dental floss or a strong thread, lace back and forth from one side to the other in a cross stitch, pulling tightly, as shown in the drawing below. Start in the center and work to one end; come back to the center again and work to the other end. Lace the other two sides in the same way, and the piece is ready to be placed in a frame and hung with pride. □

Frame assembly

- Thumbtacks
- Stretcher strips
- Muslin
- Tissue paper
- Herringbone stitch
- Design
- Ground fabric

Grain lines of both fabrics should align.

Mounting

- Fabric
- Illustration board
- T-Pins

With a cross stitch, start lacing in center and work to one end, then to other. Lace the remaining sides in the same way.

Rediscovering the Faggoting Stitch

An exploration of negative space with a simple embroidery technique

by Kitty Benton

What is negative space? It's the hole in the doughnut, the outline of a missing jigsaw-puzzle piece. It's the shape of the view you see through an arch or the pattern of the sky you see through a break in the foliage. Painters and sculptors, architects and dancers are all consciously inspired by the shape of the line that separates where something is from

where it isn't. In the realm of clothing, negative space must occasionally be remedied by patches; but necklines, lapel shapes, eyelets, laces, and embroidery stitches, like the hemstitch and the faggoting stitch, are all positive uses of negative space that enhance other design elements, like line or texture.

Of course I hadn't thought about any of this when I first came across the faggoting

stitch in a book of lingerie techniques. I was intrigued by how the simple stitch zigzagged across empty space, binding together completely separate sections of a garment in a decorative seam. As I began designing with faggoted seams, I became more aware that my choice of stitches and thread defined and gave character to the negative space in between garment or trim pieces (see photo above).

From *Threads* magazine (April 1989) 22:50-53

Kitty Benton's creations (facing page) often feature the faggoting stitch. Benton works the stitch in a variety of densities and thicknesses to give different weight to the negative space between parts of the design, sometimes leaving it as open as possible, as in the bow; sometimes underlaying the stitch with satin, as in the pillow; and sometimes filling in the stitch completely by weaving ribbon through it, as at the handkerchief edge.

Faggoting most likely developed from a form of hemstitching that bound groups of warp threads together after the filling threads were withdrawn. (see the article on pp. 71-73 for more on drawn-thread embroidery.) The resulting gathered threads resembled miniature bundles of kindling sticks called faggoting. In modern practice, even the warp threads have vanished, and the stitch is all that holds the parts together.

The variations that I've explored (drawings at right) are virtually unknown in modern sewing and are a synthesis of many names and stitches, so I've invented names for them. These stitches are all easy to execute once you've finished the edges on each side of the seam and basted the parts in place onto a stitch guide.

Preparing edges for faggoting—The faggoted seam can be a style line that you have created or an actual construction seam. In either case, you have to finish the raw edges of the seam allowances in some way. I usually face small shapes, such as collars, and line delicate fabrics, trimming visible seam allowances neatly if the fabric is sheer. Sometimes I finish the edge with a narrow machine-rolled hem or a hand-rolled edge. I let the fabric, the seam placement, and the spirit of the whole design combine to determine the edge finish I choose.

For a collar with an edge trim of faggoting and bias tubing, I make a ¼-in.-wide bias tube, press it flat and into shape with the seam on the inner edge. Then I reduce the collar pieces by ⅜ in., allowing for the bias strip and ⅛ in. for the faggoting. I cut the collar out, following the unaltered pattern piece, trim ⅜ in. from the outer edge, and stitch and turn the collar, using the standard ⅝-in. seam, so the finished size is ⅜ in. smaller than the pattern.

The handkerchief on the facing page has hand-rolled edges around the inner piece of linen, but I faced the corner medallion, creating a contrast of transparencies and covering the wrong side of the floral embroidery. I made two bias-tube strips for the outer edges, then wove ribbon through one round of faggoting stitches.

Making a stitch guide—To keep the negative space under control during the stitching and to help keep the stitching even, you need a guide onto which you can baste the finished parts. To make a stitch guide for straight faggoting, draw two parallel lines

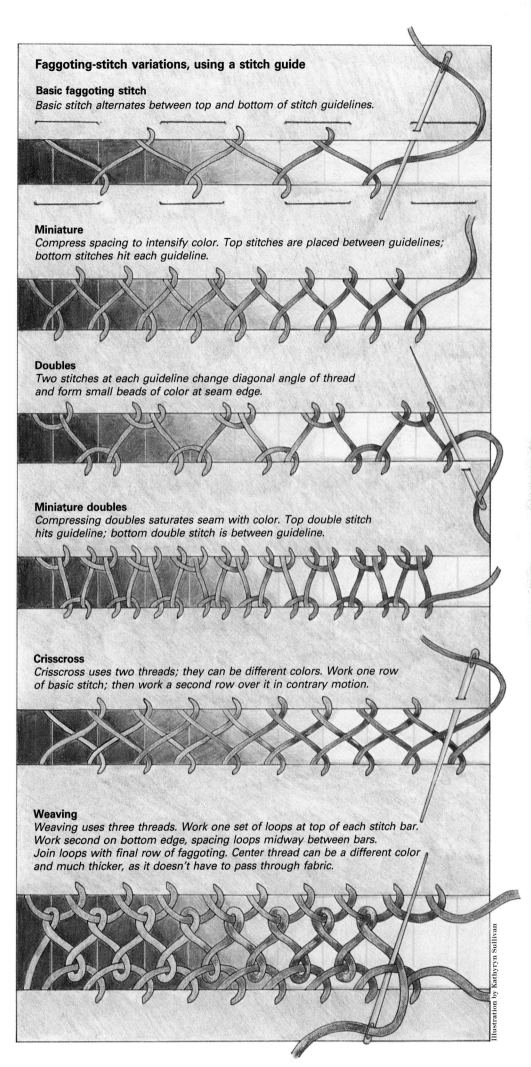

Faggoting-stitch variations, using a stitch guide

Basic faggoting stitch
Basic stitch alternates between top and bottom of stitch guidelines.

Miniature
Compress spacing to intensify color. Top stitches are placed between guidelines; bottom stitches hit each guideline.

Doubles
Two stitches at each guideline change diagonal angle of thread and form small beads of color at seam edge.

Miniature doubles
Compressing doubles saturates seam with color. Top double stitch hits guideline; bottom double stitch is between guideline.

Crisscross
Crisscross uses two threads; they can be different colors. Work one row of basic stitch; then work a second row over it in contrary motion.

Weaving
Weaving uses three threads. Work one set of loops at top of each stitch bar. Work second on bottom edge, spacing loops midway between bars. Join loops with final row of faggoting. Center thread can be a different color and much thicker, as it doesn't have to pass through fabric.

Illustration by Kathryn Sullivan

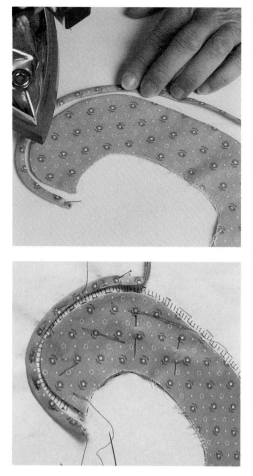

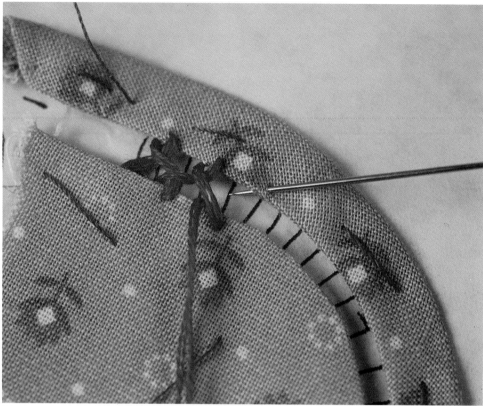

Benton shapes a strip of bias tubing around a finished collar (top left). She has pinned, then basted, the collar to a piece of stiff paper and drawn a stitching guide around the outer edge so she can see where to pin and baste the shaped strip (bottom left). Using these ⅛-in.-apart markings as guides, she loosely forms the basic faggoting stitch (above).

on a piece of fairly sturdy paper, as far apart as you want the negative space to be—usually ⅛ in. to ¼ in. Butcher paper and shelf paper both work well. Mark stitch-guide bars between the two lines, also spaced in ⅛-in. to ¼-in. increments. The guide looks like a tiny set of railroad tracks. For curved edges, like the collar in the photos above, trace around the finished edge, being careful not to mark the fabric. Then parallel the line ¼ in. away, using a French curve or drawing freehand.

Pin, and then baste the finished edges to each side of the guide, preshaping curved bias strips with an iron. If you're tempted to leave the pins and skip the basting, you'll experience the boredom of having the floss routinely catch on the head of the pins as you try to stitch and end up basting anyway. One parallel guide serves many uses, so you might consider drawing it on Pellon. For large projects, I secure the whole thing to a pressing roll with elastic bands and reposition the work as necessary.

Forming faggoting stitches—After threading a needle and knotting the floss, I slip the needle into one finished edge from the inside to conceal the knot, coming out exactly at a cross mark of the stitching guide. I work left to right with the guide positioned vertically (as in the drawings on p. 27), starting the first stitch a little in front of and outside, the edge, with the needle pointing back toward the next cross mark and coming out on the edge exactly at the mark.

I keep the thread to the right of the forming stitch so I get the left-over-right looping that characterizes the faggoting stitch. I don't pull the stitches tight; use the stitches in the photo at right, above, as an example. All the stitches in the drawings on p. 27 are slight variations of this basic stitch.

You can begin and end a faggoted seam with a normal knot or backstitch. It usually ends up in a crossing seam allowance anyway. If you have to start a new thread in the middle of your work, make a discreet backstitch right beside your last stitch. Run the end through a fold in the fabric to hide it, and resume stitching the same way. When you've finished the seam, block and set the stitches, using a little spray starch and a steam iron.

Designing with the faggoting stitch—The famous Broadway set designer Ming Cho Lee once responded, "What kind of void?" to a student who wondered why you couldn't just have a void instead of scenery in the theater. You have to learn to think like this to have fun with the faggoting stitch. If you want to see air in your void, use one strand of embroidery floss or silk and space your stitches sparsely, as in the bow in the photo on p. 26. If you want to dramatize a seam with color, use several strands of floss and a dense stitch pattern, as I did on the fronts of the shorts and pinafore in the photo at top left, facing page. Ombre floss in a complex pattern looks pleasantly like sugar frosting on a cake, while monochromatic color

schemes blend into textural designs. Ribbon backing behind the faggoted seam fills your void with light. How deep a bite you take with each stitch is another design choice, but it should be deep enough not to pull out and shallow enough not to resemble Frankenstein stitches.

The primary area of negative space is the distance between the two pieces you plan to join. You can manipulate the shape of the primary space between strips of lace or turned bias if your faggoting is planned as trim, much the way negative space is treated in Battenberg lace patterns.

If you're going to embellish a seam, the primary space will be a straight line parallel to the edges of the seam, and the secondary spaces between the stitches (determined by your choice of stitch pattern) will be uniform. Even smaller shapes occur in the interstices after the thread has passed through the fabric and crosses back over itself again. The sizes of these tertiary spaces will also be uniform in parallel situations. When the primary space has been manipulated, and the edges aren't parallel, all the internal shapes will change too.

Before I make any decisions, I think about what I want the faggoting to accomplish. Will it mask a humdrum purpose, such as lengthening a skirt, or is it part of the fundamental design? At this point, I try to analyze my ideas so that I can organize them in a way that will best reveal to someone else the beauty that I see. Some design choices are obvious; others require a con-

One design in three variations (top to bottom, above): A strong line is created by thick floss in woven faggoting; cross-stitch is mimicked by thick floss in double stitch; and a delicate two-color effect that also mimics cross-stitch is created by light floss in woven faggoting.

At right, Benton's faggoted designs include an heirloom-lace collar, a round yoke of bias strips, and a sampler bonnet that incorporates all the stitches shown on p. 27.

siderable amount of fooling with swatches and staring at the wall.

Test your stitch and floss selections on scrap fabric before starting a major project. Lift the test off the guide and block it by using spray starch and ironing it before deciding you need to change your guide's dimensions; some faggoting stitches will expand when blocked. If you've created a style line in an area where measurements are critical, such as a collar, you may need to compensate for the added width of the faggoted seam so you don't distort the fit.

There's a lovely moment in almost all of my faggoting classes when I notice that everyone seems to have gotten the hang of forming the stitch and handling the cloth on its stitch-guide backing. Things quiet down, and someone usually starts to hum softly as she works. I think it's a bit of a testimony to this unprepossessing little stitch that is so easy to make yet can have such a variety of delightful effects—all done with a little floss and lots of thin air. □

Kitty Benton was the children's-wear consultant to Laura Ashley from 1981 to 1988. Her children's-wear designs are available from McCall's patterns. Benton is the author of Sewing Classic Clothes for Children *(1981, $22.50) and* Classic Designs for Today's Active Children *(1985, $21.95), available from her, along with faggoting patterns and her* Gourmet Sewing® Design Letter with Swatches *($12.50 per year), at 285 W. Bdwy., Suite 440, New York, NY 10013.*

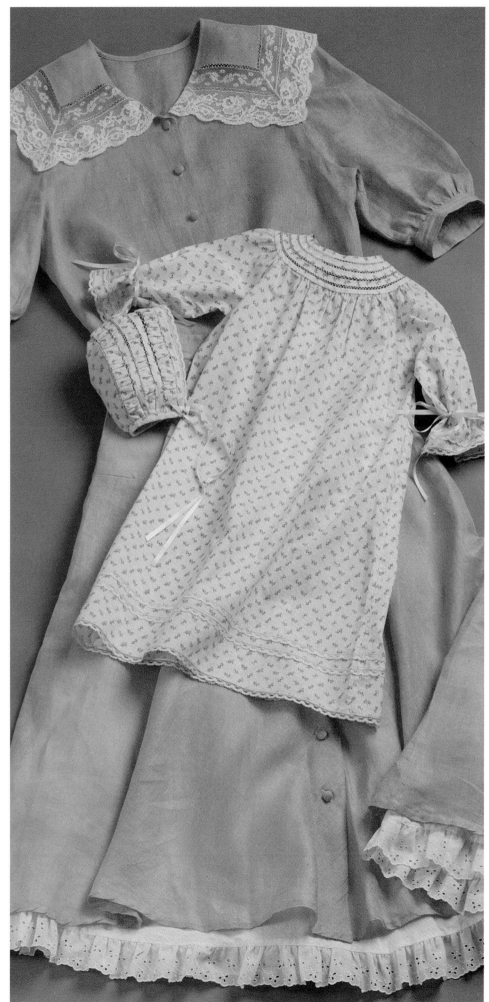

Japan's Masterful Embroideries

Fukusa, elaborate gift covers that convey appropriate good wishes

by Lilo Markrich

"The Riches of the Sea," with its grace and movement, captures the unique Japanese feeling for the bountiful sea and its creatures. Carp, lobsters, bream, and crabs all symbolize good fortune, long life, and happiness for the New Year. The lobsters are worked predominantly in satin stitches, both straight and slanted. Their shells curve imperceptibly as a result of careful padding, which also accentuates their movement in the water. The scales of the carp and bream are laid and couched, the couching thread no more than a sliver of silk. The simple waves skip and tumble by a mere touch of slanted stem-stitch outline, their rhythm stabilized by couched-gold glistening foam. This tale within a tale was made between 1757 and 1763.

In the etiquette of Japanese gift-giving, textiles play a major role. The *furoshiki,* a cloth wrapped around a gift and knotted, is the counterpart of our gift wrap. The more elaborate *fukusa,* laid over the gift to enrich its value, is offered as a symbol of regard, tribute, and affection. If it is a family heirloom, it is ceremoniously returned to the donor.

The most beautiful embroidered *fukusa* were created between 1603, when the fiercely nationalistic Tokugawa dynasty rose to power in reaction to foreign intrusion (notably from Portuguese traders and missionaries), and 1867. Known as the Edo period, these years mark Japan's enforced isolationism from the world. Only two controlled foreign trading ports linked selected Japanese merchants to Asia and the West: one was Chinese, the other Dutch.

The new rulers, having consolidated their military and political strength, placed special emphasis on the traditional Japanese values of self-reliance, honor and respect for family, authority, and cultural heritage. Unified and introspective, Japan began to prosper. In the arts, the demand grew for the more intricate and exquisite, as symbols of affluence and social power. *Fukusa,* exchanged between members of the aristocracy or given by the affluent to the more powerful, reached a rare level of charm, whimsy, and perfection in Edo Japan.

As the Tokugawa power waned, fashionable westernization threatened the traditional arts. Fortunately, many valuable textiles and fragments made during this period were collected by Nomura Shojiro (1878-1943), a descendant of Japanese silk merchants. Seeing that industrial growth was reducing the value and appeal of handmade textiles, he decided to preserve and document past skills. The *fukusa* shown on these pages are from his collection.

Every *fukusa* tells its own tale. The designs, based on images from folklore and

From *Threads* magazine (August 1987) 12:68-70

"The Old Couple of Tagasago" represents the legendary couple Jo and Uba. Jo, who sweeps out evil, and Uba, who rakes in good, convey wishes for a long and compatible marriage. Variations on couched gold lends weight to the overall composition: The moon shimmers against a deep, midnight-blue, glistening silk background; clouds gently float by; and pine trees sparkle. A golden stage setting is created for the old man with his satin-stitched balding head and wisps of white hair, and for his wife. The couple's colored silk robes with couched surface stitching are as detailed and gently padded as the finest woven ceremonial robes of the time. 1781-1788.

legend, convey a visual message appropriate to the occasion of the gift. Wishes for good fortune, long life, and prosperity are combined with gentle reminders as to the characteristics needed to achieve such goals.

But for the embroiderer, the focal point of each lustrous piece of silk must be the exquisite embroidery—the perfect control of medium and technique that gives life to the imagery within the outlines marked by the designer's hand. The stitches themselves are technically simple, well known to embroiderers the world over, and very ancient (they were probably invented in China). It is the way they have been used and placed to create mystical illusions of reality that demands examination.

The embroiderer's needle, like a Japanese painter's brush, was plied with tradi-tional restraint. By means of a simple shift in thread direction, couched-gold work was made to shimmer and recede in a deliberate play of light and shadow. Variations of laid and couched threads; the use of plain, multicolored, and padded satin stitches; and the delicate placement of stem stitch and simple straight stitches all created patterning. The embroiderer achieved a luminous backdrop for the ornamental grids and other couched-and-laid holding patterns by first laying a set of horizontal, vertical, or diagonal foundation stitches in the satin-stitch manner. (Today's less practiced embroiderer can produce a similar smooth, flat foundation for decorative work by using the false satin stitch.)

The stitchers knew that the silk they used, whether it was hairbreadth fine or thick floss, smooth or plied, turned or gently knotted, would subtly change color as the needle moved in a different direction to alter the silk's light reflection and therefore its intensity and hue. The *fukusa* were not an exercise in stitch expertise, samplers of an encyclopedic knowledge of variations. They are gentle harmonies of interaction between stitch, texture, color, and design. □

Lilo Markrich, an embroidery instructor and weaver, runs the gallery and bookshop at The Textile Museum in Washington, D.C., where The Shojiro Nomura Fukusa Collection was on view in 1987. The touring exhibition, now closed, was organized by Mills College Art Gallery, Oakland, CA. Photos courtesy Mills College Art Gallery.

Further reading

Hays, Mary V., and Ralph E. Hays. *Fukusa: The Shojiro Nomura Fukusa Collection,* 1983. Mills College Art Gallery, Box 9973, Oakland, CA. *Shows 56 fukusa, with interesting insights and historical information. Color-reproduction quality disappointing.*

Tamura, Shuji (compiler/editor). *Traditional Japanese Embroidery: Instructions for the Basic Techniques.* Traditional Embroidery Guild of Japan, Kurenai-Kai, Katoku 594, Togane City, Chiba 283, Japan. *Gives 46 basic techniques with suitable patterns. Order from Textile Museum Shop (2320 'S' St., N.W., Washington, D.C. 20008) or Shay Pendray's Needle Arts (2211 Monroe, Dearborn, MI 48124).*

Christie, Grace. *Samplers and Stitches.* London: B.T. Batsford, 1985. Distributed by David & Charles, North Pomfret, VT. *The backbone of contemporary stitchery.*

Pesel, Louisa F. *Stitches from Old English Embroideries,* Vol. 1, 2nd ed., 1921. Bradford, England: Percy, Lund, Humphries & Co. (out of print). *Documents Oriental embroidery techniques in England.*

Snook, Barbara. *English Historical Embroidery.* London: B.T. Batsford, 1960 (out of print). *17th- and 18th-century Jacobean work based on Eastern motifs.*

Stinchecum, Amanda M. *Kosode: Sixteenth to Nineteenth Century Textiles from the Nomura Collection.* New York: Kodansha International, 1984.

Hickman, Money, and Peter Fetchko. *Japan Day by Day: An Exhibition in Honor of Edward Sylvester Morse.* Salem, MA: Peabody Museum of Salem, 1977. *Life in turn-of-the-century Japan.*

Turk, Frank A. *Prints of Japan.* New York: Arco, 1966 (out of print).

Yoshinobu, Tokugawa, and Okochi Sadao. *The Tokugawa Collection: No Robes and Masks.* New York: Japan Society, 1977 (out of print).

This detail from "Three Men Laughing," one of the later pieces (1865-1867), displays a fusion of past and present. The embroidery skills are still subtle, delicate, and wondrous, but the imagery has changed. Formality has given way to naturalism; the viewer is a participant rather than a bystander and ready to share the joke. Using heavily padded and decoratively held satin stitches as well as couching, the embroiderer has created a masterpiece of portraiture.

All That Glitters

Shisha by machine

by Robbie Fanning

*i*ndian embroidery seeks to engage in a contest with the sun," said 19th-century writer Théophile Gautier, "to have a duel to the death with the blinding light and glowing sky. At all costs its duty is to shine and glitter and to send forth the prismatic rays; it must be blazing, blinding and phosphorescent—and so the sun acknowledges defeat." This battle is fought with tiny mirrors called shisha, which are held to the fabric in a cage of stitches.

No one has yet documented how these mirrors came to be used in Indian embroidery or who developed the technique. In *A History of Textiles,* Kax Wilson claims that the mirror work originated with the hill tribes of southern India, who sewed beetle backs onto wedding garments. Orthodox Hindus, disapproving of this practice, used pieces of mica instead. Eventually bits of glass or mirrors were used.

Author Jacqueline Enthoven believes that shisha was developed by clever servants who admired the jewels embroidered onto the maharanis' clothing. At first they probably salvaged chips of broken jewelry. Later, the mirrors were manufactured and practically everyone could afford them.

The most charming story is Jean Simpson's in *Shisha Mirror Embroidery.* Shah Jahan erected several buildings with rooms of mirrors, called *shish mahals* (palaces of mirrors). His wife, Mumtaz Mahal, developed the technique of shisha embroidery so the shah's beloved mirrors would appear on clothing, pillows, and wall hangings. When she died, the shah built the Taj Mahal as a monument to their love and a mausoleum where they could be together forever. Later, Shah Jahan was overthrown by a son who imprisoned him across the river from the Taj Mahal. From there, the shah was only able to view the resting place of his dead lover by gazing at one small shisha mirror embedded in the wall.

Photo by Jack Ramsdale

This long blouse is decorated with handsewn shisha and silk-and-cotton embroidery. It was made by the Harijan clan of Kutch, India, in the late 19th or early 20th century.

Shisha embroidery is practiced all over India, Pakistan, and Afghanistan. In some regions, bright-colored peacocks, elephants, and flowers are embroidered around the mirrors; in others, the designs are geometric and the colors subdued. But no matter what the variation, shisha work is always laden with mirrors, and applying them by hand is a time-consuming task.

Caryl Rae Hancock, of Vienna, VA, has devised a quick, clever way to attach shisha with free-machine embroidery. In this technique, the fabric is not advanced by the machine's feed dogs as you stitch; instead it is manipulated by hand so that you are almost drawing with thread. On a piece of organza, you stitch a circle slightly smaller than the shisha. Next, you cut out the circle's center and free-machine embroider satin stitches. Then you cut around the outside of the circle and lay the organza ring on the shisha, which has been glued to the foundation fabric. You straight-stitch to attach the shisha to the fabric and free-machine embroider again to hide the edges of the ring.

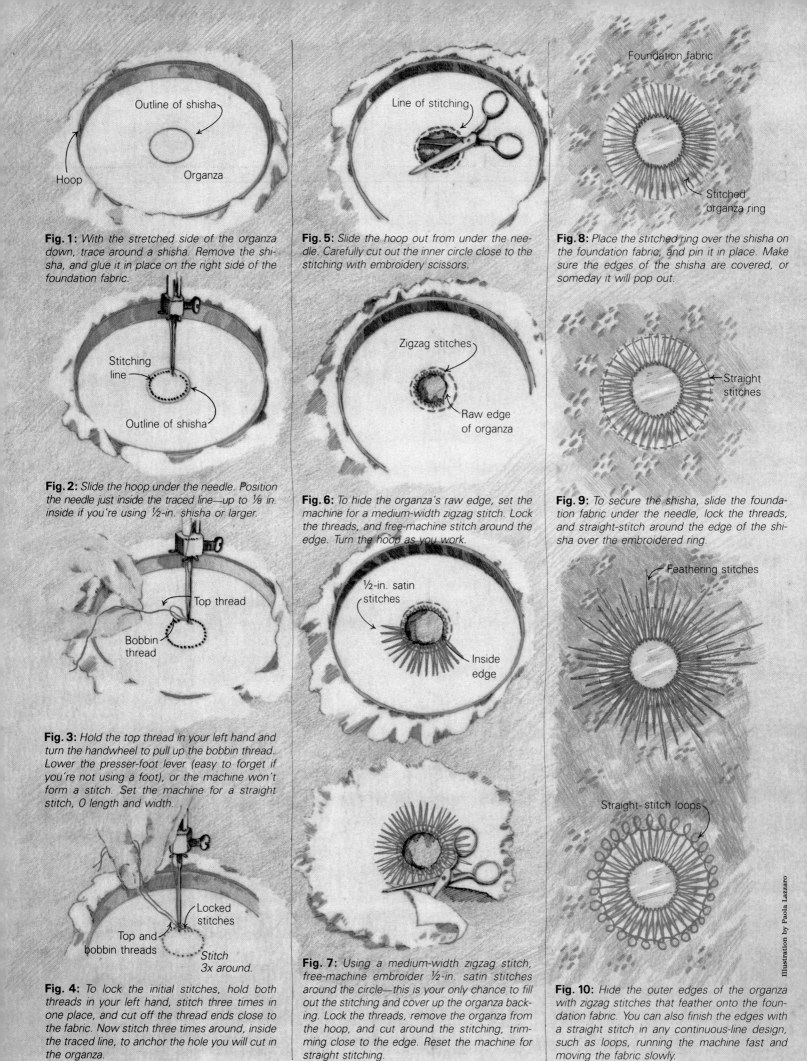

Fig. 1: *With the stretched side of the organza down, trace around a shisha. Remove the shisha, and glue it in place on the right side of the foundation fabric.*

Fig. 2: *Slide the hoop under the needle. Position the needle just inside the traced line—up to ⅛ in. inside if you're using ½-in. shisha or larger.*

Fig. 3: *Hold the top thread in your left hand and turn the handwheel to pull up the bobbin thread. Lower the presser-foot lever (easy to forget if you're not using a foot), or the machine won't form a stitch. Set the machine for a straight stitch, 0 length and width.*

Fig. 4: *To lock the initial stitches, hold both threads in your left hand, stitch three times in one place, and cut off the thread ends close to the fabric. Now stitch three times around, inside the traced line, to anchor the hole you will cut in the organza.*

Fig. 5: *Slide the hoop out from under the needle. Carefully cut out the inner circle close to the stitching with embroidery scissors.*

Fig. 6: *To hide the organza's raw edge, set the machine for a medium-width zigzag stitch. Lock the threads, and free-machine stitch around the edge. Turn the hoop as you work.*

Fig. 7: *Using a medium-width zigzag stitch, free-machine embroider ½-in. satin stitches around the circle—this is your only chance to fill out the stitching and cover up the organza backing. Lock the threads, remove the organza from the hoop, and cut around the stitching, trimming close to the edge. Reset the machine for straight stitching.*

Fig. 8: *Place the stitched ring over the shisha on the foundation fabric, and pin it in place. Make sure the edges of the shisha are covered, or someday it will pop out.*

Fig. 9: *To secure the shisha, slide the foundation fabric under the needle, lock the threads, and straight-stitch around the edge of the shisha over the embroidered ring.*

Fig. 10: *Hide the outer edges of the organza with zigzag stitches that feather onto the foundation fabric. You can also finish the edges with a straight stitch in any continuous-line design, such as loops, running the machine fast and moving the fabric slowly.*

Illustration by Paola Lazzaro

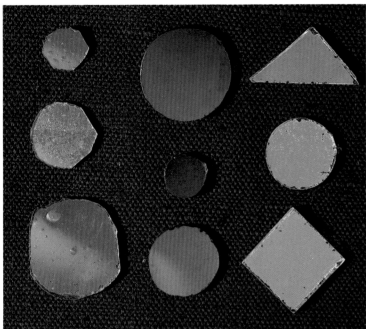

Photo by Jack Ramsdale.

There are three kinds of shisha: antique (left); rainbow (center), available in a variety of colors; and perfect (right), available in a variety of shapes.

The shoulder flaps on this 20th-century cotton blouse, or chola, *lift up out of the way so a heavy load can be carried comfortably. This garment was made by the Lambadi clan of Gujarat, India.*

To apply shisha by machine, you need a zigzag machine with a size 10/11 (70) needle and thread that matches the fabric. I use extra-fine machine-embroidery thread. The bobbin thread will show, so use the same color in the bobbin as you used to thread the machine, or choose complementary colors. You need a 6-in. to 8-in. machine-embroidery hoop or a screw-type hoop—one that's not too large to work with on your machine. You need a piece of organza, a foundation fabric heavy enough to support the mirrors, a pencil or fade-out pen, and a glue stick or white fabric glue.

Shisha mirrors are available in three forms: antique, perfect, and rainbow. They range from about ⅜ in. (9mm) to 1 in. (25mm) in diameter. *Antique* shisha are the best for embroidery because they're washable and lightweight. They are hand-cut into small disks from silvered glass blown about 1 ft. in diameter, and their imperfections—uneven edges, irregular sizes, surface bubbles—are part of their charm. *Perfect* shisha, as their name implies, are perfect. Mass-produced in round, square, and rectangular shapes, they are thicker than antique shisha. They're also not washable, so if you put them on clothing, you must have the garment dry-cleaned. *Rainbow* shisha are two-sided: a plain mirror on one side; a colored mirror on the other. Either side may show.

To apply shisha, set your machine for free-machine embroidery, as you would for darning: Use a straight stitch with 0 length and width or a medium-width zigzag stitch, as shown in the drawing on the facing page. Lower or cover the feed dogs, and either put on a darning foot or use no presser foot at all. If you loosen the top tension slightly, you will decrease the chance of dropped stitches.

Once you have mastered the techniques, you can prepare organza for four mirrors at the same time. Use a piece of organza that fits over an 8-in. to 10-in. embroidery hoop, and position the shisha so you won't stitch too close to the edge of the hoop.

Instead of organza, you could use WSS, Aqua-Solv, or Solvy—transparent, plastic fabrics that dissolve with water. After the shisha are in place, spray the mirrored areas with water. (For a moment the stabilizer will look like melting jellyfish, then will disappear.) Make sure that you've secured the zigzag stitches with the straight stitches (Fig. 9), or they will flap loose.

To create a different look, or if you don't have a zigzag machine, you can hold the shisha in place with a nonfrayable fabric like felt or a material like leather or Ultrasuede. Trace the shisha on the underside of the fabric and cut a hole slightly smaller than the diameter of the shisha. Then trim the fabric at least ⅛ in. larger than the shisha. Place the ring of fabric over the shisha that you have already glued to the foundation fabric, and straight-stitch (or zigzag) around the edge of the fabric.

You can put the foundation fabric in a hoop to make the free-machine embroidery easier, but as the fabric becomes covered with shisha, you won't be able to position the hoop without breaking a mirror. If you're decorating clothing, especially necklines or other edges, attach the mirrors before cutting out the pattern pieces. ☐

Robbie Fanning is the author of Decorative Machine Stitchery *and a contributing editor of* Threads *magazine. She wishes to thank Jerry Zarbaugh and Jacqueline Enthoven for their assistance. The historical examples are from the collection of The Museum for Textiles, Toronto.*

Recommended reading
Elson, Vickie C. *Dowries from Kutch/A Woman's Folk Art Tradition in India.* Los Angeles: UCLA, Museum of Cultural History, 1979.

Enthoven, Jacqueline. *Stitches of Creative Embroidery.* New York: Van Nostrand Reinhold, 1964.

Gross, Nancy D., and Fontana, Frank. *Shisha Embroidery/Traditional Indian Mirror Work with Instructions and Transfer Patterns.* New York: Dover Publications, 1981.

Simpson, Jean. *Shisha Mirror Embroidery/A Contemporary Approach.* New York: Van Nostrand Reinhold, 1978.

Wilson, Kax. *A History of Textiles.* Boulder: Westview Press, 1979.

Reinventing the Sampler
Old World images animate contemporary cross-stitch

by Elly Smith

It recently occurred to me that my childhood in Holland has contributed to the form and content of the needlework I do. I've inherited a storehouse of beautiful, symbolic, traditional motifs that have existed for centuries. Each of the motifs has its own history and its own story to tell. People sat on them, slept under them, and prayed in them. They are found on sheets, hand towels, pillowcases, cuffs and collars, bibs and hats.

My earliest memories of learning needlework go back to kindergarten in The Hague, Holland, where I learned the essentials of counted-thread embroidery. Our first project was a bookmark made with running stitches. I remember thinking it was hardly embroidery, certainly not like the large red cabbage roses that my older sister had embroidered on our tablecloth. I likened it more to the woven paper baskets we had made for May Day. Instead of weaving with paper, I was weaving with needle and thread. But how well I remember the concentration required to evenly count the spaces in the fabric and the pleasure I had in the accomplishment! My eyes delighted in the wonderful arrangement of colored threads.

Other forms of needlework followed. I knit a pair of socks, hand-sewed a purse and a doll's apron, and began what looked like a sampler. I worked on these projects at school, while the boys learned higher mathematics. During evenings at home, my sister, a professional seamstress, busily worked at the sewing machine. My mother was the knitter and crocheter in the family. All sorts of items magically flowed from her knitting needles and crochet hook.

Elly Smith (above) was strongly influenced by her childhood in her native Holland. Her memories are filled with images from needlework, like the traditional motif of a spinning monkey at left, from a sampler that was worked by Griet Cornelis in 1661. (Collection of F. Ex-Coenders, Amsterdam)

Rediscovering embroidery—Despite this rich background, I didn't continue needlework when I came to the U.S. in the fifth grade. Then, 18 years ago, when I returned to Holland for a visit, I bought a bellpull cross-stitch kit. Back in the states I started stitching the bellpull and suddenly discovered a forgotten fragment of my childhood. The quiet concentration reminded me of learning to write and embroider. It was fun and relaxing—like drawing pictures. The traditional motifs in the bellpull reminded me of my childhood drawings.

When I finished the kit, I looked for similar projects, but I had difficulty finding the right fabric. Also, since no ready-made designs were available, I had to draw my own on graph paper. My first effort was an embroidered pillow for a friend. It began as a simple pair of figures, but I enjoyed it so much that I kept adding things—children, dogs, cats, goldfish, birthdates—until I ran out of fabric. Someone immediately noticed that I'd created a sampler. My friend framed it. Someone else admired it and asked for one. During the next 17 years, I made many more, like the one at right, searching out and incorporating existing traditional motifs into my own designs.

Sampler symbolism—Over the years I became interested in the symbolism of folk motifs. Associations from my childhood came to mind, such as the lion holding seven spears from our national crest, a most prevalent motif in Dutch samplers. As a child, I saw the lion everywhere—on buildings, on paper boxes, and even on my teaspoon.

The angel motif in Dutch samplers has many associations for me. I love the way angels suspend themselves in midair, holding flowered wreaths or cartouches. In Sunday school we learned that angels are the highest order of creation. I assumed that, when I died, my shoulder blades would pop out and become wings, and my knobby backbone would transform into a row of buttons for my heavenly gown.

As a child, my explanation for monkeys seemed to originate from the same source. If the angels were on the top rung of creation, then the monkeys were on the bottom rung. A sampler that I inherited from my mother includes a persistent Dutch motif, the "spinning monkey," pictured in the photo on the facing page and in the sampler on p. 38, top right. He is always shown seated on a chair in from of a spindle, pulling, holding, or unwinding thread. This impish figure has multiple meanings. Since he embodies the baser instincts, one could say that he represents the devil. Scholars have also pointed out that he is an emblem of the Three Fates of Greek mythol-

Smith's "Renaissance Sampler" was loosely modeled after the 17th-century band samplers and the earliest dated English sampler, worked by Jane Bostocke in 1598.

Made in 1739, this sampler is a virtual catalog of traditional motifs. Angels (top center) float above a Dutch maiden who rests atop the garden gate, the emblem of the city of Amsterdam. To the right are the grape bearers, and in the lower left sits a mild-looking spinning monkey. (Photo courtesy of The Fries Museum)

Learning the alphabet has always been an integral part of sampler-making. These magnificent samplers (left and right), done in silk on linen, typify the Friesian love of ornate lettering, which Smith has incorporated into her own work. The eyelets surrounding each letter form characterize the Friesian style. (Photo courtesy of The Fries Museum)

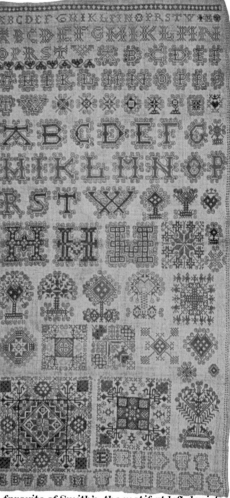

A favorite of Smith's, the motif at left depicts the five virtuous virgins, and the groom, from the parable of the Ten Virgins. Biblical motifs and other reminders that women should keep their minds on lofty thoughts commonly found their way into Dutch samplers. This motif is from a 1739 sampler. (Photo courtesy of The Fries Museum)

ogy who controlled human life. Clotho, the first sister, was the spinner; Lachesis apportioned the thread of life; and Atropos was the one who did the cutting.

I think the monkey points out the transitory qualities of life. It's a reminder to the women of those days that when they were doing their necessary, but boring, menial tasks, they should keep their minds on lofty and religious thoughts. Occasionally the monkeys wear the little black hats known as "freedom," or "liberty," hats. Prints from the 18th century celebrating the French Revolution show people dancing around a pole with a liberty cap on top. The monkey in my mother's sampler also had a little orange necktie—representing the House of Orange, the reigning dynasty in Holland.

The Dutch Maiden, another popular motif found in Dutch samplers, also visible in the 1739 sampler at top right on the facing page, is perhaps our version of Miss Liberty. I've seen several samplers where she wears the liberty hat and holds a scepter with an orange ribbon fluttering in the wind. I enjoy seeing her stand in the little enclosed garden with gate (representing the Dutch state) so reminiscent of medieval miniatures that feature a seated Virgin Mary.

It has been pointed out that the Dutch Maiden is a manifestation of Pallas Athena, the Greek war goddess. In samplers from the southern parts of Holland, she frequently is flanked by peacocks, which in my mind, represent the goddess Hera, who is associated with marriage and domesticity.

Biblical motifs—One of my favorite motifs is the Ten Virgins. It is based on the New Testament parable from Matthew 25:1-12, in which ten bridesmaids take their lamps and go to meet the bridegroom. Five were wise and brought oil for their lamps, but five brought only their lamps. Naturally, when the groom appeared late that night, the five foolish maids had to go for oil, and when they returned, it was too late; the doors to the wedding hall were closed.

From medieval days we know that the Ten Virgins was a popular "mystery" play. Traditionally, the Five Wise Virgins (see sampler detail, bottom left, facing page), who have oil in their lamps, represent the believers; and the Five Foolish Virgins re-

present the nonbelievers. As with the Spinning Monkey motif, we are reminded to keep our minds active with virtuous thoughts, and in this case, of the Second Coming.

An Old Testament motif in antique samplers is the grape carriers, traditionally thought to be Joshua and Caleb. They were the only tribal heads spared by God when they returned from the Land of Canaan with a branch of grapes. Christians later interpreted the grapes to represent the blood of Christ and its redemptive qualities.

The Friesian alphabet—Of course, lettering and alphabets are often integral parts of old samplers, since many samplers were learning tools for young women. Before the advent of washing machines, household linens were biannually sent out to bleaching establishments and were marked as a means of identifying ownership. Letter styles abound; my favorite letters are found predominantly in Friesian samplers, like the ones in the top-left and bottom-right photos on the facing page.

People of Friesland, an uppermost northern province of Holland, come from ancient stock; they were there when the Romans arrived. Their beautiful letters can be readily identified by the little "eyelets" that surround each letter. To me, they are reminiscent of the dots that surround the letters in Celtic writings, like the Lindisfarne Gospels or the Book of Kells.

Rethinking the sampler—After spending a month in Holland in 1985, studying and absorbing samplers in museums, private collections, antique shops, and a restoration atelier, I decided to no longer duplicate what had been done in the past, but to create a sampler that would be unique in a contemporary way. I tried to capture the element I find exciting in samplers: the presentation as a visual phenomenon. Dutch samplers, as cluttered as they appear at first glance, have a wonderful sense of balance. Visually, I concentrated on the scattering process, the misspellings, the design errors in borders, the didactic epitaphs, and the avoidance of scale and perspective.

In my "Contemporary Sampler" (top photo, p. 40), I tried to depict the connections between past and present sampler work and

the feelings of the artist, who is presented as a waitress in the center of the work. On her platter she carries the star, a motif that has spanned the centuries from culture to culture. Above her on the left I melded two motifs: a traditional geometric motif and a chessboard, which is my personal symbol for structure. Draped over the chessboard is a totem pole representing my various identities: mother, wife, artist, and secret child.

At the far left stands a tall, thin lady who symbolizes the historical observer. Her long, narrow shape represents a 17th-century sampler, usually rolled up for storage. The foot and the shoes stand for the new, aggressive attitude in women: "These boots are made for walking." The ladies with the bowler hats (a symbol of bourgeoisie narrow-mindedness, borrowed from the paintings of Magritte) represent the people who haven't as yet accepted embroidery as an art form. One, however, has an open hatband, so progess is being made.

The idea of using elements from the past in my current designs seems to me part of a natural process, one that my 1987 stitchery, "Till Death Do Us Part" (bottom photo, p. 40), exemplifies. In the early part of that year, we lost both of my husband's parents. As we faced the loss of two very dynamic people, their personal possessions overflowed into our little house—clothing, furniture, paintings, scrapbooks, photos, and letters. For a while I felt like a trespasser surrounded by all these personal items that had been sadly separated from their owners. I felt an internalized rage toward the process of death itself, this bad joke that nature has bestowed on us. After a while, the rage dissipated into pain.

In Holland's Sampler Museum, I'd seen a black-on-white sampler that the museum owner called a "death sampler." It was for covering the corpse's face before burial to protect and prevent the soul from escaping from the body. As an extra precaution, mirrors were turned to the wall, and curtains were drawn. The wording on the sampler was archaic Hungarian. It read, "Rest in Peace—In Your Quiet Home—The Work Now Belongs To Us Here On This Earth."

Thinking of the "death cloth" reminded me that in most cultures black is associated with death. How compelling it is when we

---

References

Colby, Averil. *Samplers.* Published in 1964, reprinted in 1985, out of print. *Check library and used-book shops.*

Eaton, Jan, and Liz Mundle. *Cross Stitch and Sampler Book.* New York: Sterling, 1985.

Kruuskes van Mine Letter Doek. Groningen, Holland: Nederlandse Bond van Plattelandsvrouwen Provinciale Afdeling Groningen, 1961.

Charted traditional Dutch cross-stitch motifs, 48pp., *English translation. Available for $13 from Elly Smith, 4111 E. Highland Dr., Seattle, WA 98112.*

Meulenbelt-Nieuwburg, Alberta. *Embroidery Motifs from Dutch Samplers,* 1974 (out of print). *Check library and used-book shops.*

Dutch museums/collection
If you are planning to take a trip to Holland and you wish to visit any of the following places, be sure to write ahead in order to set up an appointment.

Fries Museum
Gieneke Arnolli,
Curator of Textiles
Turfmarkt 24. 8911 KT
Leeuwarden, Holland
Telephone: 058-123001

Sampler Museum
c/o Mr. and Mrs. W. Rogman
Hoeve "De Waert," 6077 HK, St. Odilienberg, Holland
Telephone: 04744-1486

F. Ex-Coenders
Keizersgracht 150
1015 CX Amsterdam, Holland
Telephone: 020-255180
This shop specializes in samplers. Photographs of samplers will be sent upon request.

In "Contemporary Sampler" (above and graph on facing page), Smith tries to capture the visual excitement of the unified, but scattered, elements in old Dutch samplers. It won an honorable mention in 1986 at the biennial exhibition of the National Standards Council of American Embroiderers. "Till Death Do Us Part" (detail below) mingles Smith's personal symbols with the tradition of black-on-white death samplers. (Photos by Steve Meltzer)

realize that in some samplers the black thread, due to its chemical composition, disintegrates first, leaving only a bare patch of fabric! There is a beauty in these "threatened" samplers, as in the attempts made to restore fabric with patches. How like life itself this becomes! Are we not, as humans, constantly patching and mending our losses and our feelings of pain and grief?

Sometimes an idea for a stitchery occurs to me in a visual flash, as it did in "Till Death Do Us Part." In it I joined several ideas and images: The image of the patched black-and-white death sampler for a background; a ladder, a fear symbol for me; and my black-clothed "dream-sleep" personage, who appears in three other stitcheries. The figure is standing with one foot on a red thread, the symbolic line of life and also the mode of my artistic expression.

In this way, elements from my past and embroidery's past and my love of symbolism all find their way into my designs. For me, intellectually possessing knowledge of symbols is like having a third language, being able to utilize another form of communication. I don't consciously include traditional motifs; they just seem to fit. Perhaps it's because I view embroidery as having a history, one I find fascinating. What I do is part of a continuum, and I enjoy my part in it because it evokes an air of nostalgia for me and because I like my work to have content, meaning, and narrative. □

Elly Smith of Seattle, WA, stitches and designs commissioned family samplers and continues to make "contemporary" samplers. She also gives workshops and lectures.

One way to do counted-thread embroidery

The first question that people usually ask when they see one of my stitcheries is, "How long did it take you to make it?" I usually respond with, "Many, many pleasurable hours."

I don't draw the design on the fabric. Instead, I count it onto the fabric, stitch by stitch, from squared graph paper. Each square represents a single stitch.

There are many different counted-thread stitches. The two stitches I use exclusively are the cross-stitch and back stitch, both very basic and described in every embroidery book. Because my cross-stitch crosses over two threads on the fabric, my graph-paper squares equal half the fabric's thread count. For example, if the count is 22 threads per inch, then my graph paper will represent 11 cross stitches in 11 squares per inch.

The fabric I use has the same count per inch as my graph paper. If the fabric isn't an even weave, the results may be interesting, but a design can become too elongated or too expanded.

I use Zweigart 100% cotton hardanger cloth with a count of 22 threads per inch. Although hardanger is available in several colors, I generally use white or ivory. If I want an aged look, I soak the fabric overnight in a solution of coffee or tea.

A watercolor artist friend once said to me, "I can't become interested in embroidery because the color range is so limited." I promptly displayed my palette of 1,254 thread colors, each cross-stitched into thumb-sized squares and labeled with the appropriate color-code numbers. It took three or four large pieces of hardanger cloth to display the full range, but it's very hard to judge the colors unless you can see them stitched.

I use 100% cotton embroidery floss. It's usually packaged in an eight-meter, six-ply skein, so I split the strands in two. I keep my skeins in plastic drawer cases purchased from a local hardware store. Each drawer has a sticker with the corresponding thread number. When I need a color, I refer to my stitched palette.

I use the entire line of DMC and Anchor threads and some Coats and Clark threads. I also use Schurer, a colorfast thread from West Germany. Lately I've been experimenting with Madeira metallic thread, which comes in 200-meter spools and 30 colors. I usually stitch it with two plies. To prevent it from twisting and fraying, I stiffen it by running it over a block of beeswax.

My needle is a size 22 DMC nickel-plated, steel tapestry needle. The blunt end of the needle prevents it from snagging the fabric as I stitch, making it much easier to always stitch between the threads.

Because I'm left-handed, I work my stitches from left to right on the fabric, which I occasionally hold loosely on my knee. My right hand keeps the fabric taut, while my left hand works the stitches on top of the surface. I almost never poke from underneath—it's too time-consuming! Instead of starting in the center, as many instructors direct, I begin in the lower-left corner and fantail out from there. I don't use basting lines for reference points. I don't use a hoop or a thimble, because they get in my way. And I never care what the back of the work looks like, although people comment that it looks nice when they see it. Whether I'm stitching horizontally or vertically, all my stitches look the same and are made the same way. It probably took me six months of regular stitching to develop the rhythm that ensures even stitch tension across an entire piece.

While I'm stitching, I don't rigidly adhere to my graph, an example of which is shown in the photo above. I don't usually graph in the specific designs; I follow light pencil sketches and graph as I go. This enables me to change midway if another format or idea occurs to me.

When the stitchery is completed, I usually steam-press it and roll it up for storage on a 3-in.-dia. cardboard tube. If there are dirt marks on it, I wash it with mild soap and cold water, setting my washing machine on the delicate cycle. Then I hang it up to dry.

I leave the framing to a professional. After all the time and effort (and pleasurable hours), it's worth it. A professional framer usually mounts it and stretches it over a 100% nonacidic museum board. If there's matting, that's also nonacidic. Although some people feel comfortable having the fiber protected under glass (it should never touch the glass), I feel it loses a certain amount of immediacy. A light vacuuming (with the brush attachment) for dust and bugs once a year is all that's needed. Hanging it in indirect sunlight in a room with good circulation and an even temperature is ideal. —E.S.

Net Darning

Tracing the course of a simple stitch

by Lilo Markrich

One of civilization's most ancient and universal hand skills, embroidery is essentially utilitarian stitching honed by countless generations into luxurious decoration. It is the alphabet of a visual language, which in the hands of a visionary evolves into art. As a rhythmic, soothing pastime, it has given countless women and men pleasure as their work grew under their hands.

Nowhere is this transformation more apparent than in darning's richly textured ornamental embroideries. The basic needle-weaving technique can be divided into two groups. Cutwork is one of the earliest forms of lacemaking, where the embroiderer cuts into previously woven fabric to withdraw warp and weft threads and replaces them with a decorative darn or needle weave. There are many variations, each a display of the needleworker's ability to create positive and negative openwork, playing the transparent against the opaque.

Some of the most elaborate and delicate cutwork was created in linen-producing areas of medieval continental Europe. Often the work of nuns, it filled church treasuries as generous patrons chose such gifts to support an order or to beautify their place of worship. These imaginative embroideries, with their airiness and delicacy, were the forerunners of today's needle laces.

A very time-consuming and painstaking needlework style, this predominantly white-on-white linen embroidery carried con-siderable risk prior to the 19th century. Every piece of fine linen and linen thread was the product of skillful handspinning and handweaving. The wrong incisions, too broad or too narrow a cut, flawed tension, a worker's inability to shift direction smoothly and invisibly, or the misinterpretation of a costly design risked the waste of the carefully prepared background weave.

But with the 19th-century Industrial Revolution came the ability to produce swiftly, uniformly, and at a low cost machine-spun linen embroidery threads and fine linen yardage for sheeting, tablecloths, and lingerie. Manufacturers looked to embroiderers as a market for their mass-produced goods, recognizing that the social ambitions of the wives and daughters of the newly emerging middle classes could be profitably tied to such upper-class customs as providing brides with prolific trousseaus and dowries with enough hemstitched and hand-embroidered sheets, pillowcases, table linens, petticoats, and cambric nightgowns, all with appropriate cutwork, for at least a decade of housekeeping.

Classical lacis—The second group of needle-woven embroideries with lace effect appears to be an earlier development. These embroideries were highly prized until they were overshadowed by cutwork and laces independent of a foundation. In lacis, as it was first known, the background is airy and the design opaque—just the reverse of cutwork. And while its fashion appeal varied, its popularity was constant enough to justify its eventual imitation by a totally different technique to meet new commercial and social needs.

Lacis is worked not on a previously woven fabric, but on an open ground, a mesh hand-knotted in the traditional fisherman's way. The pattern, like a geometric silhouette, is needle-woven or darned in and out of the net's identical squares or diamonds.

Lacis was traditionally worked with handspun linen threads, the same thread serving for both the netting and the pattern darn, as shown above (or at its more luxurious, netted in silk and darned with a combination of colored silk and silver and gold threads). For altar frontals and cloths and hangings and vestment inserts, designs were based on biblical scenes and characters. Many of the surviving masterpieces were the creations of convents or princely workshops. Palaces had lacis bed hangings, coverlets, and table covers. Lacis was a favored insertion for personal linens. Pattern preference was for heraldic symbols, family crests, pictures based on mythology, heroic knights jousting, romantic maidens, and decorative repeats of floral details.

Designs were probably marked in dots or squares (one symbol equal to one net square) by someone other than an embroiderer because to transcribe a flowing linear design into a geometric, squared-off counterpart requires skill. The popularity and value at-

From *Threads* magazine (February 1988) 15:42-45

tached to the work in the 16th century are substantiated by the many black-and-white charted motifs especially designed for lacis that were published in the first printed-pattern books.

The costly pattern books were treasured and protected until they fell apart, their designs copied by generation after generation. This is one reason it is difficult to date early pieces unless they relate stylistically to new art forms. Until the 19th century, pattern books didn't provide instruction. It was taken for granted that the skill was inherent, especially netting and darning. Both were considered simple and relatively fast for meeting everyday needs. Their application for decoration was an advantage.

When world economics change, so does the way the individual lives. As the Renaissance moved beyond Italy, overseas commerce extended beyond the Mediterranean, and a burgeoning middle class increasingly prospered. It was inevitable that a demand for more complex variations of the known and the innovative would become desirable, regardless of cost. Its value after all, was as a symbol of the owner's status.

Lacis adapted to new taste. In keeping with popular art forms, new creations were added to traditional motifs and designs. Hand-knotted net has to be stretched before it is worked. Large pieces required large stretcher frames and were bulky to net. Because netting had become a popular social pastime and remained so well into the early 20th century, special attention began to be paid to designs requiring fine net, small pieces being joined to create a larger object or used as special insertions. Small, delicate netting with designs that gave a curvilinear illusion despite their rigid geometric forms was admired as classical domestic needlework.

Admiration of delicacy was, however, not enough to distinguish one piece of work from another. An artistic eye for shape and form allowed the worker to choose between two stitches for the best effect. Each stitch was simple darning; the difference lay in the way the darn was used.

The *point de toile* stitch (cloth stitch) recreates a small, even-weave cloth fragment within a square. This technique breaks up the light-reflecting properties of linen or silk; the areas worked become flat, detailed, and opaque. The second stitch, the *point de reprise*, moves from square to square in one direction—horizontally or vertically. By shifting the direction of the stitches, the embroiderer intensifies or diminishes the linen's light-reflecting properties so light and shadow interplay within the flat design.

By combining variations and skillfully directing stitches, the embroiderer can highlight certain areas within the design and achieve a three-dimensional illusion. He or she can also break up a solid motif pattern into more graceful definition by the careful use of unworked mesh squares. At its most creative, a white lacis silhouette floats on a white web, and with each washing, its luster and purity of color intensify—the mark of good linen. To enhance appreciation of the play of positive against negative, embroiderers mounted important pieces of lacis on rich silk or velvet.

Early terms for lacis, like *opus araneum* and *punto a maglia quadrata,* weren't as fashionable in Victorian days as the term *filet brodé.* This sometimes led to a confusion of the filet technique with bobbin lacework, which had emulated the early lacis and later competed against it by its extreme delicacy. *Point brodé, filet brodé,* or simply network or darned netting, became the modern, interchangeable terms for the old art.

The terms were put to good commercial use by merchants in a class-conscious society who understood that gentrification of a fashion thrives on snobbery. The educated

Some of the earliest printed-pattern books had designs for lacis. Each square represents one mesh hole. These are from Renaissance Italy.

Point de reprise is worked in one direction per square or squares (top left), as can be seen in the detail of this late 19th-century shawl. The classical piece of convent work in point de toile (above) is a fine example of turn-of-the-century lacis inserts in household linens. Filet crochet in fine cotton (top right) all but eliminated lacis.

white or colored threads in any number of thicknesses, free or cheap patterns, and a social appreciation of the worker's skill in creating something out of very little.

There was probably no home without its share of filet crochet lace, as it was generally called. Even to this day it is prized and treasured in many parts of central Europe and the Balkans for use in church or home. But in the late 1920s and mid-1930s, only the more fragile filet bobbin lace was considered appropriate and acceptable in an upper-class household. The needs of the mass market were met by low-cost hand-made darned and netted imports from the cottage industries of China and India, as a younger generation of women increasingly looked to work outside the home.

Inevitably, neglect and snobbish ridicule fade away. Somehow, somewhere, a new generation discovers past achievements, and with the decline of once-common craft skills, wonders how it was done, sometimes finding it difficult to realize that a museum piece may also have had its more banal counterpart. Frequently, the old skill seems impossible to imitate. There is often little time to experiment, and the desire to focus on one technique indefinitely is rare.

But perhaps that's one of the great advantages of lacis; it is a survivor. It is easy to try, and with a sense of fun it is not too difficult to accomplish. All inspiration needs is a trip to a fisherman's dock or a sailboat marina and a visit to the nearest ship chandler's store, where one can find unknown treasures. There are netting needles and gauges that fishermen use to repair their nets, plus countless yards of colorful ready-made fish net that even in synthetic yarn will serve the purpose. No longer does one have to think of the darning thread as having to be equal to the netting thread, and it doesn't have to be smooth. All that is needed is a blunt darning needle and whatever threads are on hand, so long as they pass in and out of the mesh singly, doubly, or trebly, and with ease. Ask yourself what would happen if you took an old design and broke it up, added outlines, and darned some doodles in the background.

A rough textured thread could be interlaced with a fine, smoother one. There could be a play of color. You could enlarge a design by translating a design square onto four blocks of mesh. And, if you're unwilling to chart your own design, remember that many a popular artist survived financially only by creating pattern books for an affluent needlework patroness, who in turn would be praised and admired for her artistry and elegant neatness of work. □

Lilo Markrich is a frequent contributor to Threads. Net-darning lace patterns and materials are available from JES Handcrafts, Box 341, Closter, NJ 07624; Lacis, 2982 Adeline St., Berkeley, CA 94703; and Frivolité, 15526 Densmore N., Seattle, WA 98133. Photos by Michele Russell Slavinsky.

supporters of the Art Needlework movement, influenced by William Morris, were a ready market for the new limited re-issues of early Italian, French, and German pattern books, specially bound and offered on parchmentlike paper. They eagerly sought handspun linen from the Balkans, deploring the use of machine-spun linen and the even cheaper mercerized cotton. They were shocked by the abundance and promotion of machine-made net (not too different from the "new" interlocked starched needlepoint canvas popularized during the late 1970s) as an adequate substitute for the original. They stressed that hair-fine thread and only the most slender of netting needles and narrow gauges were adequate tools for the duplication of good lacis.

On the other hand, most women had little money of their own. With netting a much-needed household necessity for covers and bags, not to mention summer gloves, they could spend a few extra pennies to create a "bit of trim" by following the free patterns in a newspaper or magazine.

It is therefore easy to understand that net-woven embroideries for a bride were vigorously promoted as both fashionable and valuable. Rarely did the avid readers of the description of a royal trousseau or society wedding realize that the well-to-do

generally had their embroideries worked by the family's domestic staff or a special workshop or that they ordered their more spectacular pieces from French, Italian, and Spanish convents that were famous for their needlework. The hand-embroidered linens being offered in the new department stores of London, Paris, and Berlin were the handwork of skilled embroiderers in Greece and other Balkan countries, where cottage industries were a way of life.

Changes in lacis—Popularity inevitably breeds imitation, and lacis was no exception. If you wanted sturdier yet cheap curtains, longer-lasting doilies, indestructible tea cloths, pillow trim, and antimacassars; and if you didn't know how to net, couldn't afford to buy these items, but knew how to use a crochet hook and wanted to carry your work around to eliminate any loss of precious time, inexpensive patterns for elegant copies were readily available.

Filet crochet was the brazen hussy who muscled the more graceful, hand-knotted, hand-darned lacis, or *filet brodé,* aside. Less expensive and more practical, it met the emotional needs for handwork that mass advertising for embroidery materials had created: the soothing action of the hook traveling back and forth, the availability of

How lacis is done

The net support system on which lacis is darned must be taut at all times. If it isn't, threads will work loose, the pattern darning will lose its even tension, and the design will be distorted. Handspun threads handle differently than the tighter, more precise machine-spun and twisted variety. A naturally finished thread has different light-reflecting properties than the silky sheen of artificially sized and buffed threads. The needleworker must be careful to pull and tug, adjusting the tension to the thread's inherent flexibility or stiffness. Thread supplies are relatively limited today—many types and weights are no longer considered worthwhile producing.

The frame is the backbone of the technique. Today's embroiderer will have to improvise to find a suitable frame from which the lacis can later be removed. Lacis frames were generally small and square, a little bigger than the background net, although in some European countries where oval and circular doilies were popular, needleworkers could purchase a variety of shapes. Frames were usually hand-held, unless the piece was very large, and turned when the worker shifted stitch direction. Hand-holding also enabled the worker to move the net forward and up with the fingers of the holding hand for easier darning.

The frames were metal and finished with padding—a piece of cotton batting or roving folded around the frame and carefully wrapped in silk ribbon. Each corner of the net was drawn up to a corner of the frame by a doubled piece of thread that was slung across the frame and knotted.

Next, the net was positioned evenly within the frame. One method was relatively quick. Leaving a fairly long end secured firmly to the frame, the worker would lash on the net by wrapping the working thread over and under the frame and bringing the needle up at each subsequent hole in the net. Beginning and ending threads were secured with a weaver's knot. An alternative was to stitch the net to the padded frame, which some embroiderers considered an advantage because it slightly raised one side of the net. This distinguished the "right side" and thus prevented an accidental weaver's knot join of the working thread appearing on the right side, possibly in the middle of a motif.

The simple weaver's knot is the most popular device for joining one thread to another. The embroiderer could simply darn the beginning or end thread in, but that might distort the weave, especially in the case of *point de toile*. With knotting, the needleworker must take great care to knot on the back of the work and, if at all possible, discreetly behind a grid thread.

Point de reprise—Point de reprise is a very simple up-and-down, over-and-under darning process whereby threads run parallel in an alternating manner to their predecessors. Depending on your choice of thread, you can increase or decrease the overall design's density within the net. In addition, because each set of threads runs in the same direction—vertical, horizontal, or diagonal—there are light-reflecting variations that enable you to take a flat design and break it into shapes and forms of varying values. You can use *point de reprise* worked with a full, thick thread (often silk) to outline a lacis design worked in *point de toile*.

Point de toile—The cloth stitch, just like the utilitarian darn, imitates a weave. It is more detailed, requires a fine thread, and by its very simplicity, is made perfect with practice. For designs like the printed patterns at the bottom of page 43, each pattern square equals one hole in the net grid.

Before you start, think of the background material as a mapped grid. Have a careful plan as to where to start and how to return to the same point, as shown in the two motifs at bottom right. When the working thread returns to its starting point, it has traveled over and under the earlier-laid vertical threads as well as over and under the net threads. This means that one edge of the motif will appear slightly thicker than the other.

It's a good idea to practice working corners, diagonals, and small spots for a single-hole motif before attempting a larger design. Also, before working on a large design, think it through as though it were a maze: There is an entrance and an exit. Sometimes you can successfully break up an area; other times, the overall effect will be lost if the darning has been interrupted because tension is changed and the net appears distorted.

Set yourself guideposts, and remember that if the frame is too large to hand-hold, work with one you can turn so the needle can run back and forth from more than one side. The more frequently you move your arm in the same direction, the more even the tension of your work will be.

Finally, never clamp a net into an embroidery hoop to save time. Whether it's hand- or machine-netted cotton, linen, or synthetic, the net must be stitched onto a frame to maintain its even tension and tautness. If you remember this, you can easily begin to experiment with nontraditional threads. —*L.M.*

Lacis, in progress on an old-fashioned, padded frame. The seahorse motif is being worked in handspun linen on hand-knotted linen net.

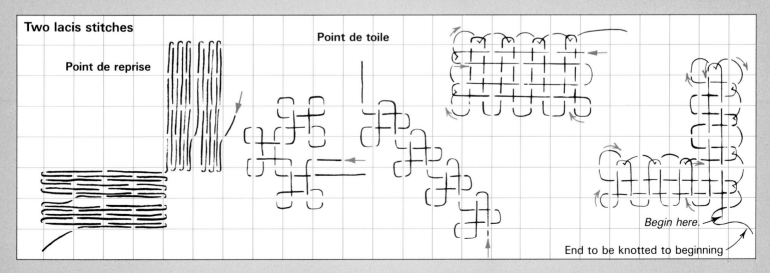

Two lacis stitches

Point de reprise

Point de toile

Begin here.

End to be knotted to beginning

Embroidery for the Goddess

Ritual fabrics wove power and beauty into women's folklife of Eastern Europe

by Mary B. Kelly

century ago one could still quietly enter the low carved door of a Ukrainian village home and find there a treasure of soft light and warm color. The flickering lamp or candle in the "beautiful corner" would attract attention first. Here, arranged on a shelf, were flowers, family mementos, and icons. The corner belonged to the woman of the house. It was hers to decorate, to enhance with needlework and weaving. Draped over the shelf, and often draping the windows as well, were soft white linen cloths, embroidered on each end with brilliant red designs. The splendor of the color, the soft glow, and the evocative aura of the objects left one with no doubt that this was indeed the most beautiful place in the house.

Here, on the eve of Easter, the woman of the house would sit decorating eggs. The work was a holy, ritual task; she worked by candlelight, late at night in the quiet, dyeing ancient designs on the *pysanka,* the egg that itself symbolized new spring life. She had embroidered these same archaic designs on ritual cloths stored in the far corner. There, the huge marriage chest was almost hidden under a woven rug, but if one could lift this fabric and the heavy lid, what an array of color and meaning would greet the eye!

This precious casket held all the clothing used for the special occasions of folklife. Here were the white linen shirts, made for the first day of the haying season, and the white linen shifts for the day of marriage, each embroidered with fertility designs around the hem, wrists, and neckline.

Here also were the ritual towels, embroidered on each end and sometimes 6 ft. long. Carefully folded, they had been used to bind the couple in marriage. They would be hung from the beam overhead for the woman in labor to pull on and would later swaddle her baby. Finally, at death, they would be used to lower the coffin into the tomb and each spring would be tied to the grave markers in memoriam.

Not only was the work of the woman of the house stored in the chest, but also her mother's ritual fabrics and clothing and her grandmother's work, for this was her wealth, her dowry. Each piece was embroidered with time-honored motifs handed down from woman to woman from the earliest centuries. Carefully repeated were the motifs of the sun and the tree of life and the image of the mother goddess, the motif most valued by women. Her figure and the accompanying fertility symbols were necessary to the growth and development of fields, crops, livestock, and family.

The *rushnyky,* or ritual cloths that overhung the icon, bore the red woven image of the pagan goddess. Bed hangings were outlined with a row of goddess motifs, each goddess with upraised hands protecting the occupants from evil. Shirt sleeves and hems were similarly picked out in protective embroidery. The long cloths show the rites of the seasons: the goddess holding birds and sun disks in the spring, the goddess overseeing the midsummer night fires and the fall harvests, and the mother goddess giving birth.

Ukrainian archaeological finds from as early as the Neolithic Period (7000-3000 B.C.) show statues of the goddess. She is slim, her hands are upraised, and she is often seen with a birdlike head. Impressed on her stomach is the fertile-field motif, so-called because it represents the way fields were plowed even in the 19th century, when ethnographers began investigating agricultural rituals. The field was plowed across the center, then recrossed from opposite sides. In each quadrant, a seed was placed. The Neolithic motif, a symbol for pregnancy and fertility, looks just the same. We find it commonly on wedding and engagement textiles in the 19th and 20th centuries. The same symbol, signifying fertility, had existed all those years.

Throughout Eastern Europe before the 20th century, the ancient folkway of life preserved many rituals from the distant past. The pre-Christian and Christian heritages existed side by side, sometimes overlaying or reinforcing each other.

At the Easter ceremonies, eggs were, and still are, painted with both pagan and Christian symbols; at Midsummer Night, when pagans went swimming in the rivers, Christians found a reason to do the same by dedicating the day to John the Baptist, or Ivan Kupala (John Bathing). At harvest time, the birthday of the goddess, traditionally September 8th, was overlaid by the Birthday of the Virgin.

In Czechoslovakian folklife, a female ritual figure is still made by village women each spring. Dressed in red embroidered clothing, she carries a ritual cloth, as seen in the photo on the facing page.

Many of the embroidered towel ends are fragments that have been removed from the long ritual cloths, and it is these that now form our legacy. In this country we are fortunate to have an early Russian collection of these samples from which the photos on pages 48 and 49 are taken. Natalia de Shabelsky began collecting textiles on her estate in Russia as early as 1850. She selected pieces with the finest stitchery and the most ancient folk motifs. Solar

From *Threads* magazine (June 1987) 11:26-29

Czechoslovakian women from the remote village of Vel'ky Lom carry a clothed goddess figure in a traditional spring ritual. The woman in the center who is wearing the wide headdress is in bridal costume. Others wear linen caps. The caps are heavily embroidered with archaic designs, and they are rolled to suggest horns. These women were photographed in 1978 by folk-art collector Helene Cincebox.

swastikas, huge trees of life, and peacock-tailed birds are all common on these pieces. But the most arresting images are those of the goddess herself. Some are squat and club-headed, reminiscent of the Paleolithic goddess figurines. Others show a horned goddess holding the reins of a horse or riding on it. Still others show her with hands upraised inside an archlike shrine.

After the death of de Shabelsky, many pieces from her collection came to the United States. Approximately 100 are available for study in Boston, Cleveland, and Brooklyn museums. Other collectors have added treasures to our store of Eastern European textiles. And, immigrant families from Czechoslovakia, Poland, the Ukraine, Hungary, and Romania have brought many ritual textiles into this country, for textiles are often among the most precious and portable of the family possessions.

The techniques displayed on samples from this early collection are varied: lacework, silk embroidery, drawnwork, and gold and silver couching. It is clear that the needle artists were accomplished. Some techniques undoubtedly derive from ecclesiastical textiles made during the same period.

Although styles differ from region to region, the ritual cloths are generally made from linen or hemp. The artist either wove the design in contrasting threads (red was a favored color) or embellished it with a variety of stitches and textures after the cloth was woven.

This spring, women of Eastern European heritage again lit their candles and drew images of the goddess, suns, and trees of life onto eggs. This ritual act echoed that long line of yearly rituals stretching back into the distant past. The women picked up their needles, carefully counting threads and outlining designs as ancient as their heritage, to make ritual cloths for their own households.

Ordinarily, textile work is done for utilitarian and aesthetic reasons. My interest was drawn to the goddess cloths when I first saw them in Moscow because it was clear that the Russian textile artists had an additional motive. They made the cloths so that they would have power, so that the fabric would make things happen. Their ritual cloths were more than technical masterpieces, undoubtedly useful, and aesthetically resplendent. The Great Goddess was embroidered over and over by women artists because she protected, fertilized, sanctified, and gave life to those who enfolded themselves in her fabrics.

Mary B. Kelly is an art professor at Tompkins Cortland Community College in Dryden, NY. "Goddesses and Their Offspring: 19th and 20th Century Eastern European Embroideries," an exhibition based on her textile research in Europe and the USSR was held in the spring of 1987 at the Roberson Center for the Arts and Sciences, 30 Front Street, Binghamton, NY 13905.

Goddess embroideries of Eastern Europe

Images of power were often layered one over the other or used side by side to reinforce their meaning. In the ritual cloth above, images of the goddess and of the tree of life promote agricultural fertility. On each side of the goddess grow large trees of life. Everything is sprouting branches. Sprouts, flowers, and birds all signal that this ritual cloth would have been made for spring festivals. Yellow silk, metallic thread, and sequins enhance its red and blue cotton embroidery.

Birth goddesses often show tiny figures within the skirt or emerging from between the legs of the central goddess figure. In the example below, embroidered in cotton on linen, the daughter of the mother goddess is riding beside her on a large bird. The mother goddess's stylized head is a simplified fertile-field symbol, shown in her skirt, her daughter's skirt, and the bird's body. A solar symbol is on each side of the mother goddess and is repeated on her shoulders and on the bird's head. Thus, the embroidery is unified, and its power is multiplied by repetition and variation.

The composition of the satin-stitched embroidery shown above, in which a strong goddess is flanked by rampant lions, recalls her title, "Mistress of Animals." It echoes a Neolithic figurine of the goddess giving birth while she is holding onto two leopards.

Without a doubt, birds are the goddess's most common familiars. Even in cases where the goddess figure has long since disappeared under a profusion of floral ornament, the birds remain to remind us of her presence. In the beautiful wool-and-cotton-on-linen embroidery above, two large birds accompany the goddess, and smaller birds perch on her horned headdress. The horns honor her association with deer and the hunt; her ability to attract deer as food was vital to tribal life. In Russian embroidery, the bird is often associated with the soul. Thus, surrounded by birds, the goddess's spiritual power is emphasized.

The embroidered sleeve panel at left shows the goddess with lowered arms, protecting the crops. At her side, two large birds seem to be sprouting branches. The lower portion has in its center the ancient fertile-field symbol of a crossed square with a seed in each quadrant, surrounded by small swastikas, or solar symbols. An abbreviated version of the fertile-field symbol can be seen in the torso of the goddess. The linen blouse from which this fragment is taken might have been worn for the Midsummer Night festivities. Photos these two pages courtesy of The Cleveland Museum of Art. Purchase from the J.H. Wade Fund. □

Easy Heirlooms

Needlepoint rugs don't demand a lifetime of skill, and they offer nearly limitless design freedom

by Beverly Dieringer

I made my first needlepoint rug, which was also my first piece of needlepoint, because we didn't own any floor coverings. My husband and I, both trained in art, were very fond of Oriental carpets, and back in 1971 we found the prospect of designing our own rug less daunting than buying one. Of course, we didn't even consider buying a kit. To this day, dozens of needlepoint rugs and pillows later, I still wouldn't do it any other way.

This isn't to say that we wanted to reinvent the wheel. We spent a great deal of time researching the many different kinds of rugs and design elements. A happy circumstance put The Textile Museum's catalog of the exhibit, *From the Bosporous to Samarkand,* into our hands, reinforcing my love of Caucasian rugs and introducing me to Anatolian design, on which I eventually based the first rug that I made. With the help of the only book I could find on the subject, Sybil Mathews' *Needle-Made Rugs* (see "Further reading," p. 54), I plunged into the task.

Before the rug was half done, *Family Circle* announced a needlework contest. My rug met the requirements, and so the race was on; but I already knew my rug was a winner. There simply are times when it doesn't pay to be modest. My husband learned to needlepoint, and together we managed to meet the deadline.

I wasn't surprised when, three weeks after putting photos of my rug into the mail, I received word that it had been chosen as one of the 200 finalists. What did surprise me, however, was that there were 60,000 entries. The "Red Rug" (so dubbed by *Family Circle* and shown above) won third

Beverly Dieringer's prize-winning "Red Rug" (above), 6 ft. x 9 ft., still looks new after 17 years of daily use.

From *Threads* magazine (June 1989) 23:36-40

prize, and it still has a place of honor in our living room. I made several small rugs and pillow tops after that and later opened my own shop, where I spent six years designing and engineering rugs for my customers, from geometrics to images of dogs and houses.

Despite all these "credentials," I feel that if I can make an heirloom needlepoint rug of my own design, anyone can, regardless of experience. I've always maintained a very relaxed attitude about the process, and I hope I can show you how easy it is.

Designing your own rug—If you want to make a needlepoint rug, you have two choices. You can go to a needlework store and buy a designed canvas and yarn. You'll probably pay a lot of money and not have much to choose from. Or you can design your own canvas and buy just the raw materials. While drawing skill can be useful in rug design, it's not a necessity. Geometric designs, the basis for untold thousands of beautiful rugs, are easy to work out on graph paper. If you feel comfortable drawing other kinds of shapes, all the better.

One way of approaching design is to think of it as a decision-making and editing skill. The problem is to cull from many good elements the ones that go together best. Having a wealth of elements in front of you from which to choose is the trick. I keep a file folder of bits and pieces that I've cut from magazines and newspapers—any snippet that catches my fancy, a piece of border here, a pattern there, or maybe a picture of an antique rug. I don't try to reason why I like a particular thing. I know only that it intrigues me, and I file it for later study.

We all have at our disposal millions of designs and motifs—easy-to-adapt graphed designs, like weaving and beading patterns, and knitting, cross-stitch, and filet-crochet charts, in addition to all the designs that are already intended for needlepoint. (Mail-order houses are an excellent source of needlework supplies.) But there's no reason not to make up your own original designs, geometric or otherwise, or to improvise on the motifs you find elsewhere.

Whether you prefer to work from charts or make up your own designs, you need to remember that the lines on graph paper *do not* represent the cross threads of the canvas. Each stitch on the rug covers an *intersection* of the canvas, but each stitch on the paper is represented by a space, so you match graph squares to canvas intersections when reading from the graph, and you count threads, not holes, when you're measuring and marking the canvas.

It's a good idea to fill up some graph paper with samples of design elements that you like, like the ones I've done in the photo at left, above. These can be copies of designs or of parts of designs, or you can just play with colored pencils or paint, inventing borders and motifs. I use graph pa-

Graph paper (above) is perfect for trying out pattern ideas for needlepoint rugs and working out corner details. At right, Dieringer works in her lap. She does all the stitches on the right side. (Photo by Joseph Kugielsky)

per a lot, but I also sketch with yarn on needlepoint canvas, and many of the pillows I've made are really ideas for rugs. Working with yarns is a better way to see the actual color relationships.

I did spend years filling in little squares on graph paper, but recently I got a computer and a program called Stitch Grapher from Compucrafts (Box 326, Lincoln Center, MA 01773; 508-263-8007), available for IBM and Apple II computers for $89.95. It's a wonderful and powerful tool. I can instantly move whole borders over a stitch or two to make proportions better, and I can lengthen or shorten an element to see if it helps the overall design.

Simple geometrics—One of my favorite design elements, honed down to its simplest form, is the dotted line and its variations. I've used dotted lines in almost all my designs. Combined with plain lines on each side, or by itself, the dotted line is great for linking other borders. Of course some border designs can be put together with others without a break to become larger designs, but this is rare. A running dotted line can be dramatically changed if the color values of the dot and the ground are reversed from light to dark and vice versa.

You could stop here and make a lovely rug just by using dotted lines in stripes across an entire rug, but soon you'd want to turn corners to make rectangular or square elements, like the corners in the photo at right, above. You need to be a bit compulsive on one hand and then be able to turn around and be very forgiving in order to resolve corners and edges. You could spend hours or even days with graph paper, working out borders so the corners all meet and turn perfectly. If it's vitally important to you, by all means do it, but I'd rather spend time stitching, so I try to solve the corners

as I come to them. I think an occasional imperfect join adds interest to the overall design and is probably not visible to anyone else. Besides, the gods of pleasing design tend to frown on the perfect, and after all, you can go back with a needle to pull out stitches. I pulled out the whole border on my 6-ft. x 9-ft. "Red Rug" (originally it wasn't red), and when my finger healed, I was very glad that I had done so.

Nongridded designs—You don't have to design on graph paper; there are other powerful tools around. Most towns have copy shops or office-supply stores with sophisticated copy machines that offer the capacity to reduce and enlarge. Say you want to make a design with hearts and handprints, as quiltmakers often do. You could trace your hand or a child's hand on a piece of paper and then make a bold outline of it or fill it in. You might want several sizes of the same thing. Make many copies, cut them out, and move them around on a sheet of paper the size of the rug. Brown wrapping paper is good for this. Make hearts of several sizes by folding a piece of paper in half and cutting out half-hearts.

Move things around until you find a placement that pleases you; then trace the pieces in place. You don't have to use all of them. Sometimes simplifying is better, and you have to design only one-quarter if your rug is symmetrical. Then all you need to do is place your design under the canvas and trace the outline directly onto the canvas with a permanent-ink marker (Sharpie pens work perfectly) or acrylic paint. Anything else is too risky. Once again, remember to mark on the intersections; that's where the stitches will go.

Quilt designs in general are a ready-made treasure trove of motifs and overall design solutions. A geometric design like Nine-

Basketweave and half-cross are interchangeable for solid areas, but to keep all the stitches slanting in the same direction, you make diagonal lines of color in basketweave (above) when stitching against the slant, and in split stitch (below) when stitching with the slant.

The underside of this rug corner shows how the folded-under edges are worked into the stitching as the top is worked.

Needlepoint-rug stitches
Basketweave

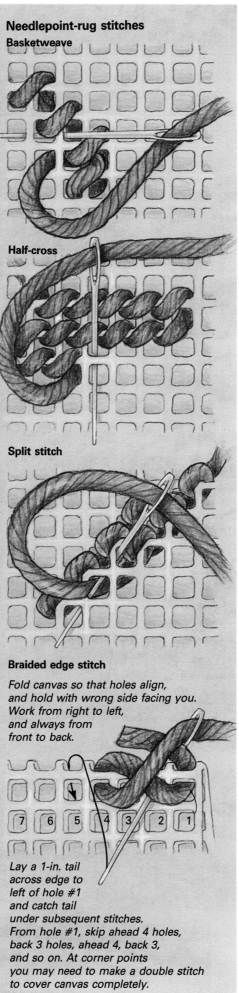

Half-cross

Split stitch

Braided edge stitch

Fold canvas so that holes align, and hold with wrong side facing you. Work from right to left, and always from front to back.

7 6 5 4 3 2 1

Lay a 1-in. tail across edge to left of hole #1 and catch tail under subsequent stitches. From hole #1, skip ahead 4 holes, back 3 holes, ahead 4, back 3, and so on. At corner points you may need to make a double stitch to cover canvas completely.

Patch or Log Cabin would be easy to work on canvas. You could work with pure color or put pattern inside the geometric areas.

Color is a very personal thing, and we all have strong preferences, so I'll just advise you not to use an excess of darks and lights. Use as many medium tones as you can to keep your designs from being too harsh, but don't be afraid to use occasional light or strong colors to spark the design.

Supplies and stitch basics—You don't need many supplies to make a rug—just canvas, yarn, and a needle. You can make a rug out of many different sizes and weights of yarn and canvas, as long as they're matched. The yarn must be thick enough so the stitches completely cover the canvas. Paternayan's and Halcyon's wool rug yarns are matched to #5 (5 holes/in.) canvas. I use these yarns interchangeably; both have colors I couldn't do without. I always get double, or lock-mesh, canvas (see photos at left) because monocanvas (single canvas) wouldn't be as stable for the simple, flat stitch I use.

The quality of your materials is of highest importance. Since you'll be putting a lot of time into your rug, you'll want it to last. A case in point is once again the "Red Rug." It has been on my floor since 1971 and has been offended by several puppies and a cat with a delicate stomach. Candle wax was spilled on it at a party. Three kids were raised on it, and it has all cleaned up. (The wax came off by being frozen and picked away at, then ironed and blotted.) The rug wouldn't have lasted a year under that kind of abuse if I had used Orlon or other synthetic yarns or even poor-quality wool. Top-quality rug wool is especially hard—it's too hard for clothing—and it has a lovely, non-reflective sheen that can't be duplicated.

I was even nervous about using cotton canvas instead of the linen recommended in older books, but I couldn't find linen anyway, and it has held up wonderfully.

One drawback of working with the highly processed, dry rug wool is that sometimes it seems to draw the oils out of your skin instead of making your hands soft, as hand-spun yarn often does. I keep Band-Aids and a good hand cream (I like Neutrogena) among my supplies. Before going to bed, I sometimes put cream on the abused areas of my fingers and cover them with Band-Aids—a small inconvenience for the growing design coming to life on my canvas.

You can also make rugs with #10 mesh and full-strand Persian yarn. Naturally, you can make more intricate designs in the #10 mesh, but a large rug could take a lifetime to complete. I wouldn't suggest anything larger than 3 ft. x 5 ft. For that matter, for your first rug, even in the #5 mesh, I wouldn't suggest anything larger than that, and smaller would be better because you'd get quicker results. Moreover, you seldom do your best work on the first rug; everything is a learning process.

I'm more interested in color and pattern than in texture, so I almost always use the basketweave or half-cross stitch (top two drawings, facing page), but the half-cross is my favorite. You do both stitches from the right side of the canvas, except for tying off the beginnings and ends of the yarn. Half-cross is the best stitch for straight lines because it won't distort the canvas, as long as you keep the stitches slanting in the same direction throughout the rug. The last thing you want to worry about is blocking a large rug that has become a parallelogram because you used the Continental stitch, a common stitch for regular needlepoint.

For years I worried that half-cross, compared with basketweave, didn't leave enough padding on the back to keep the rug from wearing thin and the stitches from breaking, but none of my rugs shows signs of wear. The half-cross also uses a lot less yarn, so the materials are more economical. Paternayan rug yarn covers #5 canvas at the rate of 2¾ sq. in./yd. when stitched in half-cross. Depending on the brand, ¼ lb. of rug wool (the smallest amount you can buy) averages about 66 yd., so ¼ lb. should cover 1¼ sq. ft. in half-cross. In theory, this means that a 3-ft. x 5-ft. rug should take about 3 lb., but you'll probably need 4 lb.

For large, solid-color areas, I almost prefer basketweave because of the pleasant rhythm that you develop as you stitch and because you don't have to turn your work as often, but only if I have plenty of yarn. Basketweave covers only 2 sq. in./yd.

The other stitch I need, the split stitch, or backstitch, is for single diagonal lines of color, which I'm very fond of. To always keep the stitches going in the same direction, you must use two different stitches, depending on whether your lines are parallel to, or opposing, the direction of the stitches. When you're going with the flow, use the split stitch (top photo, facing page); when you're going against it, use basketweave (center photo, facing page).

Except for the braided stitch (bottom photo and drawing, facing page), which is used for rug edges, these are all the stitches you'll need. As in any other needle art, you have to learn the right tension for your stitches, and you must also learn to be consistent. I try not to stitch when I'm angry, but sometimes that's just what I want to do!

Preparing and handling the canvas—Once you have the canvas in your hands and have determined the size and shape of your rug, divide it equally in quarters by folding the canvas in half and then in half again and marking the middle threads and outside edges. If you're using a graph, it will probably be divided into ten-square blocks; hence, it's a good idea to mark the canvas off every ten threads along the centerlines so it's easier to follow your chart.

Position your design so you have at least four intersections, or mesh, of canvas be-

All the techniques of rugmaking can be used for making smaller pieces, like this wall-mounted design done on #14 canvas, which Dieringer completely improvised, with the exception of the computer-designed central motif.

yond the outside borders of the design. They get folded under (bottom photo, facing page), and you'll stitch through both layers to bind them. The corners will have four layers. You must stitch through them carefully. Leave two mesh unstitched all around the outside edge; you stitch these with the braided stitch to make a sturdy edge anytime after you've stitched the border.

To control the bulk of one large piece of canvas and simplify the times when you need to flip it over to anchor your thread, use large safety pins or stitch holders from your knitting basket to hold the excess canvas. Fold up the areas you're not stitching and loosely pin them together. On large rugs, I sometimes work on the middle portions in bed with the worked parts rolled up over my legs and lap, working all the stitches from the top, and sometimes I just hold the whole thing loose in my lap, as I'm doing in the right-hand photo on p. 51. It's not as awkward as it might seem.

Working in sections—Historically, many needlepoint rugs were made in sections. For the best integrity of the rug it should be done in one piece, but canvas is often available up to only 40 in. wide in #5 mesh and 54 in. wide in #10 mesh; thus, to

make a larger rug, piecing is necessary. Many people still make medallion-type rugs a single medallion at a time. My "Red Rug" is pieced down the middle. I counted the stitches and matched the design and then went back to count them over and over, and I still held my breath when the time came to sew the two pieces together.

There are two ways to put the pieces together. When I made the big rug, I stitched up to, but not including, the last mesh from the selvage on both sides. Then I joined it by folding under the selvages and stitching through the two edge mesh, one on top of the other, as if they were one mesh, following the design. I had left out the center stitch when I worked the rug for just this purpose. This is fine for a single join, but it's better to overlap four or five mesh and stitch through double. This makes a more invisible join and is stronger.

To work squares of needlepoint to assemble later, I also use the overlap method. Whether you overlap or fold back, each corner will have four layers to stitch through. You must take great care to keep your canvas edges in good condition while stitching. Don't be chintzy about leaving wide enough edges for joining. Tape all the raw edges while you're working, and check to see that your stitches are in the same direction as the rest of the rug each time you start a new square. Canvas is woven on looms like any other fabric, and it may not be exactly square, or on grain, so don't rotate the grain of the canvas sections, or you'll have a permanently warped surface when you try to put everything together.

Blocking—I had one customer who took a steam iron to her work in progress every few days. Steam-ironing the canvas once or twice is fine, but eventually it will take all the sizing out of the canvas, and then there is nothing to help hold the shape. It's best to work loosely enough so that there is no warping and no need to block. But not everyone heeds this advice, so when you're finished stitching and you have a parallelogram, here's what to do. Find a wooden surface that you don't mind putting nail holes into or getting wet. A piece of plywood or porch floor is perfect. I've also successfully used Homosote sheets, which are like heavy-duty bulletin boards.

Mark the outside dimensions of your rug on this surface, making sure that your lines are square. Use stainless-steel pushpins or T-pins or rustproof nails, and stretch your dry rug square on this surface. Some say that this should be done wrong side up because if there is going to be any bleeding of colors, the wicking action will cause the worst to come to the surface. I think it's merely a matter of preference. Just be sure to use enough pins so your edges don't have loops or swags. Then, using a spray bottle, wet your rug, making sure the canvas underneath gets moistened because, when it dries, the sizing in it will help hold the rug square. Drying time will vary with the moisture in the air, but generally two days is a good amount of time.

Like some of New York's most experienced rug dealers, I don't believe in endless efforts to make a rug stay perfectly square. The most I expect from it is that it stay flat. Changes in temperature and humidity throughout the life of a rug will unavoidably cause it to move, shift, stretch, and shrink, and I don't believe you should fight it. For the same reason, I don't line or coat the rug's underside. Just put it on your floor in a place of honor, and enjoy a rug that is uniquely yours. Don't forget to sign and date it, as it may outlast you!

Making pillows and framed pieces—If you'd rather work small and not for the floor, you can use the same techniques (see the photos below and on p. 53). You'll just need finer canvas and wool, and you'll have to leave at least 2 in. of unworked canvas at each edge and work about ½ in. all around the design in a neutral solid color so there's some margin for error when you frame or stitch around it. Framing should be done professionally, as should the final blocking, and the framer may want to lace the edges to a backing. I decided to frame most of my pillows after I'd finished them, so I regret having trimmed off the wide seam allowances. In fact, I've even had to sew more mesh back on once or twice.

For pillows, I like to make a firm piping and machine-stitch around it with a zipper foot after sandwiching it between front and back. Sewing machines will probably balk at #5 rugs, but #10 and finer usually don't present problems. Because I don't plan to wash the pillow top, I sew up all four sides, wrong sides together, leaving a wide opening on one end, which I stitch by hand after I turn and stuff the pillow. Like most aspects of needlepoint rugmaking, nothing could be simpler. ☐

Beverly Dieringer, the owner of Dieringer's Arts and Antiques in Bethel, CT, is currently working on needlepoint rugs and designs.

Further reading

The following books contain charts and designs that you can use with or without the accompanying technical information, most of which is rather good. Those books that are out of print are available in libraries and used-book stores.

Kalish, Susan Schoenfeld. *Oriental Rugs in Needlepoint: 10 Charted Designs* (out of print). *Authentic Oriental rugs charted for needlepoint, mostly intended for finer than #5 canvas.*

Kerimov, Lyatif. *Folk Designs from the Caucasus for Weaving and Needlework.* New York: Dover Books, 1974. *One of many excellent Dover collections of charted designs, this book is perfect if you want to assemble authentic motifs into your own Oriental rug.*

Lane, Maggie. *Chinese Rugs Designed for Needlepoint* (out of print). *Lane's charts are inspired by Oriental art and are beautifully designed.*

Lane, Maggie. *Rugs and Wall Hangings.* New York: Charles Scribner's Sons, 1980.

Lane, Maggie. *Needlepoint by Design: Variations on Chinese Themes.* New York: Charles Scribner's Sons, 1981.

Mathews, Sibyl I. *Needle-Made Rugs.* New York: Dover Books, 1984. *This is an abbreviated version of my first, and favorite, how-to text. The out-of-print original is better.*

Schoenfeld, Susan. *Pattern Design for Needlepoint & Patchwork* (out of print). *This book is a thorough study of graphed geometric patterns, mostly allover and derived from Middle-Eastern artistic traditions.*

Small canvases, like these pillow tops on #10 canvas, are excellent for working out design ideas. They can be pieced together to form large rugs, or they can be mounted or stuffed individually.

Hand-Painted Charts

Choice cross-stitch florals from a collector's hoard

by Lilo Markrich

It was thanks to the simple and venerable cross-stitch that I discovered the ease of transferring a printed chart pattern from paper to cloth. I was on my last compulsory school-needlework project, a baby's romper with several kinds of fine seams, as well as decoration. Since there was no baby in the family, I had no intention of spending any more time on the project than necessary, so I took a shortcut. I chose a simple motif from one of the many color-printed DMC chart books for children's clothes. I basted a piece of cheap, cotton Penelope canvas (now known as waste canvas) across the yoke. Then I worked one cross-stitch for every printed square across the canvas, careful to stitch simultaneously through hole and cloth without catching any canvas thread. When I was finished, I used a pair of tweezers to pull away the basting and canvas threads. While my classmates were still struggling, my gaggle of ducklings marched across my romper's yoke.

Since then, my interest in pattern charts has grown. I'm intrigued by how time and again artists and craftsmen adapted designs to meet new needs and fashion preferences. My collection contains old-magazine clippings with black-and-white symbol charts typical of 19th-century thread promotions and color-printed charts for every conceivable domestic use.

But none is as appealing as the charming, hand-tinted, multishaded charts (see page 57) that were created in Berlin between the 1830s and 1860s, when the city was only the capital of Prussia and provincial compared with London and Paris. These patterns, produced and sold to meet local demand, were the work of artists who painted in the period's romantic spirit, rather than the work of designers who looked to French fashion books for ideas. They were the forerunners of a flood of pattern charts that later saturated the European needlework market until, at the end of the 19th century, the Arts and Crafts Movement labeled the work uncreative and unartistic.

The popular Berlin printed chart work enabled a woman to see in full color what she was about to stitch and helped her choose her colored threads. It was also instrumental in changing the nature of needlework, which had formerly been available to the affluent only. The style contributed to the rapid development of the needlework-supply industry, resulting in low-cost embroidery materials. By the end of the century, even the poorest woman could enjoy stitching something pretty for just a few pennies.

Aware of Berlin's growing demand for English embroidery wools and French tapestry canvases, European manufacturers capitalized on the fad. Taking into account that every woman knew how to work a cross-stitch, they developed a special double-thread, machine-sized, open-hole canvas, called Penelope, especially for chart work. It eliminated time-consuming thread counting. Special wools and cheap cotton were spun to encourage the use of the half cross-stitch as a means of cutting costs. The number of different canvases and threads increased quickly so that retailers could meet any request for fine, medium, or coarse canvas work in any price range. Thus, needlewomen could enlarge a design by working it on coarse canvas or reduce it dramatically by working it on fine mesh. Enlargement increased the amount and cost of materials but reduced working time. Working a chart on silk gauze with a few skeins of silk was time-consuming but relatively inexpensive. When manufacturers began to supply patterns, as well as instructions, to increase sales, it was a coming together of the ready-made, the affordable, and the easy—to the delight of millions.

The history of charts—The first European commercial charts in the 16th century were expensive woodcut books sold by printers to the embroidery trade or aristocratic establishments. They provided workshop owners with limited access to innovative embroidery designers' new styles, which could be copied, altered, modified, or reinterpreted. It was taken for granted that any buyer knew how to use them and that one black-marked square on the grid-ruled pattern page was equal to one stitch, loop, or pick. These charts were as useful a pattern device for a lacis, cross-stitch, or tent-stitch embroiderer as they were for a lacemaker or weaver.

In the 17th century, the new copperplate technique allowed for a far smaller pattern grid, which meant that a pattern designer had more squares available for larger and more ornate motifs. By 1660, a third tone was introduced, allowing greater emphasis on curvilinear form.

A century later, in Leipzig, Germany, hard- and soft-bound books for the wives and daughters of newly affluent men offered both charts and information about the latest French fashions, etiquette, and new accomplishments. The charts in these small "workbasket" books were no longer black and white; the small printed grid was subtly shaded with hand-painted motifs.

The most interesting aspect of the late-18th-century painted charts was the process by which an original design was reproduced. After an artist had drawn and then blocked out both design and colors on a previously printed piece of squared paper, each color was assigned a symbol. An engraver marked a squared-off plate with each delicate symbol in its correct location and number of squares. After printing, these symbol-marked black-and-white charts were turned over to the cheapest artistic labor—women, who colored each square as indicated. For the next hundred years, all hand-tinted charts were mass-produced this way.

Publishers were always searching for new designs, but toward the end of the 18th century, instead of looking to Paris, Voss and Co., of Leipzig, purchased the more eye-catching and better-painted Berlin charts of one Mr. Phillipson. His studio offered neoclassic designs and themes: arabesques, flower-and-fruit compositions, flower-filled vases, olive-branch swags, birds, funerary monuments, landscapes, and borders, which were widely used for carré (square, presumably bead) knitting. They were also popular for canvas work, a much more economical pastime than bead knitting. Borders were used above and below floral designs, which were generally worked in tent stitch or petit point on silk gauze. Phillipson's charts were the first internationally known "Berlin" charts.

With its textile industry and access to embroidery yarns and its porcelain factory and resulting surplus of artists, Berlin could easily meet the growing demand for canvas, wool, and designers. Its sudden rise in population and the expansion of the middle class in the early 19th century also provided a huge source of cheap, genteel labor—the wives and daughters of military officers, civil servants, and professionals.

The opportunity to discreetly color charts at home was one of the few ways these women could alleviate financial strain without loss of respectability. Viewed in this light, the early Berlin charts are not just pretty patterns but evidence that, for women, embroidery was as much an ill-paying trade for the underprivileged as it was a romantic pastime for the well-to-do. As the latter grew tired of counting squares and holes, women were also hired to lay chart-matching horizontal threads across canvas, today known as trammé, so that the affluent stitcher could, without counting, cross these threads with matching yarn, as shown in the photo below.

Another important aspect of Berlin work, besides its ease and affordability, was that the designs and materials lent themselves to new concepts in home furnishings. In mid-19th-century Berlin, sturdy, quality furniture with simple lines became popular, in contrast to the earlier preference for imitations of elaborate French Court styles. This "Biedermeyer" style was the perfect foil for the new, colorful canvas work.

Eventually, the popularity of Berlin work was such that more was never enough, especially when it came to include a canvas-work reinterpretation of the old linen counted-thread work. Toward the latter part of the century, a new generation of sophisticated "art needlework" embroiderers considered Berlin work less creative and less artistic than other forms of needlework because of the repetitious use of tent stitch and cross-stitch. Among them was Lady Alford, who helped found the Royal School of Needlework, which also competed in the pattern and embroidery-wool business. William Morris and his friends created special designs for these aristocratic patrons, complete with stitch and color instructions. These kits were sometimes even prestarted.

Using charts—Charts offer us a chance to experiment with color by changing a prescribed tone or hue. I've used motifs from them here and there for weaving, knitting, and stitching. For me, charts are like cooking recipes: I can add, leave something out, combine; and instead of throwing out a failure, I just rip some stitches.

I approach charts with care only when I begin to transpose a design onto canvas or linen. I first mark canvas with pencil, and linen with sewing thread, drawing or stitching in the same number of square-containing blocks as the chart. This is a nuisance, but since I start in the bottom center and work the first row from the center to the left and right, I can build each segment of a motif on top of another, confident that I won't run out of room. I'm aware that this method is contrary to popular advice, but I get more dependable results with it.

Yet, when all is said and done, the true Berlin charts are the only ones I consider art, as opposed to decorative guidelines. Those early sprays, wreaths, and bouquets were painted not only with perfection but with an artist's eye. It's easy to understand that for women whose lives were restricted and demanding, seeing such stitched flowers growing under their hands enabled them to garden and dream in the privacy of their minds. And at the same time, they gained a sense of personal, creative achievement that their everyday lives rarely offered.

Lilo Markrich is a contributing editor of Threads. *Photo below by Sandra Markrich.*

Although the chart shows a footstool suitable for cross-stitch or needle-point, the unknown embroiderer worked it as a beaded needlepoint cushion. The unfinished needlepoint rug underneath shows evidence of trammé, which spares the needleworker the chore of following a chart.

LE GUIDE - SAJOU

Journal Spécial & Complet des Ouvrages de' Dames

Novembre 1851   N° II   12

Freestyle Embroidery
New images with traditional stitches

by Caroline Dahl

*a*bout nine years ago, coinciding with a reawakening of public interest in quilting and a personal dissatisfaction with my progress as a performing musician, I began thinking of needlework as something that might be fun to do. I sat down and taught myself sewing on a Pfaff 1222 that I had inherited from my mother. In the next few months, what had started out as a diversion became a consuming interest, as I experimented with hand-quilting, appliqué, needlepoint, and embroidery.

I immediately liked the idea of making things with cloth and thread, materials that are easy for me to manipulate, inexpensive, and easy to obtain at any corner sewing-supply store. I also enjoy working with my hands. I'm a piano player and play in bands or work solo in San Francisco clubs. My hands are agile from years of playing music, which makes the intricate work of embroidery both easy and fun. I'm lucky to have good eyesight, too, and I'm fast and accurate (and well practiced), which enables me to see results quickly.

My first interest was in quilting. I made full-size quilts (81 in. by 96 in.) with lots of piecework, appliqué, and embroidery. After about two years, I found I was enjoying the embroidery more than the piecing and quilting. I wanted more of a solid, overall embroidered look rather than just embroidery stitched over seams, outlining appliquéd forms, or worked in small isolated areas as on some of my quilts. Since then, I have been embroidering framed pictures, Christmas-tree ornaments, neckties, pins, purses, and clothing.

I enjoy embroidery because of its lush texture and color and its uncomplicated nature—it doesn't require many tools or any machines. I like it better than needlepoint because it's not confined to a grid, and so the designs can be freer, thicker, and less geometric. I like it better than quilting because it's less cumbersome—you don't need a large frame, and you can work anyplace. I move around a lot and take as many vacations as possible, so I like the fact that all the materials I need can fit into a paper bag.

Materials—To start a piece of embroidery, I assemble these materials: plain white muslin, embroidery floss, embroidery needles, and a hoop. I use regular, inexpensive cotton muslin, making sure that there are no flaws in the area to be worked, and DMC cotton floss. The better the floss, the easier and faster it is to work. DMC colors are consistent, brilliant, and colorfast. The texture is smooth, and the floss lies evenly on the muslin. It twists and tangles less than other flosses and has few flaws or rough spots. The only drawback is its cost, but when you consider that floss is your only expense, it's bearable.

I usually use all six strands of floss when stitching. For details, I sometimes use just two or three, and for a very thick satin stitch, I use 12. I cut the floss to lengths of about 14 in. Strands longer than 14 in. will tangle; shorter strands are good only if you need a little bit of a specific color for a detail or small area. If the strands separate from each other or get twisted while I'm working, I just hold the piece upside down and let the threaded needle free-fall. The floss straightens itself out.

I use a wooden hoop 4 in. in diameter. To see what suits you best, experiment with a few sizes. My hands are small, so a small hoop is easiest for me to hold, although I have to reposition it around the piece more often than I would a larger hoop.

Ideas—Of course, the most important thing is the idea for the piece. If I'm about to spend hours and hours of work on something, I feel the result should be completely my own work, or else it's a waste of time. That's why I was never interested in working a preexisting design. To me, the designing is the most fun part. By designing, I mean coming up with the imagery as well as new stitches or new and interesting ways of using old stitches, and then putting it all together in a final piece.

My imagery comes from various sources: from something I did or read or dreamed, from somebody else's idea, from an exciting trip to an exotic place. A favorite subject is my Bolivian parrot, Skwabby. I also like interior scenes with angles made by intersecting floors, ceilings, and walls. Dogs, imaginary creatures, and entertainment-related imagery frequently appear in my work. I also like the humor in putting words and pictures together.

Once I have the idea for the piece, I make a rough drawing and use felt-tip pens to decide on the colors. I neaten up the drawing—or make another one—tape it to a flat surface with an ironed piece of muslin over it, and then trace the drawing onto the muslin with a pencil. At this point, I remove the tape, crank up the stereo another notch (I always work with music on), put the drawing away, find a well-lighted spot, and I'm ready to start stitching.

With the large part of the hoop over the muslin and the small part under, I posi-

Caroline Dahl's Bolivian parrot Skwabby (above) has been the inspiration for many of her embroideries. Like the real thing, his sombrero is decorated with sequins. On the facing page, Dahl models a jacket with an embroidered appliqué, also her own design.

Outline stitch

Working from left to right, keep the floss above the needle and make a series of small stitches at a slight angle. Start each stitch at the midpoint of, and slightly below, the previous stitch so that the stitches lie close together.

Satin stitch

Lay a series of long, parallel stitches close to each other, without overlapping them, to fill in the image area.

French knot

Bring the needle up from the wrong side of the fabric, and wrap the floss around it 2 or 3 times. Holding the strand taut, reinsert the needle into the fabric close to where it came up and pull it through. The more times the floss is wrapped, the larger the knot.

Couching

Knot one end of the couching floss and bring it up through the fabric at the top of the line of stitching; sink the other end into the fabric at the bottom. With a second threaded needle, secure the couching with small, even stitches.

Long-and-short stitch

Outline the image area with a row of parallel stitches, staggered in length. Fill in the rest of the image, staggering the position and/or length of alternate stitches in each row.

Fringe stitch

Make a French knot, and start a short stitch perpendicular to it. Do not finish the stitch by bringing the needle back into the fabric. Instead, cut the end and secure it with a seed stitch. Make fringe by separating the strands with a needle.

Streamer stitch

The streamer stitch is a variation on couching. Instead of laying the couching floss flat, snake it across the surface of the fabric to form curves and loops. Then secure the floss with French knots or seed stitches.

Chain stitch

Bring the needle up through the fabric and reinsert it close to where it came out, forming a loop. Bring the needle back up through the fabric a short distance below where it entered, over the loop, and pull the floss through.

Cross stitch

Make diagonal stitches on the right side of the fabric to form small x's. This stitch can be worked individually or in a continuous row.

Buttonhole stitch

Make a series of parallel vertical stitches, bringing the needle up and over the loop of floss each time to form a straight line of interlocking horizontal stitches.

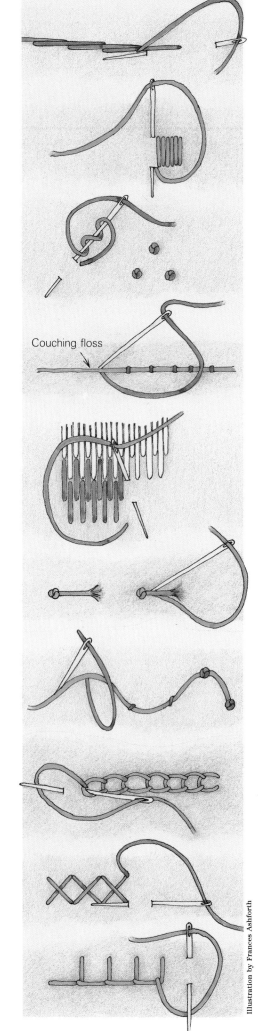

Couching floss

Illustration by Frances Ashforth

tion the hoop anywhere on the design. You don't have to start in one corner, as in needlepoint. Make sure the tension is tight enough to keep the fabric taut, but not so tight that it distorts the design. If you avoid excessive pulling of the thread and fabric when stitching, the embroidery should not need much blocking.

Stitches—I mainly use the outline, satin, and long-and-short stitches, the French knot, and couching. Sometimes I cover large areas with solid French knots to give the piece a chenille look. I also use the chain, cross, seed, and buttonhole stitches. A book such as *The Encyclopedia of Needlework* is useful if you get stuck in the experimentation stage or need help coming up with new stitches.

I've devised a "streamer stitch," which consists of a vertical cascade of floss secured every 1½ in. or so by a French knot, and a "fringe stitch"—my variation on a French knot. To make the fringe stitch in a rug, for example, I make a French knot on the border of the rug. Then I bring the needle up from underneath the muslin, immediately on the side of the knot farthest from the rug's border. I make a short stitch at a right angle to the knot, but instead of completing the stitch by going back down into the fabric, I cut the floss about ⅛ in. away from the French knot and secure it to the piece with a small seed stitch. I fan out the cut floss a bit beyond the seed stitch with the point of the needle. I frequently use a fringe stitch over other embroidery stitches.

In "One Wild Party," I used streamer stitches across the surface of the piece. I cut several lengths of different-colored floss, most longer than the height of the piece. I threaded and knotted the end of one length of floss and brought the needle up through the muslin at the very top, or near the top, of the piece. I gently snaked the floss back and forth across the surface, and with a second needle threaded with a contrasting color, I secured the streamer at 1-in. to 1½-in. intervals with French knots and seed stitches. Then at the bottom, for the first and only time, I put the first needle back into the muslin and knotted the streamer floss on the wrong side of the piece. This stitch can also be done over other embroidery stitches.

When couching, I also use two threaded needles. The first needle comes up through the material at one end of the area to be stitched and goes back into it at the end, while the other one secures the first thread at intervals with seed stitches. For decoration and pattern, I frequently put stitches on top of stitches in contrasting colors—straight or cross stitches on long-and-short stitches or French knots on chain stitches, for example.

As highlights, I often use sequins, buttons, metallic threads, or beads of glass, ceramic, metal, or plastic. Local sewing and novelty stores and flea markets have a wealth of these things from which to choose. I especially like how beads catch the light, and they give the embroidery a nontraditional look, a harder texture, and often the illusion of depth. If the bead has a hole in its center, I sew it to the piece with two or three strands of DMC floss in a single straight stitch or secure it with a French knot by bringing the needle up through the muslin and through the bead, making the knot and going back down through the bead and muslin. Then I pull the knot down on top of (not through) the bead. I use a smaller needle for the bead-work, as the eye of the embroidery needle is too big for most beads. If the bead doesn't have a hole, I simply glue it to the piece with Elmer's Glue-All. I frequently use beads in areas where I would embroider seed stitches or French knots, just to vary the texture. I used sequins on Skwabby's sombrero because that's what real sombre-ros are decorated with. Beads, sequins, stitches on top of stitches, painted paper leaves (used on several "Skwabby" pieces), fringe, streamers, and embroidered words all add up to the comfortably cluttered look I prefer. That's just what my apart-ment looks like.

I use bright colors more than muted ones. Black, yellow, and white are very

Photos this page by Caroline Dahl

dramatic colors to me, and I use them to outline shapes. I try to include lots of dif-ferent colors in one piece and aim for con-trast—dark colors next to light colors, light outlines on dark shapes, etc. I also contrast colors within stitches, as in streamer and cross stitches and couching. I don't use variegated floss, because the color change is too random. Sometimes I do shading, and sometimes I do solid areas of color. I stitch large areas of a light color toward the end of the project to minimize the chances of their getting dirty.

I work until I get tired of it, usually any-where from about 15 minutes to two hours at a stretch. Often I have two pieces in pro-gress at the same time, and sometimes I have nothing in progress.

Finishing—My pieces range in size from about 6 in. by 10 in. to about 26 in. by 22 in. I prefer a small piece because it's easy to manipulate and doesn't take forever to finish. I would like to do a large piece, but sometime in the future.

I block the finished embroidery on a large, smooth, wooden board. I leave about a 3-in.-wide margin of muslin on all sides. I get the piece thoroughly wet, stretch it a little, alternating vertical and horizontal directions, and then square it up with hammer and nails. As I work, I secure all

The piano in this detail from "Jerry Lee's Dog" (above) has decorative straight stitches on long-and-short stitches. In "One Wild Party" (below), Dahl used beads and se-quins to vary the texture. The streamer stitch is her own variation on couching.

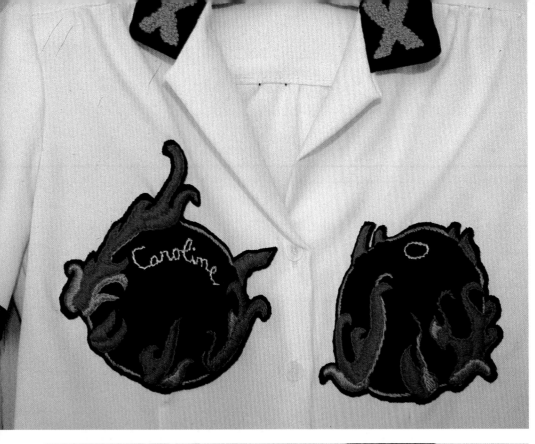

my stitches on the back of the piece with knots or backstitches. The backs are always covered with fabric, or with cardboard if the piece is to be framed. I usually have a metal or wooden frame cut to order, or I find an old frame at a flea market and frame the piece myself. When pieces have cloth-covered or multiple-opening mats, I take them to my favorite frame shop, Dow and Frosini, in Berkeley.

I don't use glass to protect pieces that have been framed. I did at first, but I found that it took too much away from the richness of the work. Instead, I now spray the piece with Scotchgard, which leaves no residue when it dries and does not affect the colors.

Sometimes I embroider directly onto clothing, but I also appliqué large, circular embroidered patches, using embroidery stitches instead of regular sewing stitches to attach the patches to the garment. Often I combine both techniques, as I did in the bowling shirt shown at left.

I make the garments as well as embroider them. First I make the appliqué patch, leaving a 2-in.-wide margin around it, and then I assemble the back of the garment. Next, I fold under ½ in. of the muslin, center the patch on the garment, baste it, and attach it with six strands of embroidery floss and a ½-in.-wide satin stitch. This leaves a neat, large circle of satin stitches on the wrong side of the garment, which you may or may not want to cover. After all the embroidery is done on, or applied to, the pieces, I finish the garment.

When I started my first embroidery, I took an experimental approach. I examined other embroidery and worked according to how it looked as though the stitches had been done, rather than learning a step-by-step method from a how-to-do-it book. I like to see results immediately, if not sooner, and I didn't have any books to refer to at the time. Also, because I'm left-handed, I'm used to jumping into things instead of reading instructions or following diagrams, which are always geared to right-handed people. Later, when I started conducting workshops, I looked at books like *The Encyclopedia of Needlework* to see if I was working in the most efficient way and to better explain the stitches to my students. Another book I liked a lot was Jacopetti and Wainwright's *Native Funk and Flash*, a colored picture book primarily of California craftwork and craftspeople. Although now somewhat dated, it was a great resource book for me, at the time still living in Kentucky and not yet having been out to the West Coast. I think the best approach in the beginning is whatever is most comfortable for you, either experimenting or following instructions from a book, and being open to what other people are doing and how they are doing it. □

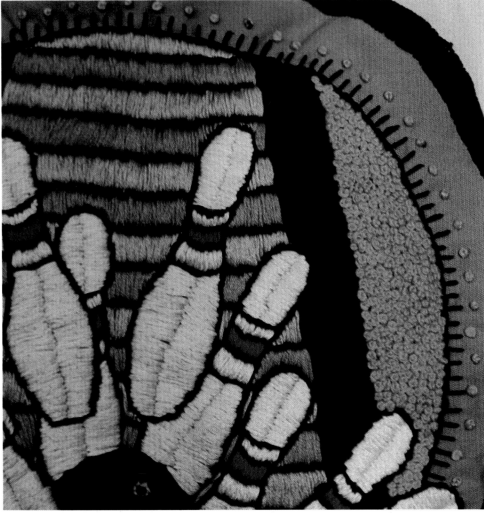

Dahl adds embroidery by stitching directly onto the garment fabric, or she attaches an embroidered appliqué. In the top photo, two 4¼-in.-dia. embroidered bowling balls are centered, pinned, and basted to the shirt front, and their edges are covered with a deeply overlapping outline stitch. Small embroidered x's are applied in like manner to the collar. The flames at the lower thirds of the balls, extending onto the shirt, are embroidered directly onto both the appliquéd balls and the shirt fabric. In the bottom photo, an embroidered patch about 12 in. in diameter is appliquéd to the back with ½-in.-wide satin stitches.

Caroline Dahl is a musician and textile artist living in San Francisco, CA.

Caroline's Triangular Purse

1. This purse is made from four pieces of embroidery: two circular pieces and two roughly triangular pieces, with the shorter sides rounded. Trace paper patterns of the shapes onto muslin, and embroider all four pieces. (The design in the photo is done in French knots and satin, outline, and long-and-short stitches.) Cut out the embroidery, leaving a 1-in.-wide margin of muslin around the edges.

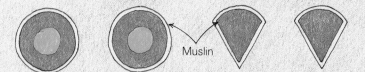

2. Position the embroidered muslin on black material, and then cut the black material 2 in. larger than the muslin. Turn under ½ in. of the muslin, and appliqué the embroidery to the black material with ½-in.-wide satin stitches. (You could embroider directly on the black material instead of the muslin, but it is easier on the eyes to work on a white background.)

3. Cut four pieces of heavyweight interfacing about ½ in. smaller on all sides than the paper patterns used to cut out the muslin. Baste the interfacing to the black material on the wrong sides. Fold 2 in. of the black material over the interfacing. Make sure that the material lies as flat and smooth as possible over the interfacing; overlap where necessary. Then pin and baste the black material to the interfacing on all four pieces.

4. To shape the pieces into a purse, fold each of the circles in half, fit one inside the other with the flat sides perpendicular, and pin the points of intersection. Then with black sewing thread and invisible stitches, sew the semicircles together where they intersect at the front and back.

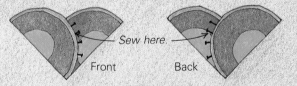

5. Pin and sew the triangles to the intersections of the semicircles on the inside of the purse, curved sides up.

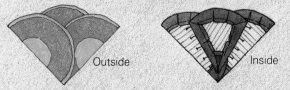

6. Embroider four circles of muslin about 1¾ in. in diameter, back the pieces with black material, and overcast the edges by machine. Sew the small circles to the purse at the front and back where the tops of the triangles meet the semicircles. (The ends of the handle will be hidden between the purse and the lining behind these circles.)

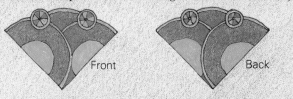

7. To make the lining, cut two triangles of black material slightly larger than the purse, and machine-sew the side seams together. Fit the lining into the purse, fold over the raw edge about ½ in., and then pin it to the purse.

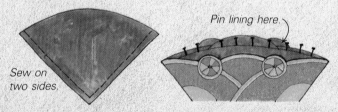

8. To make the handle, warp a table loom or warping frame 21 times with embroidery floss, in three groups of seven strands. Make one group another color. Wrap the strands with floss to form three spirals 22 in. long. For a shoulder bag, make a longer handle.

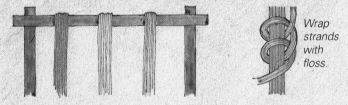

9. Cut the spirals off the loom and knot all the ends. Braid the three spirals together, and secure the braid with a few hand stitches at each end. Sew one end of the braid to the purse at the inside of one small circle. Sew the other end of the braid to the other side of the purse diagonally across from where the first end was fastened. Sew the top of the lining to the purse, over the handle ends, with black thread and invisible stitches, and then remove the pins.

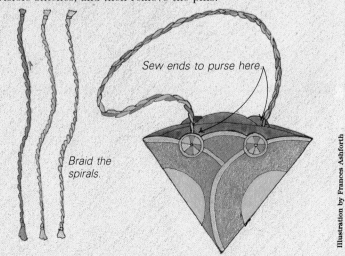

Illustration by Frances Ashforth

Decorative Ribbon Work

Folding and stitching methods for turning fabric into flights of fancy

by Candace Kling

What are they?" That's what friends would ask when they saw my corkboard full of decorative-ribbon samples back in 1980. Some of the folds were as complicated as origami. I had no idea how they were made, but then it occurred to me that if the work existed, someone must have already taught someone else how to do it.

I started my research at the library, where I found treasures in old sewing books under the heading "Decoration." I discovered millinery books and 19th- and early-20th-century women's periodicals: *Vogue, Delineator, Harper's Bazaar, Ladies' Home Companion, Peterson's Magazine.* After poring over 30,000 pages of *Godey's Lady's Books* in the "Work Department" section, I found beautifully etched illustrations with clear diagrams. (Although tempted, I didn't get sidetracked by ads for corsets, hair jewelry, candies and cookies, perfumes, and elixirs and balms, not to mention articles about suffragettes, actresses, society women, politicians, and kings.)

When I first set out on this quest, I naïvely expected to find instruction for the samples that I already had. I discovered few of them. Instead, I found hundreds more, with names, definitions, history, and whole new categories and subcategories with endless variations.

There is a pleasure and a satisfaction in discovery through research, and in being able to share it. Although there are hundreds of techniques for ribbon work, I will explain three here—quilling, a folding technique, and ruching and gauging, stitching and gathering techniques—which can be used as edgings and trims for hats, shoes, garments, jewelry, or as surface treatments.

Folding

Quilling is soft pleating. When it comes to holding up against the test of time, quills won't head the list. They're hard to store and nearly impossible to press once crushed. Despite this, they're my favorite form of vintage embellishment. It is an adventure to make them, to watch the transformation of a flat strip into a complex, three-dimensional form. I derive satisfaction from just holding it in my hand, watching the light catch the folds. Quills seem to have "old-fashioned" built into them.

In the 18th century, quilling involved laying wet, starched fabric under and over feather quills and letting it dry to shape. By the mid-19th century, it referred to intricate box, knife, and accordion pleats. Single or multiple pleats are stacked, tacked, and lifted to form fan and rosette shapes. Some are pressed; others retain their soft, rounded form. This technique gobbles up yardage. You may need anywhere from three to nine (or more) times your length in ribbon. Grosgrain works well for this style of ribbon work because you can see the grain and easily make a straight pleat. (Use ribbon 1½ in. or wider until your hands become accustomed to the process.)

Single quills—To make single quills, fold a length of ribbon into box pleats (see drawing, facing page). To create a soft, rounded effect, the top of the box pleat, that is, the distance from fold to fold, shouldn't be as long as the ribbon is wide. If the top of the box is too long, the quill will remain flat when it's lifted. For a lively fold, try two-thirds to three-quarters the width of the ribbon. You can measure the pleats or eyeball them, as I do. To make the first half of the pleat, roll the ribbon into an S-curve. As you work, secure the boxes with Duck Bill clips, Goody aluminum clips, or long bobby pins. Then roll the ribbon on the other side to make the other half of the pleat. Continue making box pleats whose sides butt up against one another. After you've made pleats for the full length of the ribbon, machine-stitch down the center of the ribbon, removing the clips as you go.

Now lift the open ends of each box so that they meet at the center, as shown in the top photo on the facing page. Pin these ends, and then stitch them in place. I use Stahl-Stecknadeln Hirsch No. 8 pins, extra long and very fine silk pins from West Germany (available from Handcraft From Europe, 1210 Bridgeway, Sausalito, CA 94965; [415] 332-1633). For an added decorative effect, you can stitch a bead or button where the fabric meets.

For a different effect, vary the space between each box, or add a thinner ribbon on top of the row of box pleats and stagger the placement of smaller boxes, as shown in

Candace Kling makes a two-ribbon variation of single quills. Her inspiring corkboard full of traditional and innovative ribbon samples is in the background.

To make a single quill, or a box pleat, make two sets of S-folds in the ribbon, and clip them in place (as shown in the drawing below). After you have folded the entire ribbon, stitch down the center. Lift the open sides of the pleats together, and pin them. Tack them, or add a bead or button for extra detail. Here, Kling has used a grosgrain ribbon, particularly good for folding box pleats because of the defined grain lines.

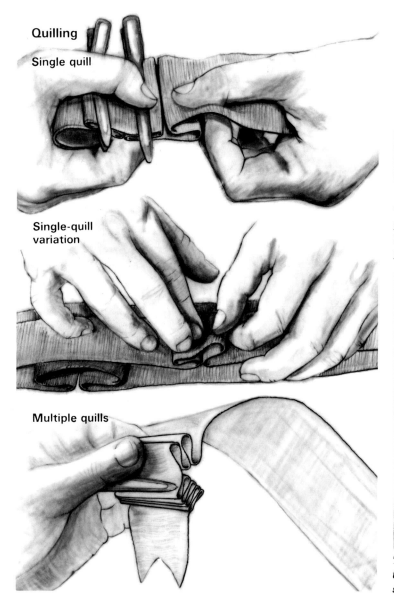

Quilling

Single quill

Single-quill variation

Multiple quills

To make a variation on the single quill (above photo and center drawing), make a length of box pleats with space between them. Center and pleat a second, thinner ribbon on top of the first. Lift the open pleats of both ribbons, pin them, and tack them with a small stitch. Vary the placement of the pleats of both ribbons to produce decorative effects.

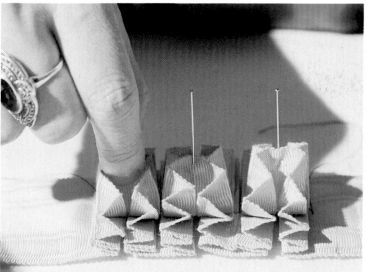

To make a multiple quill, fold the ribbon four or more times, and stitch the pleats down the center. The folds need to be narrower than for a single quill so that they will all fan open when you lift the top fold.

the center photo. Make the first row of box pleats as you would for a single row, but space the pleats approximately one and a half to two times the ribbon width apart rather than butt them together. Stitch them in place. Now center the second, thinner ribbon on top of the first, and secure smaller, alternate pleats with clips. Because there's so much ribbon between the box pleats, just sew down these boxes rather than the whole length of the ribbon. Pull the threads through and knot them on the back. Tack

the two ribbons together under the smaller boxes. Lift the open ends of the pleats in both ribbons to create the quills. You can leave the folds soft, as shown here, or you can press them before lifting for a different effect.

Several methods may be used to attach the finished quilling to a surface of a dress or hat. If you want removable trim, tack it in place under the pleats. For a more permanent application, sew the ribbons to each other and to the garment in one step, ma-

chine-stitching the ribbon center; then lift the folds and tack them in place.

Multiple quills—To create a fan effect, make multiple quills. The width of the pleats needs to be narrower than the width for single boxes in order for the pleats to fan open when lifted; if the pleats are too wide in proportion to the total ribbon width, you'll be able to lift only the top pleat.

When making multiple pleats, I find it best to hold the ribbon in my hand. Make

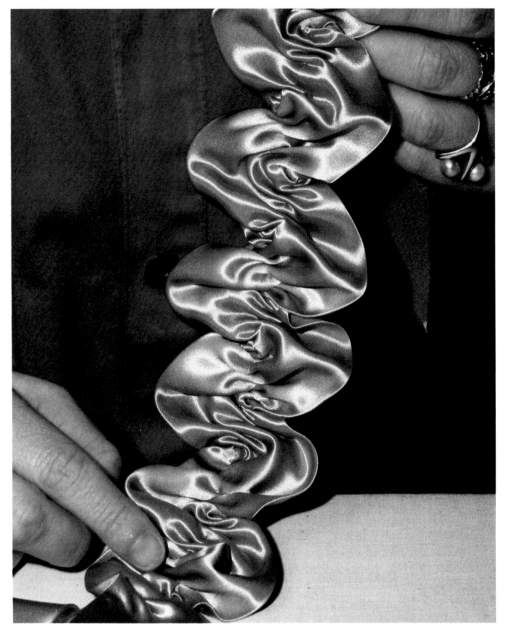

There's a ruched ribbon ruffle, a ruche that's freestanding, and a ruche that's been fluted. Confused? Zigzag gathers, snail and shell shirrings, the cross-gathered ruche, and the scallop band are all different names for the same technique.

But ruffles are the most common form of gathering. The more elaborate ones are ruches, marvels in the hands of 19th-century dressmakers. Ruches were often exaggerated in size, from massive to tiny. Different effects are created if they're made on the straight grain or bias, with a machine or by hand, with even or uneven stitches. They can be made into strip trims, which can be wound into rosettes. A variety of surface treatments can be created, too, when successive rows of ruching are made on yardage.

Ruching—To create a zigzag ruche on a bias tube, I start by sewing a tube twice the desired finished length, and I press the seam at the center back so the finished piece won't be bulky on either side. To lay out a zigzag stitching line, on the wrong side and along the edges of the tube, I mark off staggered intervals with Dritz disappearing ink, which vanishes in 24 hours. Most often, I use the full ribbon width as the interval, point to point, on the ribbon edge. You can vary the sharpness of the curve and the intervals for different effects. The smaller the interval between the points, the more the petals will cup under; the larger the interval, the more they'll ruffle.

After connecting the points with a straight edge, I sew the lines with a hand or machine running stitch. Hand stitching has a softer, more free-form effect, but several rows of parallel stitches will create a more visible center line. Machine stitches will always produce a more controlled look. Regardless of which thread you use in the top of your machine, use polyester thread in the bobbin, as it is less likely to break under the stress of gathering.

Next, I pull the thread ends as I condense the fabric. If you've used a double or triple row of stitching, make sure you pull all the threads evenly. Then work with the ruffles until they lie flat and are arranged the way you want them. Cup all the petal tips in one direction. Don't knot your threads until you've created a uniform effect. This tube can be sewn to the edge of a garment as a scalloped trim, since it bends easily around corners.

To make ruched half circles (top photo and drawing, facing page), mark off intervals on both sides of the ribbon equal to the ribbon width x 3¼. Lock the thread on the back with an overhand knot, and sew very close to the edge with a running stitch. At the end of the first interval, tightly gather the fabric and knot the thread to secure the gathers. Carry the thread across the back of the ribbon and knot it on the other side, without gathering the fabric, as shown in the top drawing on the facing page. Stitch the next interval, gather the

Ruching is a form of stitching and gathering. To ruche a bias tube with zigzag stitches, mark out points at intervals down the length of the ribbon—roughly twice the ribbon width—and connect them with a disappearing ink pen (top left). Hand- or machine-stitch along the line. Then pull the thread ends as you push the fabric to gather it for a loose or tight effect (top right). Arrange the ruffles so that they lie flat after you have secured the thread (above).

four folds, one quarter or less of the ribbon width, and clip them in place. Invert the ribbon and build the other side of the box pleat with four folds, as shown in the bottom drawing on page 65. Continue, butting boxes against one another. For pressed quills, lightly steam the clipped folds, stitch them as you remove the clips, and then re-press them. (Satin is springy, so you may need to steam every box as you work and stitch each box as it is completed.) After stitching down the center of the ribbon, lift the

open ends of each top pleat and pin them together. All the pleats below will fan open.

Stitching and gathering

I have new respect for the term *gathering*. There is plain gathering and simple shirring. There are poufs, puffs, tucks, and rucks. There is plain puffing and puff ruffling and fluffly double ruche! There are edge gathers and French gathers, which are also known as gauging. There are ruches that are twisted, corded, feathered, or poufed.

ribbon, and knot. Continue creating half circles for the length of ribbon you want.

Ruching can also be used on yardage (bottom drawing and center photo). A grid is stitched onto the fabric and then gathered two to one, that is, a 2-in. piece is condensed to 1 in. Dark velvet fabric ends up looking like poodle fur or Persian lamb.

Start with a piece of fabric two times the size of the finished piece, in all directions. Mark out two sets of stitching lines, one in a horizontal and the other in a vertical direction, to form a tic-tac-toe grid along the straight grains of the fabric. Back-tack the beginning of each row, and machine-stitch all the lines in one direction. When making the second set of stitch lines, be careful not to stitch over the intersecting lines of the first set; lift the presser foot and push the fabric so that the needle is beyond the intersection. To gather the fabric, pull all the bobbin threads for the lines that are traveling in the same direction. Use a different color bobbin thread to keep track of which threads to pull. Now pull the second set of bobbin threads.

You can create different effects by varying the amount of fabric you condense, the distance between the grid lines, and the straightness of the stitch lines. To keep the gathers from shifting, tack the fabric to a backing fabric (cut to size) at random intervals across the surface. Arrange the gathers evenly as you work.

Gauging—Gauging, another form of gathering, is used to shirr a large amount of fabric into a small space and reduce fullness, as in the waistline of voluminous skirts. It produces a decorative effect that looks like narrow folds of smocking.

Determine the height of the fold you want, and multiply by two. That number will be the interval at which you should place the individual running stitches. Mark and stitch along each edge of the ribbon, and make one or more rows in the center. (You may have to make a sample to decide how many rows of stitching are needed to control the folds. The smaller the folds, the more rows you'll need. A wide ribbon will also require more rows than a narrow one.) Make long stitches on the wrong side of the fabric and short ones on the right side, picking up only two or three threads. The stitches should be aligned under one another, and all should be the same length. After you've finished stitching, hold the ribbon in one hand, and pull all the thread ends at the same time and with the same tension, as shown at right.

More examples of artist Candace Kling's ribbon work are shown on pages 68-70. Kling often lectures about her ribbon research and gives workshops. She has also taught draping, mannequin making, and flat-pattern drafting at the California College of Arts and Crafts. Her work has been displayed at the Triton Museum of Art in Santa Clara, CA.

Ruching

Half-circles

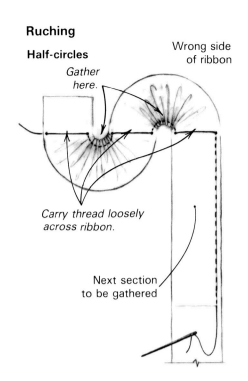

Wrong side of ribbon

Gather here.

Carry thread loosely across ribbon.

Next section to be gathered

Tic-tac-toe grid

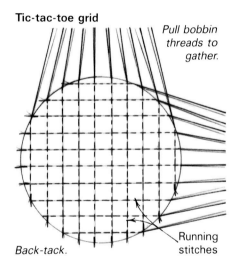

Pull bobbin threads to gather.

Back-tack.

Running stitches

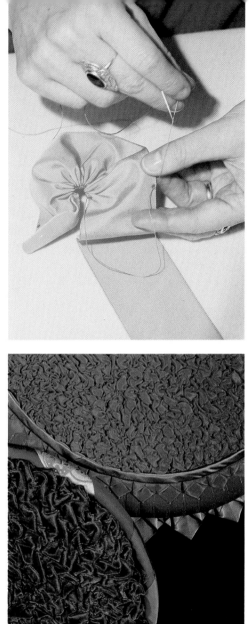

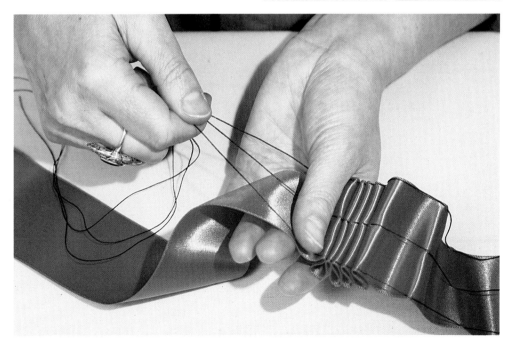

When making a half-circle ruche (top), stitch and gather one edge of the ribbon, carry the thread across the width of the ribbon, and secure it. Then gather the other side. Ruching also creates a textured surface (center). Gauging (bottom) will create narrow folds. Stitch at the center and each edge, and pull all the thread ends evenly. (Center photo by the author.)

20th-century ribbon sculptress Candace Kling

by Sandra Betzina

The sawtooth edges of "Flower in Time Lapse" (left), © 1981, are each folded from a separate square of fabric. The crinkled earmuffs are a variation of tic-tac-toe ruching (page 67). The spikes in "Dawn" (above), © 1985, each required a square foot of fabric. Each of the petal forms is made and applied individually. The purple chevron edging is a variation of a quilling technique (page 64). Photo at left by Benoit Malphettes. Above photos by John Bagley; courtesy of Sandra Betzina.

Elaborate folds are the facets in the jewellike headdresses of artist Candace Kling. "My incentive is a fascination with the medium. I am challenged by the sculptural possibilities of fabric. I explore gradations, repetitions, and variations.

"I am intrigued by how people interpret my work, what they see in it. The pieces seem to evoke a sense of past and future, a blending of cultures. That delights me!"

After studying fashion design and related arts at Parson's School of Design, the College of Alameda, and the San Francisco Art Institute, Kling graduated from the California College of Arts and Crafts in 1978 with a degree in fine arts. While she was working at an antique-clothing store, doing garment alterations and restoration, she became fascinated with the diversity of vintage-fabric details. "These were not the more traditional forms of embellishment with which I was familiar: embroidery, beading, painting, quilting, smocking, and lacework. They were details made of fabric and ribbon. I started buying some and making samples of others, which I hung on a board in my studio."

In 1980, when a friend showed her a contemporary copy of a flight helmet from the 1940's that had miniature pillows hanging from its sides, Kling incorporated some of these vintage details in her first headdress. In 1981

she exhibited eight more helmets and headdresses at Fiberworks in Berkeley, CA.

Kling uses only a handful of the hundreds of 19th-century traditional ribbon-manipulation techniques. Instead, she modifies them or invents entirely new variations. "I need techniques that are flexible. The folds have to go around corners and adapt to the three-dimensional form." As one solution, Kling has created continuous folds that move like the scales of a snake. "I piece together single increments in rows. They can be bent and twisted. Sometimes I shingle the pieces. I use forms of ruching, a method of gathering, to fill in odd-shaped areas that would be difficult to cut a pattern to fit."

Her helmets and headdresses are constructed in 50 to sometimes 100 thicknesses of ribbon and fabric. Most of them use anywhere from 5 yd. to 10 yd. of fabric. The pieces tell little about how they have been made. The final effect is one of very few stitches; yet, beneath the layers, the pieces are riddled with heavy-duty carpet thread, running stitches, and knots. These elements, while an integral part of the structure, are concealed in the finished work, which adds a bit of mystery.

After much experimentation, Kling chose a rayon-acetate satin with a milium backing as her primary medium. "There is

*The chevron forms in "Copperopolis" (left), ©
1986, are constructed of alternating colors of
folded prairie points. Courtesy of Elton John.
Photos by Candace Kling.*

*The wings of "Cobra" (above), © 1986, began
as a breastplate. The snakelike folds require
ten times their length in fabric. Courtesy of
Alex and Camille Cook. Photo by John Bagley.*

*The triangular pieces that decorate the top of
"Queen of Hearts" (right), © 1981, were made
and inserted into pleated fabric. The top was
made separately and applied midway in the
construction process. The area around the
ears (not shown) is tic-tac-toe-ruched. Courtesy of Elton John. Photo by Ed Kashi.*

a special way the bias takes the curves and the light catches the folds. It's beautiful!" Milium, a coat-lining fabric with a metal coating for insulation, comes in only a few colors, so Kling is now seeking a fabric with similar qualities—a thin, shiny fabric that will hold a hard edge when pressed. She uses buckram, canvas, and silence cloth internally to create the structure. Despite a wide color range in her work, black has always been a favorite because she feels that it forces form to come into focus. "Detail supports form, but structure is essential," she says.

Kling usually starts with a loose vision of the finished piece and one or two elements that please her. She does not do any drawing beforehand; instead, she begins the piece, letting it evolve as she works. "I find that when the fabric is in my hands, it begins to talk back. When a new idea comes, I may put it into this piece or save it for the next one. I allow myself to get sidetracked." Kling saves unused parts and experiments in a set of file drawers and frequently refers to them and to her research boards in the idea and problem-solving stages of her work, often resurrecting spare parts.

Despite her extraordinary workmanship, Kling believes that mastery of technique should set you free. Once learned, it should be forgotten. "There's a point where your technique

is like breathing. It becomes natural." Kling considers her work process sculptural, building and changing with each step. "In the middle of a project, I often become overwhelmed with loose ends. I question the original concept. At this point I force myself to continue and tighten things up; however, I won't just finish a piece to have it done. It has to work technically and please me aesthetically. Each piece must satisfy some inner sense of balance, grace, and power."

Kling frequently works on several pieces at the same time, and a piece may sit unfinished for months before she is able to come up with a solution to a particular problem. Her work style makes it difficult to determine the number of hours she put into each piece, but it is well over 150. Kling works in spurts, almost every day for months, and then takes time off. "When you work every day, there is no trauma of 'beginning.' I end in the middle. I am always in the middle. It's a continuous cycle." □

Sandra Betzina, of San Francisco, CA, is the author of Power Sewing. *For more about Kling's work, a video,* Wearable Art from California: Ellen Hauptli and Candace Kling, *is available for rent or sale from the University of California, Extension Media Center, 2176 Shattuck Ave., Berkeley, CA 94704; (415) 642-0460.*

Candy's Sampler

They may look edible, but the assorted white chocolates in this fancy box are actually folds of milium and satin fabric, coiled metal zippers, plastic and metal beads, and sequins. Artist Candace Kling buys boxes of candies, which she quickly empties and refills with fresh paper cups and sweets of her own. Thi candy sampler, plus a box of "dark-chocolate" nuts and chews, was recently exhibited at the Triton Museum of Art in Santa Clara, CA, along with eight Kling's spectacular ribbon headdresses and a corset. Above, "Candy Sample Fondant." © 1986. Photo by John Bagley

Drawn Threadwork

The art of pulling and tying threads

by Marie-Pierre Duroy

Drawn threadwork can be as simple as the ladder stitch (lower right) or as complex as the work on the handkerchief at lower left. Shown also are the trellis hemstitch (upper left) and overcast bars (upper right).

drawn threadwork is a decorative stitchery technique that can be traced to the 12th century. It was most popular in Scandinavia, where Danish hedebo and Norwegian hardanger, two variations of the technique, are still practiced.

In drawn threadwork, sections of warp or weft threads are pulled from the fabric, to leave a band of short, parallel threads. These are then wrapped to create patterns that can be very simple or as complex as lace. I especially like the ladder stitch (see top photo and drawing, page 72), as it adds distinction to an otherwise plain article. The sheets in which I fell asleep when I was a little girl and the linens of breakfast were all bordered with that subtle and delicate line, a miniature lace, discreet testimony of the countless hours my grandmother must have spent when she was still a young girl, preparing her trousseau and dreaming of what her life would be.

Fabric—Such work, such refinement in a piece of ordinary household cloth that will be soiled, abused, washed, bleached, steamed, and pressed through years of good service should not be granted to every kind of fabric. Cotton will eventually wear thin and tear. Silk, while perfect for lingerie, is too luxurious and expensive for it. And as to polyester or blended fabric, they're not worth your effort. No, only such a noble cloth as linen is worthy of the task.

Linen comes from the blue-flowered flax plant. It is strong and absorbent. Its even weave makes it particularly suitable for drawn threadwork. Linen will dry your best crystal glasses without leaving fabric particles as cotton does, it will let you sleep cool and dry during hot summer nights, and it won't irritate your runny nose on cold winter days. I like the way the fabric moves with me when I wear it, the way it folds, the sharpness of its lines, its crisp aspect. I also like the way it ages, softening with the years, like a good wine, strong and tannic at first, then mellow and rich, like a pebble rounded by centuries of dance with the waves, or like an old man, wise and quiet at the end of his life.

Whether you preserve its original crispness and shine through dry cleaning or you prefer to soften it with repeated washings, linen will look great. Handkerchief linen, the finest weight of linen, will make the most delicate lingerie, blouse, or curtains, but a fabric with a coarser weave is more suitable for towels, napkins, and

From *Threads* magazine (December 1986) 8:41-43

Marie-Pierre Duroy works a ladder hemstitch on a sample piece of linen, using thread that, for clarity, contrasts in color with the ground fabric.

sheets, and it's also easier for the beginner to work with.

Technique—Before beginning a drawn-threadwork project, preshrink your fabric by washing it in hot water; then iron it. To make sure the weave is perfectly straight, pull some threads off each edge that will incorporate drawn threadwork, until there is only one continuous thread on a side.

To work a drawn-threadwork border, pull out the number of threads that will give you the band width you want, in the location you want. Use a needle to carefully pull out the threads one at a time. You can pull out a short length of thread, such as at the top of a pocket, all at once, but you'll have to pull a longer length out bit by bit so as not to disturb the fabric's weave. In a medium-weight linen, pulling out five threads will give you a band about $\frac{3}{32}$ in. (2.5mm) wide. Thread a needle with a single strand of thread, knot the end, and secure it at the lower-left edge of the band, with the wrong side of the work facing you. The weight of the thread can match

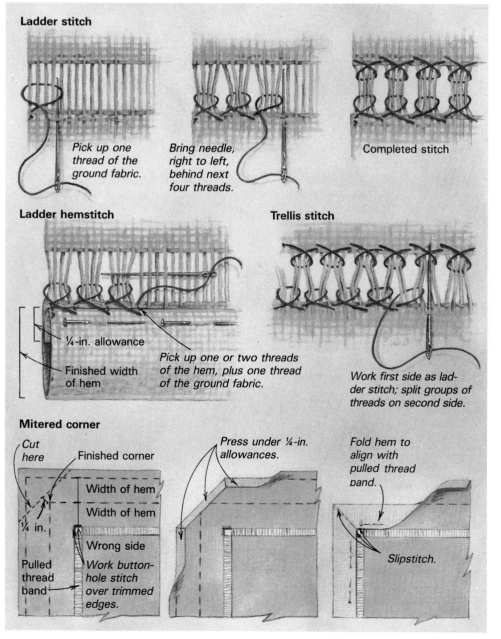

Ladder stitch

Pick up one thread of the ground fabric.

Bring needle, right to left, behind next four threads.

Completed stitch

Ladder hemstitch

¼-in. allowance

Finished width of hem

Pick up one or two threads of the hem, plus one thread of the ground fabric.

Trellis stitch

Work first side as ladder stitch; split groups of threads on second side.

Mitered corner

Cut here   Finished corner

Width of hem

Width of hem

¼ in.

Pulled thread band

Wrong side

Work button-hole stitch over trimmed edges.

Press under ¼-in. allowances.

Fold hem to align with pulled thread band.

Slipstitch.

the weight of the fabric's woven threads, or it can be lighter. I usually use heavy cotton or cotton/polyester sewing thread.

To make a ladder-stitch border, tie together a determined number of threads (four threads, for example) by bringing the needle behind them from right to left, and then out to the front of the work, as shown in the drawing on the facing page. Pick up one thread of the ground fabric near the edge of the pulled border, between this group of stitches and the next group to the right, and pull the working thread tightly enough to bunch the threads, but not so tightly as to pucker the ground fabric. Bring the needle behind the next bunch of stitches, and then back to the front. Pick up a thread of the ground fabric between the group of threads you have just wrapped and the next group. Work the length of the band in this way. Then turn the fabric upside down and work the other side.

This stitch can also be worked as a hemstitch. The top edge of the hem is positioned at the bottom of the band of pulled threads, and the working thread catches

and secures the edge of the hem. Determine the finished hem width, double it, and add ¼ in. to turn under. Measure this distance from the edge of the fabric, and pull the band of threads out at that point. Press under ¼ in. at the raw edge, and align the pressed edge with the lower edge of the band of pulled threads. Work the stitch as explained, but catch one or two threads of the pressed hem edge, as well as a thread of the ground fabric.

A variation of the ladder stitch, called the serpentine or trellis stitch (see drawing on facing page), entails splitting the clusters of bunched threads on the return side: Tie together half the threads in one bunch plus half the threads from the adjacent bunch. This is the stitch used on the robe shown in the photo on the facing page.

Corners where perpendicular bands of pulled threads intersect, leaving an empty space, need special handling. Pull the horizontal and vertical bands of threads, stopping at the corner. Trim the threads close to the two outer edges of the corner, and work a buttonhole stitch over the edges to

prevent them from raveling. Alternately you can leave 6-in. tails on the pulled threads at the corner, weave these into the ground fabric one by one for about ½ in., and trim the ends close to the fabric. If the hole at the corner is small, it can be left open; if it is large, you can decorate it.

For a mitered corner at a hem, trim the corner at a 45° angle, ¼ in. from where the finished corner will be, and turn under the ¼ in. to the wrong side, as in the drawing. Turn under and press the allowances at the two sides, and align the two pressed edges with the pulled-thread bands. Slipstitch the mitered seam edges together, then the outer edges of the hole.

You don't have to stop at decorating pillowcases or handkerchiefs with drawn threadwork. You can add an old-fashioned touch to a summer dress, hem a pair of pants, or add a simple border to a summer robe. Your imagination and your courage are the sole limits on how far you can go. □

Marie-Pierre Duroy, a native of France, lives in New York City.

Adding drawn threadwork to a garment

Incorporating drawn threadwork into a garment like the kimono-style robe shown here is both satisfying and easy to do. This robe's borders, decorated with the trellis hemstitch, complement its simple lines and fabric. A medium-weight linen is the preferred fabric, and any simple hemstitch, including the ladder hemstitch, is appropriate. Since the drawn threadwork is the most time-consuming part of a project such as this, it could be done a little at a time as a winter needlework project, with the final sewing of the robe done in an afternoon just before spring.

Prepare the fabric by preshrinking and ironing it. Only edges that are parallel to the lengthwise or crosswise grain of the fabric can incorporate drawn-threadwork borders. If you wish to add drawn threadwork to edges that do not follow the straight of the grain, you can work the stitchery on a separate band and sew it to the edge later, as I did for the front edges of the robe. To make sure that each edge is perfectly aligned with the grain, pull some threads off all sides that will be bordered with drawn threadwork (in the case of the robe, the lower edges and the sleeves, the pocket edges, and the front band), until there is only one continuous thread. Work the drawn threadwork on each section, except for the hem, before assembling the garment.

If you plan to have a horizontal band of drawn threadwork around the hem, assemble the garment before working the hem so that you can position its border at the correct height. At the side seams, pull the threads to the stitched and finished seam and cut them off close to the stitching.

Pull out vertical threads that will extend down to a drawn-threadwork border at the hem no further than 4 in. from the bottom edges. After you have established your hem length and the position of the hem's border, pull the vertical threads out further so that they meet the lower edge of the hem's border. Then finish the corner. —M.-P.D.

Duroy wears the kimono-style robe that she decorated with borders of trellis hemstitch.

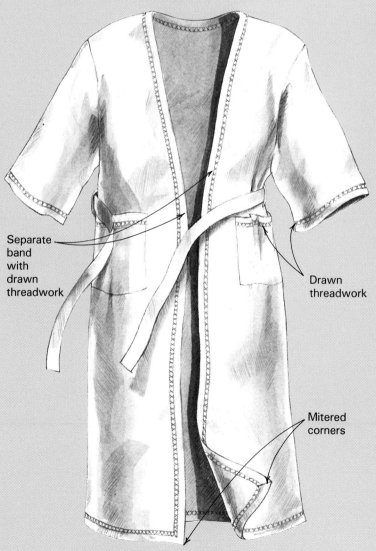

Separate band with drawn threadwork

Drawn threadwork

Mitered corners

This simple kimono-style robe's boxy shape is well-suited to drawn threadwork borders.

Banishing Needlepoint Bias

Relax and do the two-step stitch; blocking is merely a finishing touch

by Rosalie Hamer

f you've ever started a needlepoint project with a nice square piece of canvas and ended up with a parallelogram, you know how frustrating distortion can be. But biasing is easy to control once you know how.

Stitches with slanting threads on the back are the culprits, and those that slant off true bias, like the continental stitch, are the worst of all. Other stitches to watch out for are mosaic and Scotch stitches, and one of my favorites, the Milanese, which I've used in most of the samples here. Distortion that's caused by these longer and looser stitches is going to be easier to block out later than distortion that's caused by the continental stitch, but the best solution to this problem is simply to prevent it. You can't always eliminate every bit of distortion, but with the tricks you are about to learn, you can certainly minimize it.

Tension—Just as in knitting and crocheting, tension in needlepoint is an individual thing. A too-tight tension is the chief distorter, and this can be difficult to overcome. Knitters can compensate for a tight tension by changing to a larger needle; crocheters can choose a larger hook. But for needlepointers, it isn't so simple. Conscious effort is required. If you're naturally uptight, I suggest that you try a little deep breathing and a few relaxation exercises before stitching.

I've read that you shouldn't do needlework when you're angry, as your work will be too tight. I can't vouch for that from experience—I'm seldom angry; and when I am, needlework is the last thing I want to do. I'm pretty laid back and find needlework very relaxing, so I stitch rather loosely; in fact, with longer stitches I actually have to be careful not to work too loosely.

Gently firm tension is what you should aim for to make a stitch that lies flat without straining the canvas. In the sample at right, below, I purposely used a tight tension; it's not only badly distorted, but it ripples and bulges as well. This shows, however, that it's possible to change. If I can work tighter, you can work looser.

To stab or to scoop—Stabbing takes two motions: pulling the thread through from the back, then inserting it from the front. Scooping is carrying the needle in and out in one motion (photo, facing page). When I was introduced to stabbing, I thought I'd find it difficult to make the change from scooping, but I didn't. And the quality of my work has improved because controlling tension is much easier.

Some fancy stitches, such as buttonhole, chain, outline, and knotted stitches, must

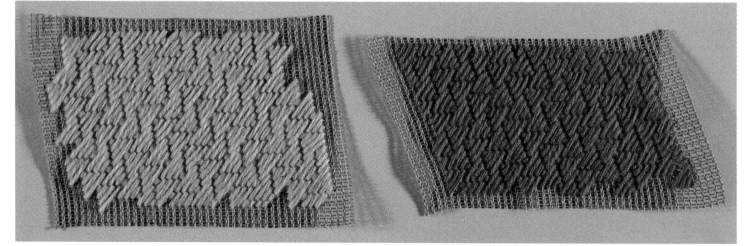

A chief cause of biasing in needlepoint is simply a stitch tension that's too tight. Rosalie Hamer worked these samples in soft tapestry wool on a firm #10 Penelope canvas. In both of them she used Milanese stitch with its long, diagonal backing threads, another contributor to biasing. Although Hamer scooped rather than stabbed these samples, she deliberately increased her tension on the one at right.

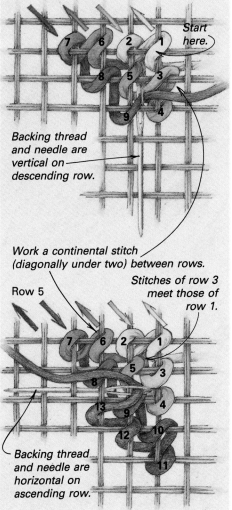

Basketweave stitch

For scooping, right-handed stitchers start at upper right; lefties start at lower left.

Row 4 Row 3 Row 2 Row 1

Start here.

Backing thread and needle are vertical on descending row.

Work a continental stitch (diagonally under two) between rows.

Row 5

Stitches of row 3 meet those of row 1.

Backing thread and needle are horizontal on ascending row.

Illustration by Christopher Clapp

Do you stab, or do you scoop? For the continental stitch, the worst distortion culprit, two-step stabbing (shown in progress on a frame), will give much more satisfactory results than scooping, where the needle slides in and out in one motion.

be scooped, but for the others, stabbing is often the best method. If a stitch goes *straight under one canvas thread,* or *diagonally under more than one,* it should be stabbed. Note that I said *under,* as it's the yarn carried on the wrong side that controls the tension.

For working on a frame, stabbing is necessary, but even for off-frame work, I recommend it. Stabbing doesn't always eliminate distortion completely, but it minimizes it, as you can see in the photo above and the top photo on p. 76. Stabbing is a little slower than scooping, but the ease in blocking makes up for that. I've made many pieces that I wouldn't have had to block (but I always do, as it smooths them out).

Which tent stitch? – If your work is all in tent stitch, the solution to distortion is simple: Don't use the continental stitch. Use the half-cross or the basketweave instead. The half-cross won't bias the way the continental does, but it will hump up the canvas into ridges unless it's stabbed. Put a needle into the canvas and bring it out in

the hole directly below, and you'll see what I mean. This take-up could cause you to end up with a smaller piece than you planned on. It's also very obvious where you've worked some rows horizontal and some vertical, as is sometimes convenient to do.

The basketweave stitch has no "bad habits" I can think of: It doesn't bias the canvas, because the stitches on the back are straight, except at the beginning of the row (shown in drawing above). It works back and forth without turning, and the needle goes into previous stitches from the top (the easier way). It also has an easy rhythm.

Individual basketweave stitches, like all tent stitches, slant up from left to right over one thread intersection. You can stab or scoop, but be consistent. There will be a subtle difference in the angles of the stabbed and scooped stitches, too subtle to show up in a photo, so you'll have to take my word for it or try it out for yourself. It won't be evident in a small area in a pattern, but it will show up in a background.

I recommend scooping while you learn this stitch, as it's easier to see where the

needle goes in and comes out. It is as simple as it looks in the drawing. Just remember to make the transition from one row to the next with a continental stitch; don't try to work a return row from the last stitch of the row just finished; otherwise, you'll come up into a full hole. After you've mastered the stitch, do it the way that suits you. If you stab, you can work comfortably from top right or from lower left.

Yarn – The heavier your yarn is in relation to the size of the canvas mesh, the more distortion-prone your work will be. If the yarn is heavy enough to fill the hole tightly, it will pull the canvas with it. I used a soft tapestry wool (similar to Rowan DK or Elsa Williams) in the samples, except for the center sample on p. 76, in which I used a heavier Bucilla tapestry yarn. The soft tapestry yarn, of medium weight, is ideal for most stitches on #10 or #12 canvas, and for many stitches on a finer canvas as well. It fluffs out and covers better than the same size in a tighter twist would. Bucilla has a harder twist and is seldom useful for

This Milanese stitch, in the same materials as in the photos on p. 40, was stabbed, not scooped. Stabbing allows much better control of tension, especially of the diagonal backing threads.

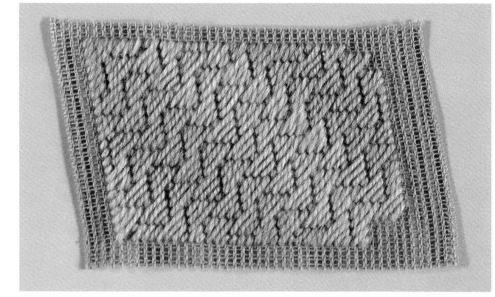

Yarn weight also affects distortion. The Bucilla tapestry yarn used in this sample is a bit heavy for the #10 Penelope. Even though Hamer stabbed, there's plenty of distortion.

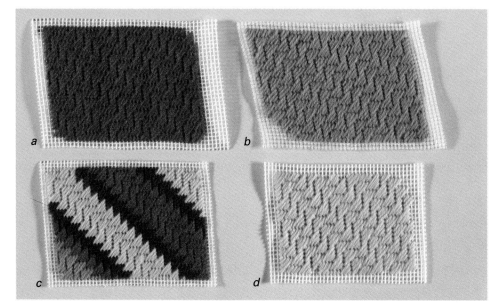

Canvas weight and structure make a difference too. The same soft tapestry wool was used in all four samples: (a) #12 mono, (b) #12 lighter-weight Penelope, (c) #12 interlock, all stabbed. With (d) #12 polyester interlock, even the scooped-stitch sample is relatively square.

finer than #10 Penelope or #12 mono canvas, both of which have larger holes. It's more difficult to pull through, and it distorts the canvas, creating ripples and bulges. The finished effect after blocking is fine, but it requires more effort both to work and to block.

My advice is to use the leanest yarn that will give you the coverage you want. Another wool that I love is DMC's Medici, which is superfine. By using multiple strands, you can get the exact size you want. Persian wool isn't fine enough to give this versatility; often two strands are too much, and one isn't enough.

Canvas—The canvas you work with also makes a difference. A firm, well-sized canvas holds its shape better than a softer one will, as you can see in the bottom photo. Regular mono is firm (top-left sample in photo), and better than a lightweight Penelope (top-right sample). The interlock mono (bottom-left sample) is even better. The ultimate in canvas is the newer Polyester interlock (bottom-right sample), which advertises no distortion and lives up to its promise. It comes in mesh sizes 3.75 (rugs) and 5 (quick point), as well as 10, 12, and smaller. It's also preshrunk and machine-washable. Of course, if you're working in wool, you won't be machine-washing.

A few more tips—Last, but certainly not least, the best way to prevent distortion is to work on a frame. Except for small pieces, I heartily recommend it. A piece of work would have to be worked very tightly indeed, or not mounted firmly, or both to show distortion when it's taken off a frame. On large pieces, stabbing goes more quickly and comfortably on a frame because both hands are working—one above, and the more dexterous one below.

One of my few "nevers" is never crush unworked canvas, as this loosens the sizing and can make it too soft for good stitching. Off-frame, the unworked canvas must be constantly rolled and rerolled to keep it out of the way. Any handling, even rolling, can be detrimental if done too much. A frame eliminates this excess handling.

Finally, I block right side down, unless there are raised stitches. Ironing on a piece of fusible Pellon interfacing while the work is pinned to the blocking board will help keep extremely distorted work from crawling out of shape again, but preventing this severe distortion (now that you know how) is, of course, much better.

Remember that if there is ¼ in. of distortion in my 3-in. swatches, there will be 1 in. of distortion in 12 in. of work. I hope that these hints will help to keep you on the straight (if not the narrow). □

Rosalie Hamer, a needlepoint teacher in Pendleton, OR, writes about texture stitches on pp. 77-79.

Texture Stitches for Needlepoint

The end of the boring background

by Rosalie Hamer

have you ever finished the central design on a lovely piece of canvas work (popularly called needlepoint) and put it away because you couldn't face the tedium of all those little background stitches? If you have, get your project out again and discover texture stitches. Since most texture stitches are longer than the short diagonal tent stitches most often used for needlepoint, they work up fast and are more fun. There's no formula for choosing the right stitch or stitches for your piece, but there are some guidelines.

What the piece will be used for is very important. For pictures or strictly decorative pillows, stitch choice is unlimited. However, if the work will take a lot of wear, as a chair seat will, for example, it requires a stitch that covers the back side of the canvas as well as the front. The friction of the often rough canvas against the thread causes the most wear in a piece of needlepoint, and sandwiching the canvas between two firm layers of thread minimizes this friction. On the other hand, if the work is to be used for clothing, in a belt, pocket or yoke, for example, a stitch with a light backing is preferable, since a heavy backing adds unnecessary bulk. Some texture stitches have heavy backing and some don't, as shown in the photos below.

Often by changing the sequence of making the stitch, you can change the amount of backing. For example, the three tent stitches look alike on the front but cover the back of the canvas to varying degrees, depending on the stitching sequence. Half cross shows a lot of canvas, so backing is light; continental covers the back well; and basket weave has the heaviest backing.

The background should enhance and set off the design, not detract from it, so the background stitches should be compatible with the design. Bold texture stitches, such as Buckey's weaving (see page 79), would detract from a dainty design; on the other hand, a dainty stitch would be lost in a bold design.

Bargello designs, which are zigzag patterns produced from vertical stitches and usually worked in several colors, are also effective in one soft color. Consider using more than one color in a background, but beware of overpowering the design. Two or more closely related shades give an attractive shadow effect, which is often desirable for the backgrounds of realistic work.

The color of the yarn also affects the appearance of the stitch. Since texture is usually lost in dark or bright colors, it's a waste of time to work an intricate stitch in a dark or bright color. Good choices for these colors are Gobelin stitches—small, flat vertical or diagonal stitches that resemble the weave of the Gobelins tapestries—and couching stitches, which are long stitches tied down with shorter ones.

Consider using a fiber different from the one used for the central design, or the same fiber in a different size for the background. Long or straight texture stitches require thicker thread than short or slanting stitches, such as tent stitches. A combination of stitches, such as tent and Scotch (diagonal stitches of graduated length), is more attractive with the tent stitches in a finer thread.

Shiny threads, like silk and rayon, enhance the texture of wool or cotton. The angle of the stitch affects the way the yarn picks up light, so a pattern whose stitches lie in several directions can positively shimmer when worked in a shiny thread.

Texture will be more obvious when worked in a thick rather than a thin thread, but the thread should not be too heavy. If you are using mono canvas (a single-thread canvas) with a yarn that is too heavy, the stitches will crowd and distort the canvas, and you'll end up without enough room for the last few stitches. On interlock canvas, whose warp threads twist around the weft threads, a thread that is too heavy will bulge on the surface, and the stitches will be too crowded for good definition—the piece will be a mass of thread. I prefer my thread leaner than most instructions recommend, as I don't like the crowded look. If three strands of Persian are recommended, I use two. Texture stitches will be bolder and have better definition when worked in a single-strand yarn, such as tapestry wool, Ostara, or pearl cotton (for finer work).

Multiple-strand yarns are versatile: They soften texture and can be mixed for subtle shading. I am partial to Medici, which is the finest wool I know. By adding or taking away strands, you can make your yarn as fat or lean as you want and thus tailor it specifically to the canvas and stitch you are using. With just one light yarn and one dark one, you can create four shades of a three-strand yarn: three strands of dark, two strands of dark and one of light, two strands of light and one of dark, and three strands of light. You can also mix colors at random for a tweedy look. One or two strands of silk or metallic yarn added to wool or cotton will add sparkle, and the colors will show up differently in each stitch.

Before plunging ahead with a new background stitch on your piece, it's best to try

If a needlepoint piece will be subject to wear, use only those stitches that cover the back side of the canvas well. Roumanian couching (left) has light backing, Japanese stitch (center) has medium backing, and three-thread basket-weave stitch (right) has heavy backing.

A history of texture stitches

Today's needlepoint stitches derive from counted-thread work that was done on a fine, even-weave canvas. Three hundred years ago, the rigid classification of embroidery stitches that we use today and their applications did not exist. It was not uncommon to find the simple` tent stitch (of today's needlepoint or tapestry embroidery) combined with textured variations of the satin and running stitches generally used for geometric-patterned embroidery on fine linen or silk (which we now call counted-thread work).

The use of texture stitches for canvas embroidery declined during the 18th century, when chinoiserie and fine silk embroidery, with their design emphasis on natural form and coloring rather than on color blocks, was prevalent. The fashionable satin-stitch embroidery on canvas—known as Florentine work, or bargello—was an exception.

With the industrialization of canvas and yarn production in the 19th century, the consequent need to promote needlework, and the mass production of a new double-thread canvas known as Penelope, the use of counted-thread canvas stitches was revived. Old designs were reused but changed to reflect the Victorian preference for these ornate textured stitches, which were now worked mainly in wool. By the end of the century, this style again faded until the 1920s in England, when the Winchester Cathedral kneeler project was organized. Textured canvas stitches were combined with standard needlepoint motifs of ecclesiastical meaning. The latter movement was enthusiastically received and became a major design influence in 20th-century canvas work.

After World War II, a younger generation of needlework designers and artists and active members of the Embroiderers' Guild in England, the founding parent of the Embroiderers' Guild of America, began to experiment with textured canvas stitches. They wished to show that the barriers between free-form embroidery and counted-canvas work could be broken down and that stitches could be used as an art medium in the manner of the medieval tradition.   —*Lilo Markrich*

For this pillow, adapted from a design of the Santa Maria *by her six-year-old daughter, Lilo Markrich has used long-legged cross-stitch for sky, French knots for clouds, and Florentine work for waves. She achieved subtle shading in the sky by combining strands of different color yarns.*

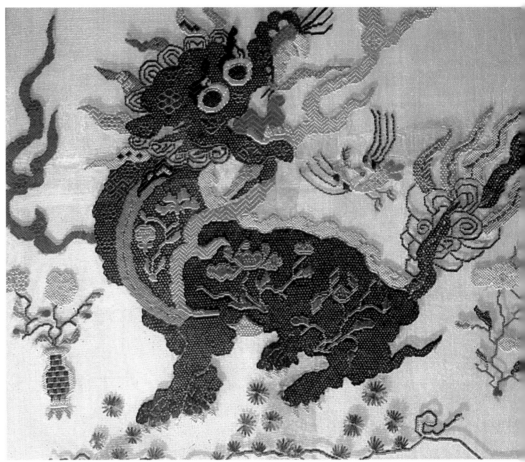

This example of counted-thread silk-gauze embroidery from 16th- or 17th-century China uses variations of satin stitches, which have since been adapted to canvas work. Photo courtesy of The Textile Museum, Washington, D.C.

out the stitch. In order to avoid damaging the canvas by too much experimenting and ripping out, I suggest making a separate swatch. You can hold the swatch against the piece to see if the background stitch is compatible with the rest of the piece.

This is also a good way to gradually build a reference notebook. A stitch sampler is fun, but even with a schematic of the stitches, it's not as useful as a notebook. For my notebooks I use the plastic sheets with pockets designed for snapshots. I usually use 2½-in. by 3½-in. pockets or larger. With the swatch, I include a note giving the gauge of the canvas; the type of thread; the number of strands, if a multiple yarn; a diagram, if the stitch isn't obvious; anything I like or dislike about the stitch; and the book or article from which I got the stitch, in case I want more information later. When you've just made the swatch, you may think all this information is superfluous, but will you remember it a year later?

When testing for a specific piece, use the same canvas and thread, in the same color, that you are using in your work. All of these make a difference in the appearance of the stitch. Even if you already have a swatch of the stitch in a different color or yarn, make a new one and add it to the same pocket. I never consider the time spent on my notebooks as wasted, since I learn from making the samples and get to know the stitching rhythm and personality of the stitch. Although a picture can give you an idea, you won't know the stitch until you try it. I almost passed up one of my favorite stitches because the picture didn't intrigue me; now I try them all.

Rosalie Hamer, of Pendleton, OR, has been teaching needlepoint since 1970.

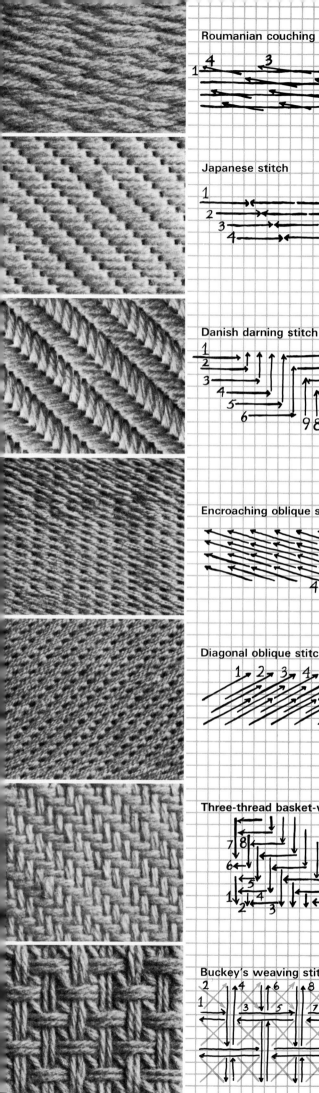

Roumanian couching stitch

Japanese stitch

Danish darning stitch

Encroaching oblique stitch

Diagonal oblique stitch

Three-thread basket-weave stitch

Buckey's weaving stitch

Texture stitches

Almost any stitch can be used for backgrounds, so I'll explain just a few of the lesser-known texture stitches I especially like. Diagrams and photos of the stitches are at left.

Roumanian couching stitch—Couching stitches are simply long stitches tied down with shorter ones. In Roumanian couching, the tying threads are slanted and of random length and spacing. Roumanian couching works up very quickly and has a natural, free-form look. The laid thread can run the length of the piece or the area to be couched, or it can be worked in short sections. After laying the thread, bring the needle out below the laid thread, in the same row, and stick it back through the canvas above the laid thread, further on in the same row. Part of the charm of this stitch is the unevenness of the length and the spacing of the tying stitches, which also add to the speed, as there is no counting. Don't pull the laid stitch tight; it should not sag, but if it's too tight, it will pull. The tying stitches should be firmer, but still not tight, as they are not meant to be obvious. It may take a little practice to get just the right tension. Roumanian couching can also be worked in two closely related shades of the same color. For two colors I use two needles, leaving the unused color on top of the canvas so it won't get tangled. Light backing.

Japanese stitch—Also very simple, Japanese stitches consist of straight horizontal stitches worked over four canvas threads. Each row is offset one canvas thread to the right of the row above it, creating diagonal rows. Medium backing.

Danish darning stitch—The first row is worked the same as the Japanese stitch, with the next one and subsequent alternate rows worked in vertical stitches. This is effective in shiny thread or in two closely related shades of the same color. Medium backing.

Encroaching oblique stitch—This stitch, which covers one canvas thread vertically and four threads horizontally, slants up to the left. Threads are skipped between stitches but not between rows. Heavy backing.

Diagonal oblique stitch—This stitch, which slants up to the right, is my own variation of the encroaching oblique stitch. It crosses two threads vertically and four horizontally. Each row is begun one row below and one row to the left of the previous row, for a diagonal ribbed effect. Note that the stitches of row 3 meet those of row 1. This requires more concentration than the others and is not a fast stitch. To minimize distortion, work in a stabbing method (push the needle in on one side of the canvas and pull it out on the other side), use lean thread, and keep the tension gently firm so the thread lays flat but doesn't pull. This stitch is best worked on a frame. Heavy backing.

Three-thread basket-weave stitch—I developed this as a variation of the back of the basket-weave stitch. It is a terrific stitch for shading, as there are no hard edges. For shading, I work with two or more needles so I can complete a row, leaving the unused needles on top to avoid tangles. I like to work this in Medici for maximum variation. Heavy backing.

Buckey's weaving stitch—Another stitch that works up fast, this looks good in one color or more than one. First work cross-stitches over two threads, skipping one thread between crosses and between rows. Work the straight stitches from the lower left of one cross to the lower right of the next, across the row, and then a second line of horizontal stitches in the row directly below. Work the vertical stitches in the same manner as the horizontal, turning the work sideways if desired. Light backing.

—*Rosalie Hamer* ☐

From the Workshops of Sultan Süleyman

Analyzing art treasures to enrich contemporary needlework

by Virginia Churchill Bath

From *Threads* magazine (April 1989) 22:38-43

in the summer of 1987, I conducted a workshop at the Art Institute of Chicago, concurrent with the show, *The Age of Sultan Süleyman the Magnificent.* The workshop was based on the idea that a close study of first-rate work from a period of superb design would be inspiring and useful to modern-day designers. I certainly found it so, and I'd like to relay some of the discoveries I made and show some of the work that grew out of them. The geometric basis of many of the designs in the show suits them perfectly for a variety of needlework. Perhaps a look at how we analyzed them will help demonstrate how any body of design ideas could be used in the same way.

None of us in the group made exact copies from the work we saw. We were looking for unfamiliar compositions, motifs, and techniques to enrich our own work. Still, an opinion persists (unique to our modern culture) that such a use of art history is questionable. While working for Museum Education at the Art Institute of Chicago, I observed hundreds of gifted grade and high school art students as they developed. Almost all of them began by copying. At the time, I discouraged this. Today, however, I feel that copying is an ideal way to handle form without having to wrestle with content, and analyzing a work in order to copy it is certainly a good way to understand how it was created. Knowing the historical background of a given body of work (in this case, 16th-century Ottoman) isn't essen-

tial, but it can be useful in the analysis, and it helps put the designer into the spirit of the work at hand.

I participated in the lecture-workshop in much the same way the other members of the group did. We made sketches directly from the objects on display, refined them into working drawings, made samples (many of which failed and were discarded), and finally made needlework pieces of various sorts. Like the other members, I've scarcely begun to utilize the ideas suggested by the work that came from the show, but I do have a notebook full of drawings for other projects. We also took full advantage of Estin Atil's excellent catalog, *The Age of Sultan Süleyman the Magnificent* (Washington: National Gallery of Art, 1987, out of print), in which every object was shown in color. A sampling of the pieces I completed appear below and on p. 85. As time passes, and I go back to my own ideas, I'm aware that something of Ottoman art occasionally filters into my work.

Süleyman the Magnificent—Süleyman I, born in 1494, inherited his realm in 1520 and by the time of his death in 1566 had doubled it. His empire stretched to the borders of Algeria, Ethiopia, Poland, and Iran. Süleyman lived at the famous Topkapi Palace in Istanbul, where his family residence, or harem, required an impressive 350 rooms.

Despite the fact that the business of Süleyman's reign and the focus of his energies

was warfare, Süleyman was a renowned patron of the arts, and his imperial studios employed hundreds of men. Artists from all parts of the realm were welcomed, the best of them forming the Ehl-i Hiref, the Community of the Talented. The career of the great architect, Sinan, flourished during Süleyman's time. Buildings at Mecca and Jerusalem were renovated.

Ottoman art during Süleyman's reign—The art produced during Süleyman's time can be divided into three categories: art based on motifs already traditional when Süleyman came to power; art produced after 1530, which shows a new interest in naturalism; and fantastic art in a style called *saz,* produced after 1540.

Western art seems to have had little impact on the Ottomans. They collected it, and Western artists worked in the court workshops, but the Renaissance experiments with form and space don't seem to have influenced Ottoman art to any extent. The Ottomans belonged to the Sunni sect, which didn't allow depiction of human beings in public art. Perhaps this helps to explain their lack of interest in spatial illusion.

Of the five or six traditional motifs that appear in all Ottoman arts and crafts, I chose three: the *rumi* scroll, the *hatayi,* and the cloud band (drawings, p. 82) to develop into needlework designs.

The *rumi* scroll is the counterpart of the acanthus scroll, so important in Western art. The *rumi* is a long, split leaf, its sweep-

This embroidery by Virginia Bath was inspired by the 16th-century shield at left. Ottoman artists created the conventionalized tulips and carnations by wrapping silk around the shield's wicker structure. (From the Topkapi Museum)

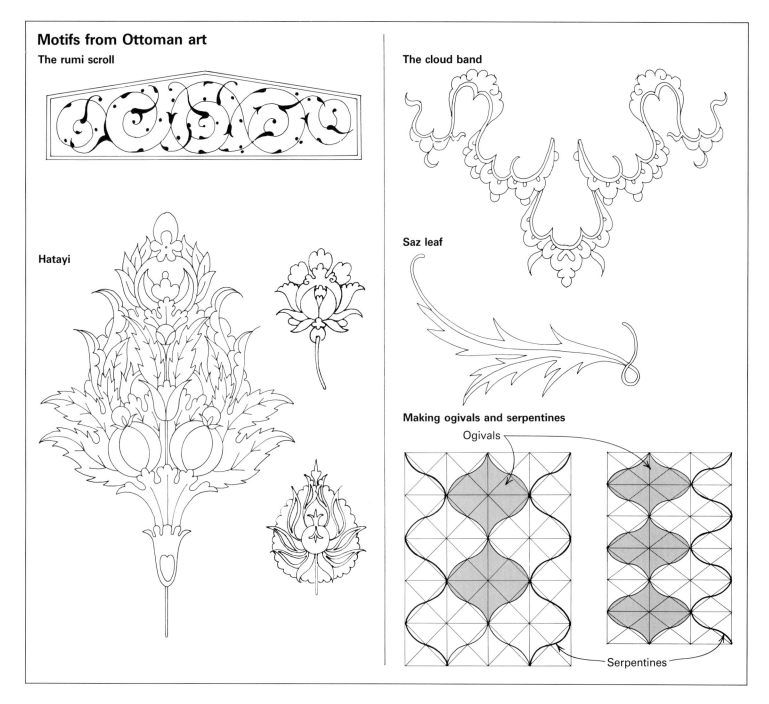

Motifs from Ottoman art
The rumi scroll

Hatayi

The cloud band

Saz leaf

Making ogivals and serpentines
Ogivals

Serpentines

ing curves usually uninterrupted by scallops or serrations. Often, the design is of the utmost simplicity.

The *hatayi* is a conventionalized flower. In *saz* work it is very elaborate, but in the earlier, traditional designs, it is a flat, stylized, symmetrical design with paired petals, some of them downturning, overlying a basic oval or circle.

The cloud band is a motif adapted from the Chinese. In Ottoman art, it is usually symmetrical, formed of convex and concave scallops, embellished at intervals with curlicues that retrace themselves to merge into the next scallop. It is used in scrolling and intertwining configurations, as well as in borders and as single devices.

With these and a few other motifs, the Ottomans produced an enormous variety of amazingly complex objects. They habitually designed with one scroll or spiral overlying another. Other designs, especially textile

designs, were built on one or more ogivals on serpentines, or half-ogivals (drawings at bottom right, above), or on ogivals overlying spirals. Equally popular were reciprocal patterns, usually used for borders. In these, the motif, almost always symmetrical, is turned upside down in alternate repeats.

Geometry, naturalism, and the fantastic— In the 1530s, natural-looking flowers and recognizable varieties of flowering trees joined the cloud bands, *rumi* scrolls, and *hatayi* in ornamenting calligraphers' verses. These flowers are still linear, designed as flat patterns and shown without a spatial rendition of the background, but they weren't always drawn with the geometrical symmetry of traditional *hatayi*s.

The tulip and carnation, which decorate the wicker shield in the photo on p. 80, were the most popular flowers; but cornflowers, hyacinths, irises, roses, and other

flowers also appear. Pine cones, cypress trees, and plane-tree leaves are distinctive in other pieces.

It is paradoxical that, to the Western eye, *saz* work, which in subject matter is imaginary and fantastic, is the most naturalistic of the Ottoman styles. Ottoman painters drew large, undulating, serrated leaves with washes of delicately shaded ink so that depth seemed to be created. Within this suggestion of a fantastic forest lurk dragons and other mythical creatures, all drawn with intricate precison.

The long, twisting leaf shown in the brilliant fabric in the photo on the facing page

The stylized leaves and elaborate flowers, call hatayi, *on this silk fabric from a royal kaftan, are in a style called* saz. *Bath created a needle-lace version of a* hatayi, *shown in the top left photo on p. 85. (From the Topkapi Museum.)*

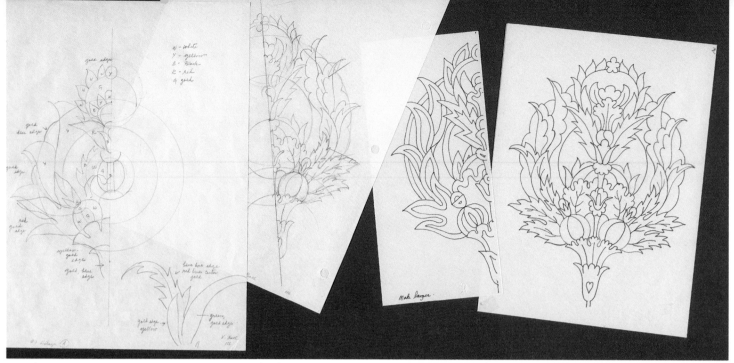

Working sketches for Bath's hatayi *evolved (left to right) from schematic notes through a traced refinement and a discarded double-line treatment to the final working outline. Bath made her* hatayi *(top-left photo, facing page), 10 in. x 12 in., from assorted metal threads that are held together through a variety of buttonhole stitches in plied silk, DMC Coton Perle, and cotton floss.*

is characteristic of *saz*. It became a popular motif in metalwork, textiles, and ceramics. The *hatayi*, elaborated by *saz* painters, was rendered by craftsmen in an endless number of compound versions.

Despite the predominance of floral themes in the art of Süleyman's time, there is geometry at the base of most of a great many designs and motifs. The *hatayi*s, seemingly freely drawn, emerge from a basic pattern of circles. Stars are at the center of many compositions. The much-used ogival pattern is based on diagonals upon which are set two identical, but reversed, curves.

Limited color schemes are typical of Turkish textiles also. Colors were never shaded. For textiles, red was the favorite color, with blue and green in second place. Gold was used a great deal, often as a neutral.

All Islamic art, including Ottoman, combines the second and third dimensions in interesting ways. The design of the compound *saz hatayi*s cannot be said to be two-dimensional. Shapes overlap, curl, and display other indications of one shape behind another, but the overall impression of the designs, because of their stylization, flat color, and decorative outlines and fillings, is two-dimensional.

Possibly, color was so important to the Ottoman people that they did not care to make three-dimensional forms, because that would mean graying some of their tones to create the illusion of space.

Adapting a *hatayi*—A single *hatayi* in gold needle lace (photo at top left, facing page) seemed a good choice for my first project. (For more on needle lace, see the article on pp. 119-121.) The *hatayi* design from which I adapted my pattern is from a remarkable kaftan of silk-and-gold fabric that was worn by one of Süleyman's sons, the

fabric for which is shown in the photo on p. 83. This large kaftan has no repeats and is a tour de force in both weaving and design. I chose one of the *hatayi* blossoms and made a sketch of its basic format, adding color notes, which in the end I didn't use. It was necessary to draw only half the design, since this conventionalized flower, like many *hatayi*s, was symmetrical.

However undulating the various flower petals and the leaves may be, this symmetry keeps the overall effect of the *hatayi* static. Often, there is a circle of petals, leaves, or scallops under the design's main part, simplifying the contour. Over this, smaller circles are arranged. Since my choice clearly was based on a foundation of concentric circles, I began my work with compass-made circles (see sketches above).

Reference drawings can be simple or elaborate. I make hurried little sketches in galleries or from books on file cards or sheets of typing paper folded in quarters for stiffness. A small sketchbook probably would be better, but if I'm on my feet, I like to travel light. I use an HB pencil and an eraser, since museums don't allow people to use pens in the galleries.

The initial sketch is an exercise in analyzing another artist's work, in finding the basic structure of the design. I try to reduce the finished work to an organization of rhythms, shapes, colors, and other formal elements. My first drawings are rough and free, fragmentary, and full of inaccuracies and awkwardness. Only the essence of the design appears, with perhaps a tiny detail of a texture or contour. Often, the page includes more written notes than drawing.

The *sine qua non* of the designer is tracing paper, which makes corrections and second thoughts quick and accurate. I traced half of my original sketch, folded

the paper at the centerline of the design, and traced the opposite side. The first version usually needs improvement, but tracing and retracing eventually will produce an acceptable pattern.

A mirror is a helpful tool. Holding the first sketch against the mirror along the centerline shows how the full pattern will look. By viewing your design in the mirror, its image reversed, you'll often notice problems with balance. Turning the design upside down can also refresh your vision of it.

Other Ottoman-derived pieces—Next, I made a series of pieces in techniques that could be finished more rapidly. Using a paint marker and stem stitch in DMC No. 8 Coton Perle on natural muslin, I worked out a pattern for an ogival design (photo at top right, facing page), the format so beloved by Islamic textile artists. I closely followed the pattern of a fabric in the collection of The Metropolitan Museum of Art, simplifying it and changing the shape of the ogival. The motifs—tulips and pomegranates—are naturalistic, according to the Turkish conventions.

Using the same technique, I worked out another design (photo, p. 81) in the naturalistic genere, using acrylic paints and chain-stitch embroidery on natural muslin. I adapted my straight border pattern from the tulips and carnations in the circular border of the shield. (photo, p. 80)

I adapted one piece from a silk-and-gold embroidered linen headband that belonged to Hurrem Sultan, Süleyman's wife. I designed it with the simplest of interlace patterns, which were much loved by the Ottomans and often used for thread-counted embroidery. I worked my border (center photo, facing page) with cotton floss on loosely woven linen, using the same stitches

The tulip and pomegranate motifs, held within an ogival, in Bath's embroidery are based on Ottoman standards of naturalism. Bath painted the blue areas and outlined them with stem stitch, in DMC Coton perle on muslin.

as the original; but the scale is much larger, there is no gold thread, and some details have been eliminated. The intriguing aspect of this embroidery is not the interlace, but the fact that thread-counted embroidery is combined with fagoting.

I also made two pieces designed to be used as quilt blocks. The first piece (photo at bottom left) was to accompany some blocks with large stars that I had already made. Since I would have to make several of the new blocks, I decided to keep the design simple. I looked through the show for a pattern with a star as the central element and found a set of hexagonal tiles in blue-and-turquoise ware. The first step in the adaptation was a change from hexagonal to octagonal format; the stars that I had already made were eight-pointed. Surrounding the small central stars of the tiles, alternately, are *rumi* leaves and *hatayi*s. I reduced these to basic skeletons and changed the color scheme to match the large stars. I appliquéd the block with printed cotton, embroidered it in red DMC Coton Perle, and quilted it with blue DMC floss and white cotton thread.

My other quilt block (photo at bottom right) is based on the border of an illuminated title page of an Ottoman manuscript and is composed mainly of cloud bands. I made a four-way design, greatly modifying the motifs, but using the delicate underlying scrolls that often appear in these designs. I worked this embroidery on white muslin with DMC floss in various colors.□

Interlaced motifs, like these entwined squares, were popular subjects for Ottoman embroidery, here rendered by Bath in cotton on linen, instead of the silk and gold of the original linen headband, made for Süleyman's wife.

Virginia Churchill Bath, Conservator and Assistant Curator of Textiles at the Art Institute of Chicago from 1968 to 1971, is the author of Needlework in America *(1979). See pp. 124-125 for additional examples of her work.*

These two quilt blocks are simplified versions of traditional Ottoman motifs, the rumi scroll on the left, and the cloud band on the right. The rumi scroll is cotton appliqué, embroidery, and quilting; the cloud band is painted and embroidered. Both are on white muslin.

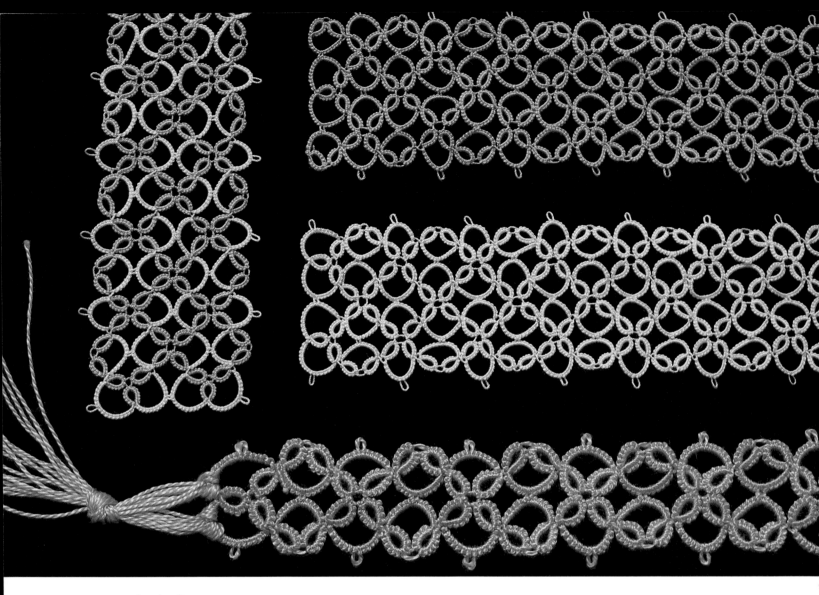

Tatting

Poor man's lace that is really elegant finery

by Betty Suter

atting is a knotted lace. Known as a "popular" lace, it has been in and out of vogue throughout its history. Less time-consuming to produce and more durable than bobbin laces, it has been called "poor man's lace" because it has sometimes been used to imitate fine handmade needle and bobbin laces. Some people don't even consider tatting true lace because it is knotted.

Tatted lace is made of a series of double half-hitch knots over a core of thread. Called double stitches, these knots are formed into two basic structures—rings and chains—that are combined to make lace patterns. Loops between the double stitches, used decoratively or to join the rings and chains, are called picots. Even tatting done in very fine thread is firm and strong. For this reason, tatting was used in everyday items—purses, collars, cuffs, edgings, buckles, bonnets, and curtain pulls—where finer laces would have been unsuitable.

For those of us who learned tatting before learning to make other laces and who are enjoying its current popularity, tatting is an intriguing lace. As is true of other laces that are making a comeback, the survival and development of tatting depend on its becoming more than just a trimming on a handkerchief or decoration for a table. Yet, while trying to elevate lacemaking to a fine-art form, many tatting artists are emphasizing traditional techniques. Current exhibitions feature everything from exact reproductions and traditional uses to three-dimensional sculptural and abstract lace forms. In this article I'll show you the fundamental techniques—how to make the ring and chain and how to join them.

Tatting developed during the early 19th century, primarily in England and Europe. Works on the subject have been published in English, Spanish, French, German, and the Scandinavian languages. The few references to it prior to 1850 are sketchy; some suggest that it was developed from knotting techniques popular in 16th- and 17th-century Europe or from macramé. Today, the history of tatting and its techniques are being provided to us through reprints (see page 92). The how's and why's of subtle techniques and shortcuts, however, are often not written down, leaving this information to be discovered by the determined or passed on from one lacemaker to another. This creates a pleasant opportunity for lacemakers to seek each other out in order to learn and share the art.

Shuttles

In tatting, a shuttle holds and carries the thread. Stitches can be formed by the manipulation of the thread with the fingers, but the shuttle makes working easier and the storage of thread more convenient.

Shuttles are made from a variety of materials. Metal shuttles are heavy. Gold, Ger-

Suter made four bookmarks in a traditional pattern to represent the Four Worlds of the Kabballah, the mystical aspect of the Jewish religion. Rows of alternating connecting rings and chains create the pattern in varying widths. The short bookmarks have four rows of MEZ Spitzengarn size 80 cotton thread. The longer one is two rows of size 8 DMC Pearl Cotton.

The lace centerpiece at right was made between 1914 and 1924 by Florence Hawes, of Ishpeming, MI, with size 100 cotton thread. Property of Frances Suter, Ft. Defiance, VA.

All tatted lace is made up of a series of double stitches (double half-hitch knots) and picots (loops). These two structures can be combined, as in the photo below, to produce lace that consists of just chains (top), just rings (center), or both rings and chains (bottom).

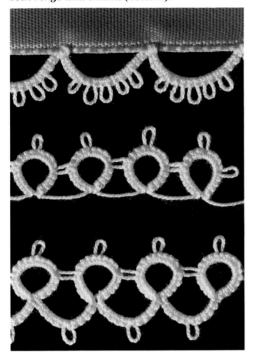

man silver, and steel shuttles will not tarnish. Sterling silver and brass shuttles tarnish easily and may soil the thread. Bone, horn, shell, and wooden shuttles vary in weight and are aesthetically pleasing. Bakelite and plastic shuttles are lightweight and versatile. All are suitable, so long as they're comfortable for the lacemaker's hand.

Some shuttles have a sharp point or hook at one end, which is used to join rings; otherwise, the tatter needs a pin or crochet hook. I prefer plastic shuttles with fine, sharp points. They were made in the '40s and '50s, and I comb antique shops for them.

Seventeenth-century knotting shuttles were about 4 in. long, elaborately decorated and open at the ends. The shuttles adapted for tatting, and those made today, are about 2 in. to 4 in. long and have closed ends, which prevent the shuttle from unwinding if you drop your work. The closed ends also cause the thread to feed out with a pleasant ticking sound. Shuttles may have a fixed shank in the center around which the thread can be wound, or they may have a removable bobbin. The fixed shank should have a hole in it so the thread can be inserted and tied before it is wound. A shuttle with a removable bobbin holds a larger amount of thread, but one with a fixed shank is easier to use, as you can wind and unwind it without having to put down your work. When the shuttle is wound, it should appear as in the left photo on page 88, with the thread extending from the right back of the shuttle.

Threads

The quality of the lacework is greatly affected by the type of thread. Although cotton and pearl-cotton threads were traditional, colorful silk threads were also used. I have an 1860's Corticelli Color Chart of Silk Sewing Thread with 72 brilliant colors. Today, however, silks are extremely hard to find, and they're difficult to use because they're very fine and slippery.

Tatting requires a round cord of moderately tight twist. Cotton is most often used. Rayon threads come in a variety of textures, but are slippery, so if you use them, secure the last stitches with a drop of fabric glue on the back of your work. Metallic threads add glitter, but can cut your hands. They should be round and worked slightly looser than cotton cords. Polyester-wrapped cords produce a dull, firm, waxlike quality. Threads may be obtained from local needlework and fabric shops; from The World in Stitches, 82 South St., Milford, NH 03055; and from The American Needlewoman, Box 6472, Forth Worth, TX 76115.

Except for a few foreign cotton and novelty threads, I prefer DMC cotton threads. DMC Cordonnet Speciale, a 100% cotton crochet cord, has a soft sheen and produces a firm piece of lacework. It comes in white and ecru in sizes 10-80 and size 100.

Slightly softer, DMC Cebelia Crochet Cotton produces a moderately firm lace and comes in 20 colors in sizes 10, 20, and 30. Pearl cotton is available in many colors and produces a soft, lustrous quality. I prefer size 8 pearl cotton, which is equivalent to a size 20 or 30 thread. DMC tatting cotton, size 70, traditionally used for handkerchief edgings, comes in about 40 colors.

MEZ Spitzengarn, a German cotton tatting and crochet cord in size 80, is sold by The World in Stitches in 59 colors, many of which are not available in DMC tatting cotton. It is a very fine thread and yields a delicate, colored lacework.

J & P Coats's Knit-Cro-Sheen or a size 10 thread is best for learning. When you've mastered the double stitch, use a size 20 or 30 thread. When you've mastered the basic tatting motifs, try sizes 70 and 100.

In her 1854 book, Ann Stephens recommends that: "Tatting should always be done with a very cool, dry hand, as a moist hand can soil a beautiful piece of lace in the making." I wash my hands or fingertips often with a mild soap and dry them with a cotton towel, and I wipe the surfaces of the shuttle with a moistened towel. French chalk or powder is hard to get out of the work.

Working position

Here's the basic working position for making double stitches for the ring and chain. Unwind 15 in. to 20 in. of thread from the

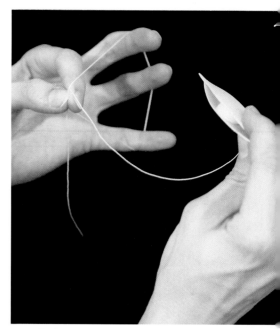

A shuttle should be wound so the thread feeds out from the right back end (red shuttle). From top: Two plastic shuttles without points; plastic shuttle with point; steel shuttle with bobbin; brass Art Deco shuttle with cap to separate shuttle points for winding; German silver shuttle with point; novelty shuttle with openwork design and hook; Lady Hoare's shuttle, of buffalo horn. Suter made the 2½-in.-dia. emery cushion at right with Size A Belding Corticelli Silk sewing thread. This type of cushion is used for polishing and cleaning needles.

1. This is the basic working position for tatting. Hold the knotting shuttle in the right hand and wrap the thread clockwise around the fingers of the left hand. The thread in the right hand is the shuttle thread. The working space is the triangle formed by the thread between the left index and middle fingers.

shuttle. Hold the shuttle in the right hand between thumb and forefinger. Pick up the end of the thread with the left thumb and forefinger. Wrap the thread clockwise around the remaining fingers of the left hand to form a circle, meeting again between the thumb and forefinger, where both threads are held securely, as shown in photo 1.

The thread around the left hand is the knotting thread. The thread in the right hand is the shuttle thread. The section of thread between the left index and middle fingers defines the working space.

The little finger of the left hand is used to catch and hold the thread against the palm of the hand as you work. The middle finger of the left hand should be very flexible. It is used to lift the thread to form the working space and to lower the thread to relax the tension. Hold the hands parallel at a comfortable level for seeing the work.

Making the double stitch and picot

To form the first half of the double stitch, wrap the shuttle thread around the right hand, or lift it with the right middle finger so that you're holding it above the work (photo 2). Pass the shuttle under both the raised shuttle thread and the thread of the working space. Bring the shuttle around the thread of the working space and back under the shuttle thread held taut by the right middle finger, or right hand (photo 3).

Release the tension of the knotting thread by lowering the left middle finger. Draw the shuttle to the right, holding the shuttle thread straight and taut—a position you must keep until the first half of the stitch is complete (photo 4). Hold the knotting thread firmly between the left thumb and

forefinger to prevent it from sliding as the shuttle thread is drawn to the right.

Drawing the shuttle thread to the right causes the stitch to jump, or transfer, from the shuttle thread to the knotting thread. At first, the shuttle thread loops around the knotting thread, but when the shuttle thread is pulled taut and straightens, the knotting thread loops around it instead. This action is instantaneous and hard to see, but look for it, as the stitch will be successful only if the transfer has occurred.

Increase the knotting thread's tension by raising the left middle finger, sliding the thread loop to the left. The first half of the stitch is now formed and held between the left thumb and forefinger (photo 5). If it's been formed correctly, you'll find it easy to slide the knot along the shuttle thread while holding the stitch between the left thumb and forefinger.

To form the second half of the double stitch, reverse the process you used to form the first half. Hold the first half firmly in place, and let the shuttle thread form a loop below the work. Pass the shuttle over and around the thread of the working space (photo 6), then back through the shuttle-thread loop beneath the work (photo 7).

Again, release the tension of the knotting thread by lowering the middle finger of the left hand. Draw the shuttle thread to the right, holding it straight and taut for the remainder of the stitch. The stitch transfers once again to the knotting thread.

Increase the tension of the knotting thread by raising the left middle finger and sliding the thread loop to the left, against the first half of the stitch. If the knot has been formed correctly, the completed stitch will

slide along the shuttle thread as you hold it between the left thumb and forefinger.

Continue making double stitches by alternating the first and second halves of the stitch. When the circle of knotting thread becomes too small, slide the stitches to the right along the shuttle thread or pull the knotting thread to the left of the stitches. With practice, the entire process of making the double stitch becomes a natural hand movement and takes a second to execute.

The picot is a loop used for decoration and for joining rings and chains to each other. To form a picot, simply leave a space of thread between groups of double stitches. When you slide the stitches close together, the loop is formed (photo 8).

Forming and joining rings

The ring most often forms the basis of the tatted-lace design. In the pattern at center in the left photo on page 87, each of the rings is made from four sets of five double stitches, each separated by a picot. When you've made all the double stitches and picots for the first ring, hold the last stitches securely between the left thumb and forefinger and pull the shuttle thread until the first and last stitches meet to close the ring at its base (photos 9 and 10).

Before starting the second ring, leave a space of thread. The second ring will be joined to the last picot of the first ring.

Make the first five double stitches of the second ring, and bring the final picot of the first ring close to the working-space thread. Release the tension of the knotting thread a little by lowering the left middle finger. Use the point of your shuttle, a tatting hook, a crochet hook, or a pin to draw

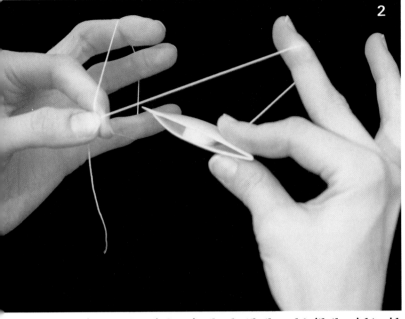

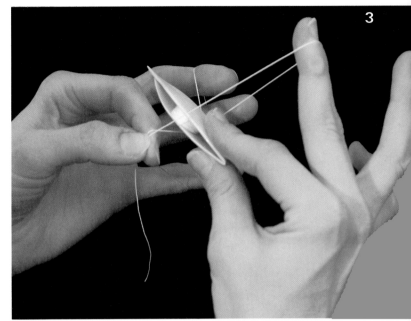

2. To begin a double stitch, raise the shuttle thread (with the right middle finger) and pass the shuttle under it and through the working space.

3. Bring the shuttle around the working-space thread and back under the shuttle thread. Let the raised thread slide off the finger.

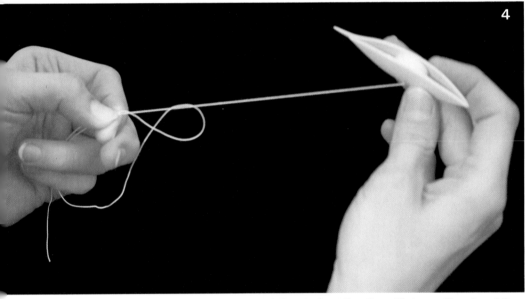

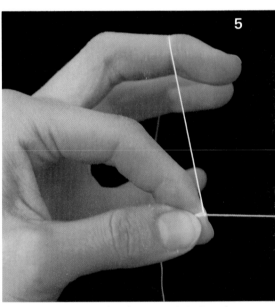

4. Lower the middle finger of the left hand. Holding the knotting thread between thumb and forefinger, draw the shuttle to the right. Raise the middle finger of the left hand to increase tension.

5. The thread loop will slide to the left, forming the first half of the stitch.

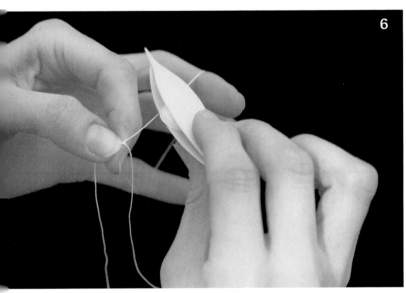

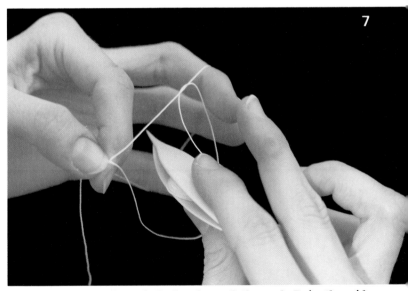

6. To form the second half of the double stitch, reverse the process. Let the shuttle thread fall in a loop below the work. Pass the shuttle around the thread of the working space.

7. Draw the shuttle through the loop beneath the work. Raise the middle finger of the left hand and draw the thread loop to the left, as when forming the first half of the double stitch.

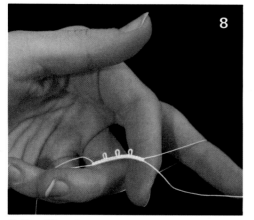

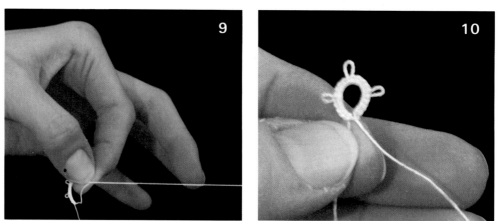

8. To add a picot to your work, leave a space of thread between groups of double stitches. When you slide the double stitches together along the core thread, the picot is formed.

9. The ring, composed of both double stitches and picots, is the most common element in tatted-lace designs. After you have made enough double stitches and picots, pull the shuttle thread, holding the stitches securely with the thumb and finger of the left hand. **10.** The first and last stitches will meet to close the ring at its base.

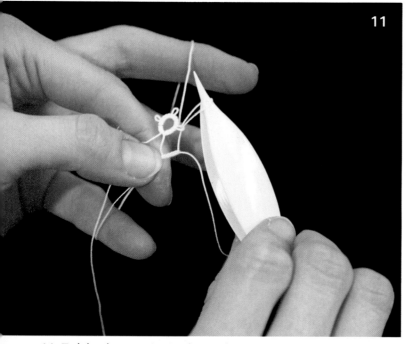

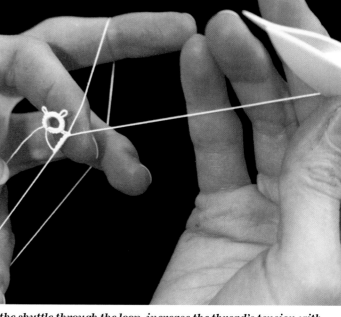

11. To join rings, make the first series of double stitches for the second ring. Then with the shuttle point, a pin, or a crochet hook, draw the knotting thread through the picot of the first ring to form a loop.

12. Put the shuttle through the loop, increase the thread's tension with the middle finger and the little finger of the left hand, and slide the loop against the previous stitch.

the knotting thread through the picot from back to front to form a loop (photo 11).

To make the join, put the shuttle through the loop and draw it to the right, holding the thread taut. Reduce the loop in the knotting thread by increasing the thread's tension and sliding the loop against the previous stitch (photo 12).

Now make the second half of the double stitch in the usual way. Together, the join and second half of the stitch serve as the first double stitch of the next group of double stitches. When you have made all the double stitches and picots, close the second ring, leave a space of thread, and proceed with the third ring of the pattern.

As shown in the drawing on page 92, you can make variations of this basic tatted edging by adding more picots to the ring, by reversing the work after completing each ring to form a double row of rings, or by eliminating the spaces between the bases of the rings to form a round, or rosette.

(See tatting abbreviations in the box on the facing page.)

Forming and joining chains

Although you can create designs of just rings, some patterns require chains of double stitches. Chains can be formed between rings or added on in separate rows to increase the lace's width. Picots are also used in chains for decorative effects and joining.

For a design made from rings and chains, you need two thread sources. As your second source, you can use the ball of thread from which you wound the shuttle; just don't cut the shuttle thread away from the ball. You can also wind two shuttles and attach the first shuttle's thread to that of the second (it's best to use two different color shuttles so you don't confuse the threads). The most common method for adding a second thread source, however, is to tie the end of a ball of thread to the end of the shuttle thread. This method is al-

ways used for making two-colored lace, and usually, the same size thread is used.

To add a chain to a ring, reverse the work (that is, turn the ring upside down). Place the ball thread, or second thread, which serves as the knotting thread, over the fingers of the left hand and wrap it around the little finger to control the tension. Make the chain of double stitches and picots according to the pattern, and draw the stitches to the left so they lie close together and against the base of the reversed ring (photo 13). This makes the work firm and eliminates empty spaces of thread between stitches. The stitches in the chain should be even and consistent with the double stitches in the ring. Drop the ball thread, reverse the work, and use the first thread again to form the next ring.

Fixed joining—Adding a chain as a separate row across the top of a row of rings requires a fixed join. This join is made to

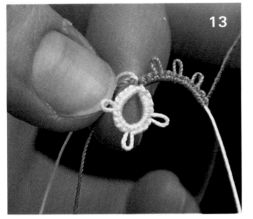

13. *To add a chain to the ring, tie on a second thread at the base of the ring. The second thread serves as the knotting thread for the chain. Reverse the work, wrap the thread around the little finger to control tension, and double-stitch to form the chain. When the chain has been completed, drop the second thread, reverse the work again (so it is now right side up), and make the next ring, using the original thread as the knotting thread.*

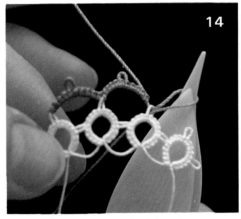

14. *Adding a row of chaining to a row of rings requires a fixed join, made with the shuttle thread. Before winding the shuttle, thread the second thread through the top picot of the first ring from front to back. Make the chain. Then with the point of the shuttle, draw the shuttle thread through the top picot of the next ring to form a loop. Bring the shuttle through the loop, and increase the tension to fix the join. This join won't slide like a regular join.*

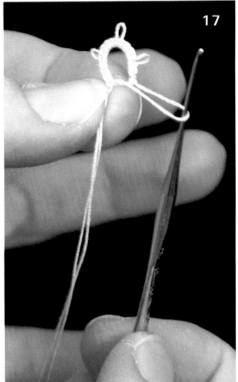

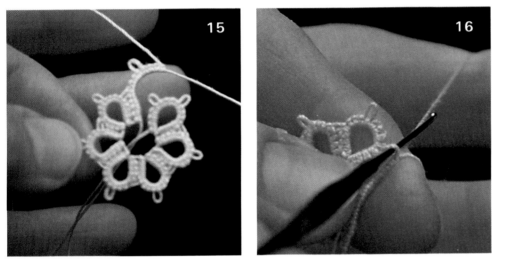

15. *To make a reverse join, hold the rosette as shown.* **16.** *Fold the first ring so that the back of the work faces you. Twist the top picot of the ring upward and backward, and insert a crochet hook to complete the join. When the ring is unfolded, the work will lie flat.*

17. *To reopen a ring to fix a mistake, hold its base firmly, and with a pin, needle, or crochet hook, pull the core thread (from at least two stitches above the ring base).* **18.** *Open a large enough loop to correct your work.*

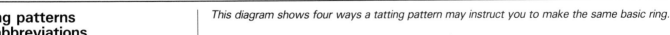

Tatting patterns and abbreviations

The abbreviations below are common to the various forms of tatting instruction.

Ring	r	Short picot	sp
Large ring	lr	Separated	sep
Small ring	sr	Close	cl
Double stitch	ds	Space	s
Picot	p	Chain	ch
Long picot	lp	Reverse work	rw

Reversing the work means to turn the work upside down. Some instructions will indicate where you should "turn the work over to the left" or "turn the work over to the right." Often these directions are eliminated altogether, and you must figure out how to turn the work in order to continue the pattern.

If you're having difficulty with the instructions, have someone read them to you as you work, or watch another person implement the design as you read the instructions aloud.

This diagram shows four ways a tatting pattern may instruct you to make the same basic ring.

R 5ds, p, 5ds, p, 5ds, p, 5ds. Cl R.

This translates: Make a ring of 5 double stitches, picot, 5 double stitches, picot, 5 double stitches, picot, 5 double stitches. Close the ring.

R 5ds, 3p sep by 5ds, 5ds. Cl R.

This translates: Make a ring of 5 double stitches, 3 picots separated by 5 double stitches, 5 double stitches. Close the ring.

5-5-5-5

This instruction gives the number of double stitches to be made; dashes indicate a picot.

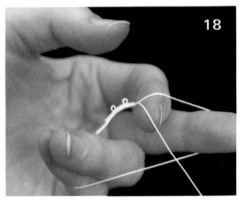

In this graphic instruction, the number of double stitches to be made is indicated in each section of the ring. Short lines extending from the ring indicate a picot.

picots that lie to the right of the work, rather than to the left, as when rings are joined. Therefore, the join is made with the shuttle thread rather than the knotting thread because that thread is closest to the work. The chain can be joined to the picot of a ring, to the picot of another chain, or to any other joining point through which you can still insert the crochet hook.

A fixed join won't slide as a regular join will, so you must be sure the spacing of the chain stitches is even and equal to the stitches in the rest of the lace before joining. You can make adjustments only by picking out the joining knot and stitches, or by cutting out large amounts of work, which is time-consuming and may damage the thread and lace.

Before winding the shuttle, thread the ball thread through the top picot of the first ring from front to back. Attach the end of this thread to a shuttle and wind the shuttle, pulling the thread through the picot. Use the ball thread as the knotting thread, and make the required number of double stitches and picots. Adjust the chain

to the correct length. To make the fixed join, use the point of the shuttle or a crochet hook to draw the shuttle thread through the picot from back to front to form a loop (photo 14). Put the shuttle through the loop and draw up the loop to fix the join.

Reverse joining—Reverse joining is necessary whenever a regular join will twist the picot (as when the first and last rings of a rosette are joined) or when a fixed join is impossible because the picot isn't near the shuttle thread. With experience, you'll quickly recognize points in your work where this join is needed. This method is attributed to Mary Konior, author of *A Pattern Book of Tatting* (London: Dryad Press, 1985).

Hold the rosette with the first ring to the right. Fold the first ring over to the left so the back faces you. With your fingers, half-twist the top picot of the first ring upward and backward (photo 15), and insert a crochet hook from the front (photo 16). Complete the join as usual. (With practice, you'll be able to flick the picot backward with the hook as you insert it.) When you unfold

the ring, the picot won't be twisted but will lie as flat as the other joining picots.

Correcting work—Before it's joined, a chain can easily be pulled out and corrected. Later, to add, remove, or correct stitches, the work must be cut out and replaced. A ring can be reopened easily. This method, provided by Rachel Wareham, of Ludlow, MA, is more successful with coarse threads, as the core of fine threads splits easily. Insert a pin or crochet hook between the stitches, at least two stitches above the base of the ring, to locate the core thread (photo 17). Hold the ring at the base, and pull the core thread out to the right to form a loop. Enlarge the ring enough to add stitches or correct your mistake. To remove stitches (photo 18), loosen them with the pin or crochet hook, and feed the shuttle in the reverse direction from that which you used to form the stitch. □

Betty Suter, of Waterbury, CT, is a home economist and social worker. She has been tatting since 1969 and teaching, publishing, and designing since 1982.

Variations of basic tatted edging

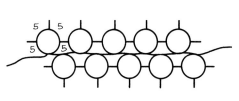

Additional picots are added to the ring.

Work is reversed after the completion of each ring to form a double row of rings.

Spaces between the ring bases are reduced or eliminated to form a round, or rosette.

Tatting publications

Encyclopedia of Victorian Needlework, 2 vol., by S.F.A. Caulfield and B.C. Saward. *Reprinted in 1985 by Dover Publications, 31 E. 2nd St., Mineola, NY 11501.*

Originally published in London in 1882 as *The Dictionary of Needlework,* this is an extension of *Beeton's Book of Needlework* (1870). Both books contain designs and suggested uses for tatted lace and were developed from the works of Mlle. Eleonore Riego of England, who is credited with having written 11 tatting books between 1850 and 1868. *A Ladies Complete Guide to Crochet, Fancy Knitting and Needlework,* by Ann Sophia Winterbotham Stephens (New York: Garrett & Co. Publishers, 1854), confirms that tatting had developed at the same time and to the same level in this country.

The Complete Encyclopedia of Needlework by Thérèse de Dillmont. *Published in 1886 and reprinted in 1972 by Running Press, 38 South 19th St., Philadelphia, PA 19103.*

In the 1880s, as tatting's popularity declined in England, it grew in France with Mlle. Thérèse de Dillmont's multilingual work, an extension of Riego's work. Dillmont is known for her use of two shuttles, combination patterns of crochet and tatting, frequent use of colored threads, the half ring or partially closed ring, and the introduction of the Josephine knot, a ring of single stitches.

The Art of Tatting by Lady Katharin Hoare. *Published in England in 1910 and reprinted in 1982 by Lacis Publications, 2982 Adeline St., Berkeley, CA 94703.*

While the French continued to produce significant work, the next major development in tatting occurred in Roumania. The queen and her friend Lady Katharin Hoare worked in silk and metal threads, incorporated pearls and gems into their work, and developed a more creative use of the chain than as a connector of rings. Lady Hoare also invented a new-style shuttle, more useful to her blind mother than the traditional one. This book is more of a photographic record than a teaching manual, as it contains no technique.

Tatting Books 1-3, Old and New Designs in Tatting and Crochet Braids, A Collection of Many Novel and Interesting Varieties of Tatting, 40 Original Designs (1982). *The House of White Birches, Box 337, Seabrook, NH 03874: Learn to Tat (Coats and Clark's Book No. 240); Tatting Patterns by Julia E. Sanders (1977); Tatting Doilies and Edgings by Rita Weiss (1980); Classic Tatting Patterns by Anne Orr (1985). Reprinted by Dover Publications, 31 E. 2nd St., Mineola, NY 11501.*

Tatting flourished in the U.S. around 1915 with the regular publication of patterns in *Needlecraft Magazine,* in booklets by The Priscilla Publishing Co. (1909-1915), and in the booklets of Mary Fitch, sold by the

F.W. Woolworth stores. Collections of patterns were also published in booklets by The American Thread Co. (Star Books of Tatting) and the J & P Coats Co. between 1935 and 1950, featuring the work of Anne Orr and others. The Priscilla Books included instruction in technique, such as incorporating cords, braids, and beads into lace; extended use of the chain; metal thread; and variations of the basic double stitch, such as the lattice stitch, twisted stitch, knot stitch, roll tatting, cluny petal, and tatting with a shuttle and needle. *Learn to Tat,* sold by many needlework shops (including Lacis and The World in Stitches) for under $1, is excellent for beginners. It contains patterns and information on laundering, blocking, and finishing lacework.

Tatting by Elgiva Nicholls. *Reprinted in 1984 by Dover Publications, 31 E. 2nd St., Mineola, NY 11501.*

Nicholl's book, based on the 1850-1868 Riego texts, was first published in 1962. It contains a valuable and extensive history of tatting and tatting techniques.

The DMC Corporation (107 Trumbull St., Elizabeth, NJ 07206) can supply additional pattern books. Lacis (2982 Adeline St., Berkeley, CA 94703) is a mail-order lace specialty shop that carries a variety of shuttles as well as domestic and foreign tatting books.

Fabric Collage

Bits of patterned cloth, machine-sewn in layers,
capture the essence of people's faces

by Deidre Scherer

From *Threads* magazine (April 1988) 16:68-72

i don't know what to call what I do. Sometimes I feel I offend any category I lean into. One time while in Boston I took my work into an art gallery and a crafts gallery on opposite sides of the street. Each one sent me across to the other gallery. Work like mine lands on the yellow line. It's a hybrid art form that confounds people.

People call me a fiber artist, but I'm not always comfortable with that. There's a way I ignore the medium. It's an illusion; it's a picture of a head, a face. Often the illusion is so strong that people don't perceive right away that it's made up of stitched cloth. So, to make it plain that it is fabric, I started leaving the edges raw and mounting my work on a cloth background.

You've had fabric on your body all your life. You know how it feels. When your eye hits a surface of fabric, you feel it. That's why people can't resist touching my work—it pulls them in. I don't like having to frame the pieces behind glass for exhibitions.

I love the fact that they're fabric, the feel of them. You can say something with fabric that you can't say with paint. The closest thing to working the way I do with fabric is collage—using found objects that have their own textures and colors. The prints and textures of the fabric can be limiting, but you can push against the limitations. I revel in that.

The cloth—A lot of my cloth has a history. There's a piece of my great-grandmother's shroud in one picture. Sometimes it takes me a year to gather the fabric for a project. Sometimes I ask people for the very shirts off their backs. "When you're ready to give up that shirt," I say, "I want it."

One time I'd had a vivid picture in my mind for quite a while—two women in flowered dresses sitting on a flowered sofa. Then some friends had a housewarming. When I walked into their home, the first thing I saw was the sofa, covered in the very print I had envisioned. They had a few scraps of fabric left over from the upholstering, and I grabbed them.

My cloth needs are very specific. It's just not feasible for me to sort through bags of cloth scraps, yet a special piece of yardage saved and sent by a friend can instigate a new project. I use a lot of teeny textures and florals, plaids, and stripes. If a fabric looks particularly versatile, I'll buy a few yards of it. Sometimes I go to New York City or Boston and spend a day at cloth stores. Jan Norris, who runs Delectable Mountain Fabrics, a little shop in Brattleboro, VT, has a great collection and supplies me with most of my cloth.

In her fabric collages, Deidre Scherer strives to capture an essence of life, not to portray specific people. For her, older faces are an inexhaustible source of rich imagery. Opposite page, "Map of the Year One Hundred," 23 in. x 22 in., 1987. (Photo by Jeff Baird)

My fabrics are more than paint. Besides what paint has, I have the printed pattern, the texture of the weave, and the way light reflects off the thread. I use both sides of the cloth. Because the "wrong" side can be lighter or darker or a muted version of the printed side, I always think that I'm really buying two pieces when I'm buying a piece of material. By alternating right and wrong sides, I can make areas appear to come forward into light or recede into shadow.

My challenge is to break the rules. A finer pattern sits back, a larger one comes forward. So, there's a rule I can try to break. Blue is a cool color, and it goes back. Red is hot, and it moves forward. It'll add up—the density of the pattern, the color value, the hue. Every tiny piece influences how the eye is guided across the surface of the work.

Even with opaque materials, one color sewn over another makes a third color. Silk voile makes a transparent overlay for a water jar, a glass window, light hitting a surface. Laces are usually too precious, though I have used them. When I use lace, I have to cut it, sew over it, knock it back, and it's ruined as lace. Usually I can't bring myself to do it.

Drawing with the scissors—I rarely work entirely from imagination, but usually from a drawing or a photo or a picture in a book or even from the actual thing. I always have a theme, an idea, but then it happens as I work it out. Often I'm surprised.

I don't pencil lines on the cloth. I draw with the scissors, cut the layers and move them around, and cut some more until I get it right. Sometimes I hold the scissors in the air and steer the cloth into them with my free hand. Sometimes I have to cut in reference to the other layers on the table, so I twist myself over the work, steering the scissors along the line I want.

Nobody else uses my scissors. I have three pairs—one pair for cloth, one at the sewing machine for thread, and one for paper. And I've bought scissors for everyone in the house, so no one touches mine.

Usually I have three pieces going at once. That's enough busyness for the size of the room I work in. I can't live with a lot of my pieces facing out at the same time; it's too noisy. I have to turn their faces to the wall or put them under the table. I think of some of them as swing pieces. There's something in a swing piece I don't understand. So I keep it, don't show it, and return to it to try to figure it out.

I don't do portraits for anybody. It's confusing, it stops me. The purchaser of a portrait becomes a third person, an intermediary between my subject and me. My pieces are essences, interpretations, so I will sabotage the likeness for the spirit.

Sewing—The first time, I draw with the scissors; the second time, with the sewing machine. With the scissors you make the mark in line with your hand movement. With the sewing machine you place your hands on each side of where the mark is being made.

I usually work from background to foreground. I cut and piece a few layers of my collage, pin it, then sew it down, then move to the next layers. I pin the pieces and let them flow into place and smooth it all into place as I sew. I pin every inch and a half or so, using extra-fine silk pins. A bulkier pin makes the fabric bunch up.

Scherer, 43, works through the nights in an attic room atop her old house in Williamsville, VT. She sorts her cloth by color, pattern, or texture and stores it in bins along a wall of the studio. As she chooses fabric for a new piece, she inevitably makes piles of yardage that suggest new color ideas. An entire work can be based on one key fabric. (Photo by Jeff Baird)

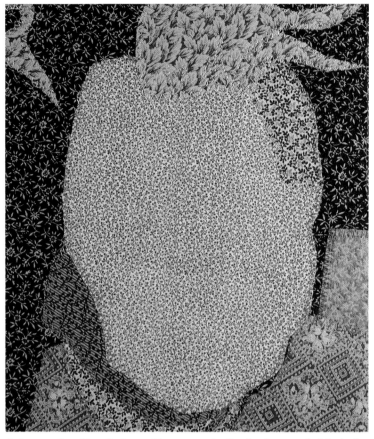

A layer of unbleached muslin supports the background fabric for "The Peace," 12 in. x 9 in., 1987. The first sewing, a wide and long zigzag, fastens the rough shapes in place and catches the raw edges.

After considerable moving and looking, Scherer pins the eyes and nose in place. She refines their positions and attitudes by layering the inner shadows and highlights. She pins the hand and sleeve last.

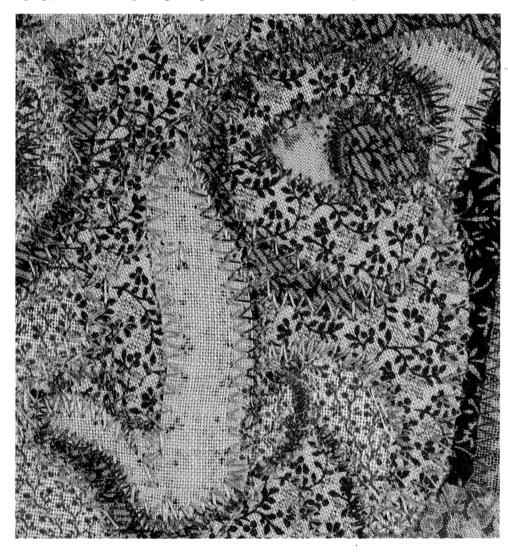

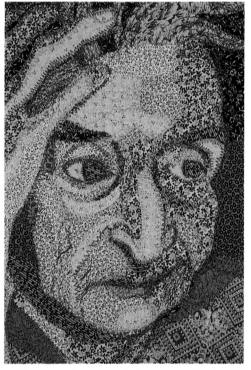

In the second sewing, Scherer goes back and forth over all the edges, frequently changing stitch dimensions and thread color (left). "The Peace" is finished (above). The tiny mouth parts are the last to be sewn in place. New highlights model the cheek, chin, and hand, and a red collar frames the face. Scherer has also adjusted the background to the right of the face. Oversewing with a straight stitch softens and shades such features as the corner of the mouth. (Photo sequence by author)

Detail photo (near right) reveals the depth and intricacy of Scherer's sewing. She is concerned only with the needle-thread color and does not attempt to manage the bobbin color on the reverse side (far right).

I never baste and rarely handsew. Basting doesn't let the cloth move enough. With pins you can let it go, slip the pin out and release it, let the layers ride and settle without puckers. I know the fabric is going to move when I sew it, and maybe my secret is just letting it. If I know a nose is going to walk under the pressure foot, I cut it in a little to compensate.

The first sewing is structural, to place and hold the fabric. It catches all of the raw edges with a zigzag stitch, gets all of the pieces fastened in place. The stitches are long and wide. The second sewing is far more intricate. I go over many of the edges again, and I go across the pieces too. I might sew over a line two or three times more. Sometimes I cut a piece that's just too small, and the sewing needle disintegrates it. But I hardly ever rip out. That leaves the cloth bruised and holey. I just sew more layers on top.

I used to make a heavy satin stitch, but that creates a harder edge. Now I find that a looser and wider stitch allows the areas to melt together. You can see the fabric through it. I change the length and width of the stitch constantly. You have to get the pedal action down too. You have to use the pedal so it just jabs the needle in, then stops. Pivot the cloth on the needle, and then sew.

I carefully consider the color of the thread. In earlier work I used black thread, which gave everything a stained-glass feeling. Now the thread becomes shading, melting the colors into one another, making transitions between colors and textures. I had a section in one of my pieces where the thread color was too dark. I took a lighter shade of thread and ran a few stitches through it to lift the color and keep it from falling behind the surface. I don't do anything with the color of the bobbin thread. I just use whatever is in the machine.

My machine is an old Pfaff, at least 17 years old. Once I tried a computer machine. You punched in the stitch length—1, 1.5, 2. I couldn't get in between those numbers. It was very frustrating. The machine automatically set the force of the pressure foot, and it grabbed the work hard, but with all these layers of cloth I have to be able to adjust as I go along. The foot pressure has to be very loose; you can't allow the machine to walk the fabric. I fought that computer machine all the time. I love this old machine. Pfaff even found another

Scherer really gets her teeth into her work: She steers the fabric with her left hand and adjusts the dials for stitch length and width with her right hand, while carrying the weight of the bulky cloth roll in her mouth.

A photo in an old book was the source image for "Pink Kitchen," right (photo by Jeff Baird), 24 in. x 21½ in. A second version emerges on the cutting table, above: The head and shoulders have been sewn; the hands and foreground are cut but unpinned. Tiny patterns, many of them florals, create depth and texture. The woman's scarf is modeled with both front and back sides of the fabrics, as are her face and hands. On the right side of her bodice the large star-paisleys are covered with blobs cut out of the background motif, causing the right side to recede into shadow.

"Maria in Memory" (left) was so extensively sewn and resewn by machine, especially around the head, that the needle finally broke in the thickness of thread. "Maria" (23½ in. x 19 in., 1983) travelled with the Vermont Council on the Arts exhibition and was on show at Castleton State College in the spring of 1988.

one for me, the exact same machine, so now I have a spare. It's not as loose as the original, though.

The old people—In 1971 I made a fabric picture book for my daughters. It consisted of a series of patchwork pictures without words, and I remember feeling challenged by the fact that these things could get more narrative and more illusionistic. In 1980, I was working with symbolic images from playing cards, making a series of fabric wall hangings. I wanted more depth and character in the heads of the queens, so I visited a nursing home, looking for wise, queenly figures to draw. I became fixated on the richness and experience in an older face. Each face has an essence of life, and if I get it right, I can bring out that essence.

You need courage to have a vision of where you want to take yourself, to struggle past the limits of your skill. When I began to work with the old people, to communicate the impact their faces were having on me, I had to push my technique beyond my traditional conceptions of appliqué.

After 90 years of life, our faces have visible layers of feeling, of opposites. The mouth can smile; simultaneously the mouth can turn down. The eye can look forward as it looks deep inside into the past. But it's not only the old people themselves, their faces showing how they've been shaped by their lives; it's also the issue of aging itself. When I started to think about what I wanted to say about aging, I realized that I hadn't talked to myself about it yet.

I'm a baby boomer, and I think it's difficult for my generation to see itself as old.

We don't envision ourselves as dying of old age. We die young of disasters, of cancer, or we don't die at all. People are afraid of getting older and dying.

I think that my soft medium allows the eye to touch and absorb these images, to move past the fear and admit the wonder, the awe, the unknown of life. While cutting, piecing, moving the fabric around, and sewing it, I'm engaged in a visual dialogue, a long conversation. I'm encouraged when I see that conversation going on between my work and other people. □

Deidre Scherer's work can be seen at the Harbor Square Gallery in Camden, ME; the Gayle Willson Gallery in Southampton, NY; the Woodstock Gallery and Design Center in Woodstock, VT; and at the Beside Myself Gallery in Arlington, VT.

Costumes of Royal India

The last hundred years of an extraordinary textile tradition

by Betsy Levine

In 1866, while artisans in India were producing many of the exquisite garments shown on these pages, J. Forbes Watson finished a report for the India Office in London, which was bent on increasing the Indian market for British cloth and so destroying the indigenous industry of India. The 18-volume work included 700 cut samples of Indian textiles, each annotated and presented so the entire cloth could be reproduced by a British manufacturer.

Watson analyzed, measured, and categorized in detail both loom-shaped and cut-and-sewn Indian garments. The vast majority of clothing was (and remains) simple lengths of cloth, which leave the loom ready to wear. Much of the cut-and-sewn clothing is made from rectangles woven for the purpose, with integral borders, edgings, and decorative details.

A *sari,* the rectangle of cloth that a woman can wrap around herself in many ways, might be 8 yd. long by 1½ yd. wide. Depending on how it was to be worn, it would have one or both ends and edges decorated. A turban, wound around a man's head for protection from the sun, might be 9 yd. long by 20 in. wide. The *choli,* or bodice, though sewn, was often woven to size (perhaps 38 in. by 33½ in.) with decorative borders at top and bottom.

Besides reporting on the many garment types and their variations, Watson described the various textile-manufacturing processes, including elaborate brocades and embroi-

These late-19th-century men's coats, or cho-gas, from Jaipur (far left) and Benares (near left), are silk with gold brocading. They were custom-designed and shaped on the loom: The position and size of the decorative borders and motifs were predetermined and woven to fit the owner's arm, chest, and torso. Adjustments were made at the shoulder, under-arm, and side seams. The turbans are fine cotton—lightweight, yet bulky and porous. Coat at far left lent by Bhawani Singh of Jaipur; coat at near left lent by Shrimati Gouri Parwati Bayi of Trivandrum.

deries (with little hope that England could produce them more cheaply, but rather as a lesson in taste). He advised:

> . . . the British manufacturer must not look for his customers to the upper ten millions of India, but to the hundreds of millions in the lower grades. The plainer and cheaper stuffs of cotton, or of cotton and wool together, are those which he has the best chance of selling, and those which he would be able to sell largely, if in their manufacture he would keep well in view the requirements and tastes of the people to whom he offers them.

But Watson believed that some fabrics would always be best produced by hand, by countries with the necessary attributes: cheap labor, intelligence, and refined taste.

In fact, for 4,000 years India has produced some of the world's most sought-after cotton. It was often so fine (and worth its weight in silver) that weavers worked in damp caves to keep the threads moist and unbroken. Gauzy cotton muslin was sometimes embellished with gold-and-silver embroidery, in a heavy, elaborate manner (*zardozi*) or in a lighter, simpler style (*kamdani*). Silk, first imported from China, then produced in India (*tussah* was their wild silk), became available in early Christian times. With it began the tradition of silver-and-gold brocading on silk. In some districts, brocading was reserved for borders. Others specialized in diapered figures (overall, small-scale designs) or stripes. *Kincob,* meaning "happy hunting ground," was the name given to the highly ornamental animal-figured brocades.

Starting with the 8th-century Mohammedan invasion, and especially in the 16th through 18th centuries, the Moslem influence and its assimilated Persian artistic traditions became strong. Akbar, the great Mughal emperor, united much of India in 1556. He set up court workshops, where Persian and Indian artisans could collaborate in a grand style. Cut-and-sewn garments became more prevalent. Because they were restricted by religion from wearing

pure silk, the Muslims developed blends of silk and cotton, such as a satin weave of silk weft on a cotton warp that they called *mashru,* meaning "permitted."

In 1600, attracted by this rich culture, the East India Trading Company began to make its presence felt. India continued to produce great quantities of dyed cotton for export well into the 19th century. But by 1877, when Victoria became Empress of India, the economic policies that followed England's Industrial Revolution gradually supplanted India's handloom industry.

The Indian textiles that were produced from the mid-19th century on necessarily reflected the changes wrought by the British. But India, not England, would clothe her own upper ten millions. The royal Indians shared with the royal British a penchant for pomp and ceremony and an indulgence in clothing themselves as befit their wealth and power. The traditions of embroidering and brocading in gold and of producing the finest cottons and thick, closely woven silks survived.

Probably the most oft-heard exclamation about the garments at the Metropolitan Museum Costume Institute's "Costumes of Royal India" exhibition was, "Imagine how much time and energy went into their making!" The Indians have always believed that: "Each task is a dedication.... Each man is born to his ordained work, and through that alone can he progress spiritually" (see Kamaladevi Chattopadhyaya, "Further reading," page 103). Society func-

"Costumes of Royal India," exhibited at the Metropolitan Museum of Art's Costume Institute from December 20, 1985 through August 31, 1986, was organized by Diana Vreeland and coordinated by Stephen Jamail. It was one of 39 separate exhibitions in the U.S. during the cultural exchange known as "Festival of India," agreed to in 1982 by President Reagan and the late Prime Minister Indira Gandhi. Thanks to Jean L. Druesedow, associate curator in charge of The Costume Institute, for her cooperation and help.

The horses and elephants on this yellow silk-satin ghagara (skirt) from Kutch are embroidered with silk thread and a hook in chain, or tambour, stitch. At first glance, the fabric looks printed, so calculated are the repeats and so precise is the work (detail of right and wrong sides below, left and right, respectively). The skirt was probably one of several commissioned by a mid-19th-century prince for his courtesans to wear on a festival day. The skirts would have been made, on fairly short notice, by a professional workshop. Lent by Smt. shad Kumari (New Delhi).

tioned on a code of personal relations, and work was seen as a duty handed down, not as a system of contract and competition.

Guilds, though weakened by British rule, regulated not only the hours spent and the quantity produced by textile workers but also the quality of materials and workmanship. Membership in the guilds was hereditary but not completely caste-bound. Boys were apprenticed young, but the training was not formal.

The tailor, or *durzi,* stitched sewn garments by hand, overcast minute bits of appliqué, and sometimes embroidered. Embroidery was traditionally done by women in the home, and it was also a profession practiced in large workshops by men with varying degrees of expertise. Printers stamped the designs on the cloth with a woodblock dipped in red-earth pigment mixed with mucilage, which would easily wash out. Young embroiderers stitched outlines, and very old, skilled men did the fine, detailed work. They sat together on the floor with the cloth stretched over a horizontal frame and cut the ends of their threads with a bit of glass or china. The embroidery from Kutch, in far western India (see photos, facing page), with its characteristic elephant, peacock, and mango motifs, is essentially folk art.

Kashmir, which also produced exquisite needle embroideries, is probably best known for the woven *shal,* whence comes the word *shawl.* The *kairy* (mango) motifs—later called paisleys when imitated in Scotland—were woven with many tiny weft shuttles called *kanis.* One half inch of a 48-in.-wide fabric might be woven in a day. The fabric was called *jamawar* because kings and courtesans bought it by the yard (*war*) to make a gown or robe (*jama*). The jamawar detail in the photo at top right is from a late 19th-century coat.

Gold and silver were worked into all costly loom-shaped garments and into piece goods, whether they were woven as tissue with a fine-silk warp or weft, brocaded directly on the loom, or embroidered on the woven cloth. In 1866 in Bharatpur where the garment in the photo on page 102 was made perhaps 50 years later, there were nearly 400 "gold-thread weavers."

More than 1,400 people were engaged in making gold thread, which was also supplied to embroiderers. To make this thread, artisans began with a bar of silver about the size of a finger and wrapped it three times in gold leaf (the heavier the gold, the yellower the thread). The wrapped bar was heated until the gold diffused with the silver. The gold remained on the surface as the bar was beaten to the size of wire, drawn through ever smaller holes, and flattened with a steel hammer. It could then be used flat, or it would be wound on a core of lightly twisted silk thread. Gold tissue woven with this thread was often stamped in a raised pattern and used as a decorative edge for saris and shawls. The

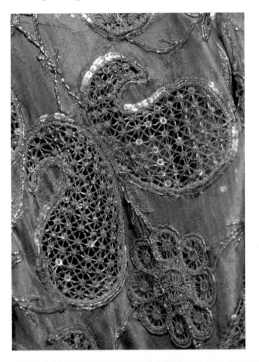

Detail from a late-19th-century Kashmir achkan, or long coat (right). The natural resources and wealth of each region were reflected in the ruler's dress. Fine Kashmir wools in cream shades are enhanced by the traditional kairys *(paisleys), woven in indigo, madder, and yellow weft yarns. Lent by Safdar Ali Khan (Patna).*

Two early-20th-century Muslim women's costumes. Each three-piece ensemble consists of Farshi pyjama *(a very long, loose culotte), a* kurta *(tunic), worn under the matching, filmy* duppata *(veil). Emeralds, rubies, and gold are worked in celestial themes on the cream chiffon* duppata *from Rampur (garment below, left). Gold cutwork and appliqué edged with gold sequins are worked in paisley and floral motifs on fine silk tissue from Lucknow (detail at left; garment, below right). Lent by Mrs. Hamana Khatoon (Pirpur).*

This early-20th-century women's costume (above) from Bharatpur, south of Delhi, consists of three pieces, which were woven from red, gold, and green silk: an odhini (shawl), a choli (close-fitting bodice), and a ghagara (skirt or petticoat). The ghagara is often simply a length of cloth, joined at the ends, with a band running along the top edge and housing a drawcord for fastening. To achieve this full skirt without a bulky waist, the weaver placed the hem border warpwise on the loom. The fabric was woven so that the brocade panels formed horizontal triangles pointing to the waist, with open warp between. When the open warp was cut away, the garment seams shown in the detail at left were sewn. The skirt was still so full, however, that half of it went to the recipient's sister. Lent by Tikka Rani of Nabha.

border would be removed when the garment was washed, and then reattached. Gold sequins and spangles were also in demand by embroiderers (left photo, facing page). Any mirrorlike surface would repel evil spirits, who can't look at their own image.

Color and motifs from nature are as significant to the meaning and worth of a garment as the dedication of purpose that brings it forth. Colors are chosen to supplement and enrich one another: pink with emerald green or purple, yellow or red with purple or green. Violet may indicate the fruit of the jamon tree, which symbolizes the holy scriptures of India. The *kairy* motif is believed to bring the wearer abundance, good health, and good character. The body owes a debt to the clothing and must be worthy of it, just as the clothing owes a debt to the body that displays and enlivens it.

"As a man changes his old garments for new ones, even so the soul migrates from one corporeal frame to another in a perennial chain of births and deaths." (From a *Divine Song,* quoted by S. N. Dar in *Costumes of India and Pakistan,* Taraporevala, 1969). □

Betsy Levine is an associate editor of Threads.

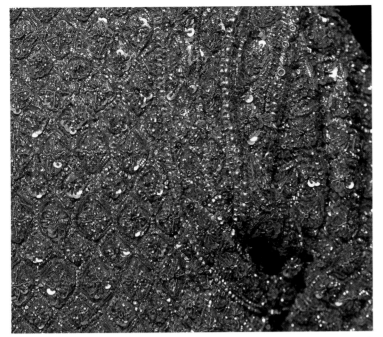

From early-20th-century Hyderabad in southern India comes a gold-encrusted coat, known as a chaubaghla. *The gold fabric, shown above in detail, is embroidered with gold beads and sequins, and the motifs are highlighted at their centers with beetleback. Weighing about 40 lb., the coat required great fortitude of its wearer and repaid him in prestige. Lent by Begum Naheed Fazaluddin Khan of Hyderabad.*

A relatively small group of handweavers survived 20th-century British mill building, and, after independence, the Indian government has begun again to support and encourage that heritage. The Handicraft and Handloom Export Company of India commissioned the fine-silk and gold sari at right, made in Karjipuram in 1985 for this exhibit. One length of unstitched cloth wraps both the upper and lower body. It may be tied twice about the waist, gathered in front, and held by a belt that is stitched to an undergarment. The other end is then taken over the left shoulder—over the head of a married woman—and draped over the right shoulder and arm.

Further reading

The following sources on the history and philosophy of Indian costume and textiles may be found in a university library or in the library of an art museum.

Bhushan, Jamila Brij. **Costumes and Textiles of India.** Bombay: Taraporevala Sons and Co. Private Ltd., 1958.

Birdwood, G.C.M. **The Industrial Arts of India,** 2 vol. London: Chapman and Hall Ltd., 1880.

Chattopadhyaya, Kamaladevi. **Indian Handicrafts.** New Delhi: Allied Publishers Private Ltd., 1963.

Dar, S.N. **Costumes of India and Pakistan.** Bombay: Taraporevala Sons and Co. Private Ltd., 1969.

Irwin, John, and Margaret Hall. **Indian Embroideries.** New York: Orientalia Art, Ltd., 1973.

Jamail, Stephen. "India's Native Princes." **FMR,** Vol. IV, Dec./Jan. 1985-86, pp. 44-48.

Olson, Eleanor. "The Textiles and Costumes of India: A Historical Review." **The Museum New Series**, Vol. 17, Summer-Fall 1965. The Newark (NJ) Museum.

Patnaik, Naveen. **A Second Paradise.** New York: Metropolitan Museum of Art and Doubleday, 1985.

Sethna, Nelly H. **Shal, Weaves and Embroideries of Kashmir.** New Delhi: Wiley Eastern Private Ltd., 1973.

Watson, J. Forbes. **The Textile Manufacturers and the Costumes of the People of India.** London: Eyre and Spottiswoode, 1866.

Crewel Gardens

Joanna Reed stitches seasonal wildflowers in wool

by Anne S. Cunningham

Joanna Reed looks up from her herb garden, wipes her hands on already grimy pants, gathers an armful of clippings, and shoves them into a crowded wheelbarrow. "About my curtains," she says, "some of the flowers are gems; others are just stitches."

Reed's crewel curtains are the work of a master artisan. Augmented by an artist's eye and painterly use of needle and wool, the stitching reveals her passion for horticulture. Details of embroidered flowers, pods, leaves, and cones are crafted as knowledgeably and meticulously as are the massive gardens outside her 18th-century Pennsylvania farmhouse.

Reed's skill and interest in gardening have brought her prominence in the horticultural world, as president of the Herb Society of America and designer of a Specialty Herb Garden at the National Arboretum in Washington, D.C. She is now a hearty 69, but in the 1960s, Reed developed severe osteoarthritis and had to stop gardening temporarily, so she turned to crewel work, a skill she'd always admired but had never had time to learn. "I took it up as a self-taught project while visiting friends," she says. "My hostess told me about classes—what she was really telling me was that I should take lessons."

Reed signed up for classes at the nearby Wallingford Crewel Studio, where crewel is taught as a highly refined technique, able to pass for oil painting. Her artistic instincts (she had spent two years at the Philadelphia Museum School of Industrial Art, now The Pennsylvania College of Art) came out, and she decided to tackle a major project: living room curtains—four crewel panels representing the four sea-

Inspired by her gardens, Reed translates the changing view from her window into meticulously executed, realistic crewel work. In the detail from the curtain panel entitled "Fall," French knots stitched closely together, color variations in the yarn, and careful shading create the fluffy effect of golden yarrow.

From *Threads* magazine (August 1986) 6:48-51

Joanna Reed, crewel artist and horticulturist, works on the "Fall" panel (right). In the photo above, the curtain panels "Spring" (right) and "Summer" (left) are shown in place on one of the living room windows in her 18th-century Pennsylvania farmhouse.

sons. She had planned to make elaborate, imaginative Jacobean gardens full of fancy stitches, but her husband persuaded her to stitch realistic gardens instead because of her vast knowledge of plants.

"Winter" was the first panel. Reed took the curtain on trips and picked native flora that attracted her. A scrub oak branch from Colorado, a wild rose and meadowsweet from Maine remind her of faces and places in her past. As she recovered from her arthritis, she resumed gardening and began the "Spring" and "Summer" panels. Reed always works from models. "Spring" shows the fruit pod of a skunk cabbage and a cabbage moth. She was also able to include a realistic bee "that had the courtesy to die mid-flight." The "Spring" panel took almost two years to design and stitch; "Winter" and "Summer," about one year each.

With the model before her, Reed stitches freehand and never works top to bottom. At the start, she roughly bastes tree trunks and large branches with a long running stitch to remind herself where they should lie. If there is an outline in her work, it's only because it appears in nature.

Shapes are distinguished by intricate variations of color rather than by outline. A catkin, for example, evolves from subtle shading and unedged laid work. Instead of filling in a flat, outlined sketch, Reed almost literally paints the object with wool. She creates her scenes that way too, choosing a flower that interests her, adding touches of color as she goes along. A leaf may look as if it falls across a branch, but she never embroiders one pattern on top of another. Keeping the work light allows the curtains to move freely, enhancing the illusion of a breezy garden.

The work along the bottom of the 72-in. by 36-in. panels occasionally resembles traditional, stylized Jacobean stitching, but Reed usually doesn't plan these areas; she makes them up as she goes along. She puts on special touches, then determines the rest by the need for visual or color balance, interest, and focus, or by the need to use up thread scraps.

Reed knows just how the morning light strikes a flower, the texture and feel of each petal. She picks a flower and sketches it on paper to become familiar with its

lines and contours. "It helps to know the plant," she says. "As much as I look at flowers, I'd never think of [stitching] petals falling down the way they do when they're almost over. I like to have one in full bloom, one going by." Then she puts the sketch away. If her stitching takes longer than a flower lasts, or if she wants to record its characteristics, Reed draws the subject and notes the colors with arrows to the appropriate areas. Notations like "dark, dark blue-green" are clearly those of an artist who wishes to re-create precise shades.

With the flower in front of her, she holds the wool up to it, noting the colors that appear—not those she expects. While planning a lilac for the "Spring" panel (see photos, page 106), she was surprised that no yarn matches the lilac's color precisely, so she decided to "make it interesting, if not accurate." She used several shades of blue, purple, gray, and white.

Reed's realistic renditions limit the number of stitches she can use. With more than 100 stitches possible, she uses fewer than 15 simple ones, like chain, regular and detached buttonhole, Cretan, and cor-

Reed created the lilacs in the top part of the "Spring" panel (left) with lazy-daisy stitches, tacking down the loops and adding a French knot in the middle of each floret. With stitches made close together in several shades of blue, purple, gray, and white, the flowers have a three-dimensional and massive quality. Reed stitched the main trunk and roots at the base of the "Spring" panel first (above), then filled in with fanciful laid work to create solid textures and convey the impression of foreground and background.

al stitches. Reed works single strands of wool on Belgian linen twill fabric, with only an occasional double strand for a French knot. To depict a chestnut, she uses turkey work, in which large, secured loops of wool are cut across the top to create a fuzzy effect similar to that of a pile rug. However, most of the crewel is not raised; this way the stitches can withstand being repeatedly pressed under a hoop. She occasionally adds a dark dot to make a cone or pod look three-dimensional.

Shading, particularly soft, gradual shading within one color is Joanna Reed's greatest skill. She uses as many as eight values within each shade of color. Appleton wool, an expensive yarn made by Appleton Brothers of London (up to $1/30-yd. skein), gives her a very subtle progression of colors. There are more than 400 colors on numbered cards, grouped by color family (available retail from American Crewel and Canvas Studio, 164 Canal St., Canastota, NY 13032; wholesale from Appleton Brothers of London, W. Main Rd., Little Compton, RI 02837). The yarn is popular for fine shading because the tones in its numbered value system are very close. For instance, different intensities of rose pink range from #750, the brightest, to #759, a deep, almost violet. The colors are sophisticated, subdued old-world European hues. Detractors, when you can find them, complain that Appleton is a little "fuzzy."

Pat Allen, Reed's instructor (Reed has taken classes intermittently for 17 years), teaches a group correspondence course for the Embroiderers' Guild of America. Allen insists her students use Appleton yarn even though they complain it's hard to find. She describes Appleton as "very thin single-ply wool, almost as fine as French wools. Then there's a big jump to Persian wools, the standard needlepoint kind. A single strand of Persian (divided, because it's usually three-ply) is still heavier than Appleton, and Appleton looks superb when used on fine needlepoint canvas." Allen recommends using lengths of only 10 in. or 11 in. at a time so the strand won't tangle. "Crewel was once called the Queen of Needlework," Allen says. "There are no holes, no counting. It's not regimented, and the best way to get that elegant three-dimensional look is to use a yarn with a palette as broad as Appleton's. Of course it helps to be as artistic as Joanna Reed...."

When Reed finishes a curtain, she washes it and steams it from the back to press the fabric and set the stitches. When she steamed the first panel, she covered the wet curtain with wet towels and ironed it on top of towels on the dining room table. It didn't look too good, so she washed and steamed it again. The curtain came out beautiful, but she ruined the table. She steamed the second panel on the floor, starting in the center of the curtain and working out to the ends. The panel came out well pressed, but lopsided. Reed finally asked her woodworking son-in-law to make her something like a giant sock stretcher. Serendipitously, when she went to his house for dinner, a guest who knew of the mother's and daughter's love of stitching brought a turn-of-the-century curtain stretcher as a gift. This device—four pieces of slotted wood, adjustable thumbscrews, and hundreds of pins used at regular intervals to secure the material—solved her problem.

After pressing and drying the panels, Reed backs each one with cotton fabric, adding a flannel lining between the crewel work and the cotton lining to protect the work from fading. The moss-green border stitching, not so protected, has faded over the years; in winter, when the trees are bare, the sun comes through the windows with great intensity. The combined effects of the sun and the closed house (when fireplace smoke and cigarette tar collect on the fabric) convinced Reed to take her curtains down in winter. Sometimes she stores them, sometimes she exhibits them at horticultural institutions or crewel-studio shows.

Now that the last panel, "Fall," is almost finished, Reed is looking forward to making bed hangings. She's still out in the garden, and cooking great herb-based meals, and lecturing, and writing; crewel has become yet another passion. But she enjoys having several projects going at the same time so that she can work on whatever fits her mood instead of having to force herself through a tedious problem before she's ready to conquer it. "In theory, I should finish one thing before I go on to another," she says, "but I never do. I always have at least three things going on at once. In the end, I think I get more done that way." □

Anne S. Cunningham is a free-lance writer in Devon, PA. Photos by Chew & Co.

This close-up of the wild rose of Maine from the "Spring" panel (facing page) and the pink azaleas below it reveal Reed's appreciation of flowers in each stage from bud to bloom. The feathery gray artemisia at top right is a fine example of her characteristic soft shading.

Color Blending in Needlepoint

A technique that does away with distortion and dye-lot matching

by Lloyd Walton Blanks

Soon after threading my first needle with a colorful yarn and working it into a square of canvas, I knew that at last I had found my medium—simple, old-fashioned needlepoint. I was no dilettante looking for something to busy idle hands during the evening while waiting for bedtime, but a serious artist in search of serious artistic expression. I was already past my 50th year, schooled in design, and experienced in painting and sculpture.

I had never been completely happy with any of the traditional media of the artist. In my New York apartment, for which I had exchanged the great expanses of West Texas, I found oil paints unpleasant to live with, wasteful, and annoying, as they dried too quickly or too slowly. A painting could be pushed just so far, and then it had to be set aside to dry, usually when creative fervor was at its highest. Finished canvases were rather fragile, subject to punctures, scratches, and sticking together.

Wood sculpture was not only hard labor and slow to emerge, but the clack of the chisel and mallet disturbed the neighbors. After years of turning out highly finished pieces and selling mostly to friends, I had filled my available storage. When I could no longer find seasoned blocks of wood in Manhattan, it seemed useless to go on.

Discovering needlepoint—Visiting one evening in the home of a friend, I found a small canvas with a mound of colorful yarns. The image on the canvas didn't interest me, but the yarns did. I asked my friend to show me a stitch, and I received the extent of my instruction in needlepoint—how to bend and tighten the yarn for insertion into the needle's eye, how to tie in the yarn for the first stitch, and how to do the continental stitch. She suggested that I turn the canvas upside down when I reached the end of a line, but that bit of information remained an unexplored confusion to me.

It did not take me long to learn that I did not like the continental stitch—the distortion it brought to the patch of canvas and the excessive amount of yarn it left on the reverse side. I set out to find the stitch that would suit my requirements, realizing it was unlikely that I'd invent a new stitch for such an old medium.

I stitched, inspected, and removed, while very slowly it became clear to me what I wanted. I began to do what I later learned was the vertical half-cross, merely stitching upward on one line and downward on the next, not turning the canvas as I began a new line. I liked the way the stitches lay against each other and how little yarn was retained on the back. The canvas distortion was less, though it had not disappeared completely. An instructor could have shown me the stitch in two minutes.

I now urgently needed a rack or an easel. I had cramps in my left hand, and my eyes soon tired from trying to keep up with their moving target. Most important, I could not work fast enough to produce the large pieces I expected to do. I looked at the commercial offerings and found nothing to suit my needs, so I made my own rack from found objects—a large, flat board; some sloping moldings; and a heavy cast-iron lid left over from the repaving of First Avenue, which became a weight to keep the rack from tilting into my lap. Some discard barrels offered up angled pieces of wood. I cut the lumber and put the pieces together into a remarkably workable table rack with rounded bottom corners, shown in the photo at bottom right on the facing page. While pushpins held my canvas in place, I had both hands free to work through the 17-in. by 15-in. frame. I attached the soft-pine

moldings with screws so that, when they became riddled with pushpin holes, I could replace them easily. I adjusted my rolling secretary's chair to the proper height and for back support to ensure long and comfortable hours of work.

I was exhilarated. I could find so much pleasure and so little to object to. It may be the world's slowest medium, but it is clean and accessible at all times. There is no "putting away for the day," not even for company. Work progresses steadily.

My workday would begin about 7 a.m. and last until 9 p.m. There would be breaks, of course—to eat or to walk the dog—but the needlepoint rack was never far away, and I returned to it like a homing pigeon to its loft. Long after I would have been too tired to stand around a painting or too weary to chip away at a block of wood, I sat at my table rack, pushing and pulling the needle. I continued to turn out pieces for the joy of the medium. Each piece seemed to be an individual concept, but my output was held together by a thread of regional subject matter, a throwback to my younger days and the West Texas I knew then.

I felt compelled by inner forces to complete a concept, only to be unprepared for the letdown that came with the finishing stitch. It was then that I quickly started a new piece. As my pieces began to accumulate, I rolled them to insert them into muslin sleeves—and I had no storage problem.

Refining my technique—When friends asked what I was doing with my time those days and I told them I was spending long hours on needlepoint, some became silent and looked the other way. I wanted to say, "Not *that* kind of needlepoint—mine is creative." I think subconsciously I began to try to make the stitches uneven, not round and smooth and perfectly drawn. Instead of flat areas, I

From *Threads* magazine (April 1987) 10:24-29

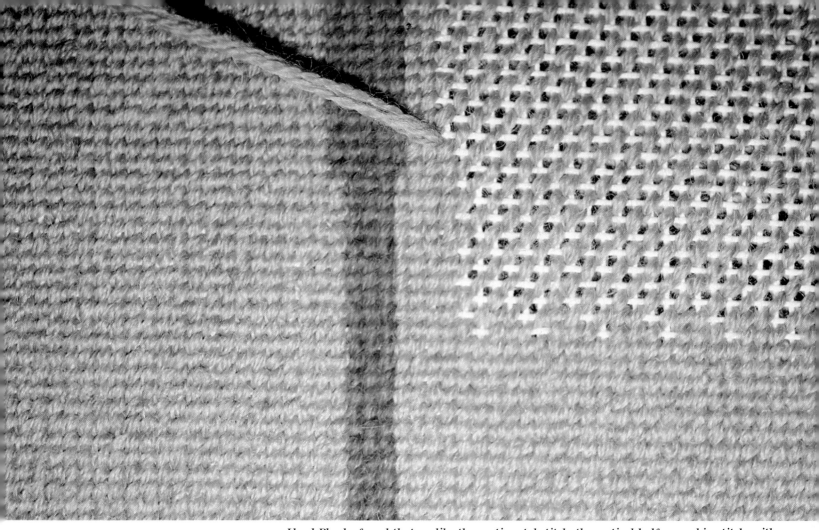

Lloyd Blanks found that, unlike the continental stitch, the vertical half-cross skip stitch, with rows worked alternately top to bottom, bottom to top, gives a smooth, distortion-free surface (above) with no excess yarn on the back of the canvas (left). All photos by author, except where noted.

Blanks (below) can comfortably work a 12-hour stitching day at his homemade table rack. Constructed of scrap wood and moldings, the sloping 17-in. by 15-in.-wide frame is counterweighted. Blanks attaches the canvas with pushpins, and both hands are free to work the top and bottom of the canvas. Staff photo.

Vertical half-cross skip stitch

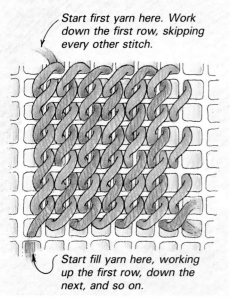

Start first yarn here. Work down the first row, skipping every other stitch.

Start fill yarn here, working up the first row, down the next, and so on.

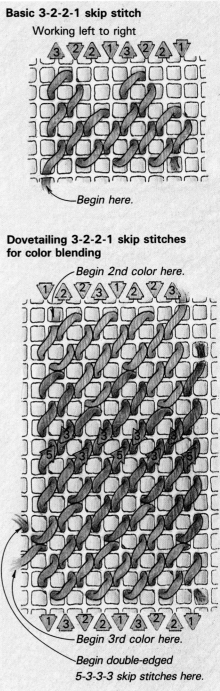

Basic 3-2-2-1 skip stitch
Working left to right

—*Begin here.*

Dovetailing 3-2-2-1 skip stitches for color blending

—*Begin 2nd color here.*

—*Begin 3rd color here.*

—*Begin double-edged 5-3-3-3 skip stitches here.*

A fill yarn will cover the canvas.

For subtle color changes, Blanks needle-mixes plies of three different colors and works his vertical half-cross skip stitch in small areas that dovetail together. Then he fills in the skipped areas with a slightly different blend of plies, depending on the effect he wants.

wanted to see something happening, not just in the relationship between the color areas, but some vibrations taking place within each single field. I worked one color of yarn on a line, skipping every other hole, and then brought in a second color to fill the remaining holes. It produced a more dynamic effect. Depending on the colors I selected, the effects were hard and glaring or soft and subtle; and the areas seemed to breathe. I combined yarns closer in hue, value, and chroma, skipping not one hole but two, three, and four holes, and then filling in with other related colors. But too much yarn built up on the reverse.

Soon I began needle-mixing the yarn: I split a strand of yarn into its three plies and combined one ply with plies of two other yarns. Using the vertical half-cross stitch and skipping every other hole, what

I call the "skip stitch," I lay in a strand of yarn composed of three colors. Then doing the same with three other yarns, I returned to fill in the remaining holes. Here was an area containing *six* different yarns, and on the reverse all stitches lay neatly side by side, all going in the same direction and as neat as the front, except for the tie-ins and tie-outs. To my pleasure, the canvas lay as smooth and squared as it was originally. I had eliminated from my work two great concerns of all needlepointers: distortion and worry about different dye lots.

Today I am on my 102nd needlepoint canvas, 12 years after I began. Changes have come slowly. I still work almost exclusively in the skip-stitch method, putting six plies in an area in two separate applications. The six plies need not all be different. It depends on the desired effect.

Often I change only one ply in the second application, which causes subtle vibrations. Too much contrast in the second set of yarns produces a disturbing diagonal pattern. I may choose to work the canvas as a whole from left to right, top to bottom, or vice versa, or to switch between areas. But within these choices, there is little, if any, stitching at random.

For example, as shown in the drawing on p. 109, if the area to be covered has an odd number of horizontal lines and I choose to begin at the top-left corner, I skip the first horizontal line and place the first half-cross-stitch to cover the second horizontal line. At the bottom of the first row, I move down one horizontal line to place the first stitch of the second, ascending row. At the top of the second row, I drop down one horizontal to place the first stitch on the

Mounting and framing

In working out my system for mounting and stretching my work, I have relied on information from textile conservators at leading museums, especially Mary W. Ballard, Senior Textile Conservator at the Conservation Analytical Laboratory at the Smithsonian Institution in Washington, D.C. It was pointed out to me that canvas that is stretched too tight will one day break somewhere. I came to the conclusion that the canvas must be pulled tight enough to eliminate sloppy sags, but no more. It was also suggested that perhaps pieces should *not* be mounted and stretched as a permanent condition, in consideration of future dismantling for cleaning or other reasons we can't foresee. Certainly the fewer the staples used, the more easily a canvas may be unstretched and removed, and the less likelihood there is of breakage and damage at the borders. My eye has now become accustomed to the idea and no longer requires that extremely taut look.

Here is my method: My mounting boards are ¼-in. white Philippine mahogany plywood, cut to size. Mahogany is lightweight, low in acid content, and not prone to warping. Birch is a good substitute. I sand the edges of the boards before applying a first coat of polyurethane to one side and the edges. The following day I turn the boards to coat the other side and the edges. I suspend the boards with pushpins and short strings from a rope stretched near the ceiling. When a month is up, I apply a second coat and rehang for another month to ensure that the boards are completely dry and that harmful fumes have evaporated.

As an extra precaution, I place a piece of acid-free (nonligneous) tissue paper on the sealed and seasoned board. I fold it around to the back to cover about 3 in. on all sides, holding it for the moment with adhesive tape. Over the paper I lay a piece of unbleached muslin, again

folding about 3 in. to the back. As I square the corners and pull to stretch the muslin across the face of the board, I use a staple gun on the back. I set in only enough staples to hold the muslin firmly over the paper. Monel metal staples are a must, as they will not rust or corrode. This provides a rigid mounting base for stapling and holding the needlepoint in its display position, while keeping the cotton canvas out of contact with the acidic wood.

On top of the prepared mounting base I place the piece of finished needlepoint, which I have lightly pressed on the reverse side with a steam iron and allowed to dry. The borders are about ¹⁄₁₆ in. smaller than the mounting board so that there will be no puckering when the frame is attached later. I position the corners first and then work out toward the middle of the edges. I strive for a consistent ⅝-in. border from the edge of the board to the first row of yarn. I staple, checking constantly with a ruler and an L square. Nothing is more irritating to me than seeing a line of stitches disappear off the edge and under the frame.

My frames have a wide lip to cover the ⅝-in. border. The face is 1¼ in. wide, flat, painted white, and unadorned. I repeat the polyurethane treatment on the raw wood that is not painted white. I screw a stretcher to the back of the frame to hold the mounting board securely in place, but it can be removed easily.

Pieces that may be exhibited once or twice a year spend most of their time in storage, stacked flat, in their unbleached muslin slipcovers, in a well-ventilated room. Between the large pieces I have placed sheets of nonligneous tissue paper. Over the different stacks are thin covers, as additional protection from light and dust. I let no more than four months elapse before rearranging, airing, and inspecting. —L.W.B.

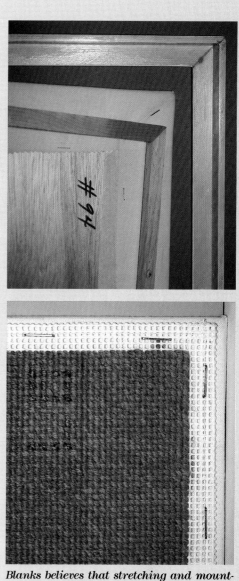

Blanks believes that stretching and mounting should finish and protect the needlepoint but not seal it in permanently. He covers the polyurethane-treated mounting board with acid-free tissue and muslin, then sparingly uses Monel staples to attach the piece to the board. The frame's lip covers the raw canvas.

---

third, descending row, and so forth, until the first application is completed.

To fill in the skipped stitches, I begin at the bottom-left corner. This plan, in addition to mixing the colors, ensures that on the reverse all stitches run in the same direction and lie flat without causing distortion of the canvas. I do not go into the same hole with two consecutive stitches, as it produces knots on the reverse side.

For an area with an even number of horizontal lines to be covered, I work the area as described above but leave the bottom line until last. I complete this line separately with a skip-stitch horizontal movement, left to right and back to left.

A color area that is too large to be worked at one time may be broken down into sections that can be managed on the rack. Using the 3-2-2-1 skip-stitch pattern (three

skip stitches in the first row, two in the second, etc.), I make sections with zigzag edges that dovetail together, thus avoiding objectionable division lines, as shown in the drawings and photo on the facing page.

I use the same 3-2-2-1 skip-stitch pattern for blending colors to develop the illusion of space and distance—to make areas recede toward the background or advance into the foreground. Blending, a movement toward a different hue, value, chroma, or all or any combination of the three, also establishes mood and atmospheric effects.

I introduce vertical blending in horizontal bands. With each new color band, I incorporate a new ply or strand of yarn that leads the color blending in the desired direction, using a variation of the 3-2-2-1 pattern that will dovetail properly with the previous band. The eye must tell if the grada-

tion is effective. Just as a painter may not try to conceal his brush strokes, I may not try to conceal my blending bands. In fact, a visual hint of the bands and the technique contributes to the pictorial structure.

My materials and tools—After finding some undesirable characteristics of nonfraying, interlocking canvas, I have come to use 10-gauge, 40-in.-wide mono cotton canvas. The strings of mono canvas are not actually interlocked in weaving, as is the case with interlocking canvas, so they are less rigid and will give easy access to needle and yarn. Mono canvas has more fibers per string and is heavier than interlocking canvas. It is less subject to breakage with age. Mono's slightly thicker strings make the holes in the canvas slightly smaller, so coverage is more nearly complete, and I

seldom find those little glints of white canvas showing through the yarn.

After I cut the mono canvas to my planned sizes, I protect the edges from fraying by machine-sewing straight down the first string on each edge of the canvas to secure it to the crossing strings. I use all-cotton thread and about 20 stitches per inch.

As far as I am able to determine, there is no right or wrong side to these canvases, but the position of the selvage does make a difference in the ease of manipulating the yarn. I keep the selvage to the sides, not at the top or bottom. When cutting the canvas into smaller portions, I indicate the top or bottom for future reference.

To prevent the yarn from snagging on the raw edge, to ensure against raveling, and to strengthen the borders, I hem the canvas, turning it back between the fourth and fifth lines and machine stitching.

On the front, I machine-baste ⅝-in.-wide cloth tape over the borders to keep them clean while I'm working, having learned well the obnoxious qualities of masking tape for this purpose. Later, I usually remove the cloth tape with a razor blade. Tape on the borders can constrict the corners during stretching and prevent the canvas from lying perfectly flat (see "Mounting and framing," page 111). On the other hand, if left in place, the tape becomes a cushion and guard between the canvas and the staples, an especially helpful protection if the staples will be removed later.

It is very possible that I have the distinction of being the only needleworker of more than ten years who has never lost a needle. After five years of good and faithful service, still in its prime and showing no wear, my first tapestry needle was retired to an index card for my files. I replaced the sec-

ond one, simply and without ceremony about two years ago: I came across an extra-long needle, a No. 16 darner's needle, which I filed to bluntness. I am comfortable with the way it goes in and out of the canvas, and it suits the size of my hands better than a regular tapestry needle.

The first yarn I bought was Paternayan Persian wool, and I have continued to use it exclusively. The color range meets my needs, it is mothproof, and the strands can be easily divided into separate plies. For future reference, I keep a card file of 1-in. samples of color combinations that seem particularly effective.

Building a body of work—There is, in this most deliberate and regimented medium, the satisfaction that comes from watching work accumulate slowly, stitch by stitch. It's like plowing the land round by round

or row by row, looking behind at what's been done and ahead at what remains.

In June of 1979 I began "Front Gallery Series" and am now doing the 56th piece in that series. Some are as small as 11 in. by 12 in.; others are as large as 69 in. by 38 in. In all of them I, the viewer, look out toward the horizon from a sheltering porch.

My paternal grandmother called the long porch that curved across the front of the farmhouse the "front gallery." I was born in that West Texas house, just before the days of the Dust Bowl. My grandmother would sit, looking up the north road, watching for signs of rain, and I learned to look at the horizon also, to watch the land and sky under all atmospheric conditions. Under the Texas sun, summer after summer, the land lay parched, and nothing green grew. When no rains came, the winds whipped the topsoil of Oklahoma and the Panhandle into the sky, and in the noon darkness the cows came up for milking, chickens went to roost, and at night we slept uneasily with wet cloths across our faces.

I saw the first haze in the fall indicating a blue norther, and I watched the clouds gathering in the northwest to come up after dark as storms, which sent us racing to the cellar, hopeful for rain, fearful of wind and hail and a twister. We waited out the storms while they raged and tore above our heads. When the southeast rumbled and quiet had returned to our land, we laid back the cellar door and came out to nights of stars.

To that West Texas I return for statements that will stand clear and valid, spanning and uniting my years. Front gallery, land, and sky are the psychological symbols in the pictorial language I know, a formalism of structure with the atmosphere of color, in needlepoint, my chosen medium. □

Lloyd W. Blanks was born in 1922 near Abilene, TX. He moved to New York City in 1951, where he studied art and worked at the New School for Social Research. In 1985, he retired to devote full time to his needlepoint. He has exhibited at the New School, Marymount Manhattan College, Marcoleo, Ltd. Gallery in New York City, and The Textile Museum in Washington, D.C. He is represented in Needle Expressions '86.

Blanks began the "Front Gallery Series" in 1979. "Prairie Moon" (above), 18 in. by 10 in., is one of the first of 56 needlepoint pieces that explore the same theme: the horizon seen from a sheltering porch. Owned by Helene Breban, NYC.

In "Night Cloud" (top left), Blanks renders the quality of the atmosphere against the barely discernible elements of the porch through subtle color blending. 17 in. by 18½ in., 1986.

The image is abstracted to a few elements (facing page): the porch floor, pillar, and roof, the horizon, and a cloud. Color blending within each contained area creates vibrations and an illusion of movement and distance. "Dry-Weather Cloud, III," 16½ in. by 18½ in., 1985.

Embroidery from Japan's Snow Country

Simple running stitches make complex *sashiko* patterns

by Hiroko Ogawa

When I was growing up in Kiso, in central Japan, my grandmother, who was from the northern region of Tohoku, taught me the simple running stitch, *unshin* ("carrying the needle"), which is used for all Japanese handsewing, including the style of embroidery called *sashiko* ("doing stitching"). This was my first exposure to *sashiko* patterns (see photo, facing page). The dynamic patterns look complicated but are merely lines of running stitches that never touch one another. Later, my mother, a professional silk embroiderer, taught me how to do grid-based *sashiko* (*hitomezashi*), in which the running stitches are long and fill in square units.

I started collecting *sashiko* patterns from books, old documents, antique pieces, and modern kimonos and have over 300 patterns, each of which has its own name. Now I do *sashiko* full time and am constantly inspired by the work of Japanese embroiderers, dyers, and weavers, as well as by the free spirit of southern California and the U.S. I like to stitch *sashiko* patterns onto indigo-dyed cotton, Japanese ikat, nubby cotton or silk, dyed and discharged cotton, or cloth rewoven from old fabrics. I also like to make garments that follow traditional Japanese style lines but that have a contemporary flair. *Sashiko* is dynamic, yet it's easy to learn and offers many creative possibilities. My style of *sashiko* is rooted in Japanese tradition but is influenced by Eastern and Western cultures.

History of *sashiko*—*Sashiko* was used in early times all over Japan, although it flourished most beautifully in the northern farming regions of Tohoku. During the Tokugawa shogunate (1603-1867), only people in the ruling class could wear or use silk and wool. Common people made fabrics from wild plants, such as willow, wisteria, and paper mulberry, and from cultivated plants, such as hemp or flax. After it was introduced to Japan from southeast Asia and India in the 17th century, cotton was also allowed but remained precious because northern Japan's climate was unsuitable for growing cotton.

Wives of farmers, fishermen, workmen, and artisans developed *sashiko* as a means of strengthening or thickening the precious fabrics of work clothes. They used running stitches to quilt two or three layers of fabric together. Besides using *sashiko,* people also dyed fabrics with indigo because the scent protected cloth from moths.

White thread showed particularly well against the shades of indigo dyes and inspired the imagination and creativity of the snow-country women. They adapted the printed patterns from forbidden silk kimonos—flowers, ocean waves, birds, bamboo—into beautiful geometric *sashiko* embroidery patterns and stitched these onto their plain indigo cotton or linen fabrics. Ordinary work garments were transformed into elegant, artistic creations.

Grid-based *sashiko,* with overlapping layers of stitches, was developed to reinforce garments much more strongly than regular *sashiko*. In the north, people wore

Patterns for the Japanese embroidery called sashiko *are often stylized images from nature. At left, Fan and Ocean-Wave patterns decorate the pillow, and imaginary flowers grace the purple tunic (courtesy of Miko Miyama). The quilt displays family crests (courtesy of Mr. and Mrs. Katsunori Watanabe). All work is by Hiroko Ogawa. While doing a running stitch, Ogawa (right) keeps only her thumbs on the right side of the fabric. As she pushes the tip of the needle up through the fabric with her right index finger, she pulls the fabric down over the needle tip with the fingers of her left hand.*

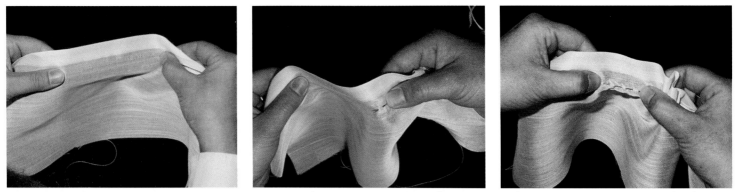

Running-stitch sequence: Push needle tip down; pull fabric up (left). Push needle tip up; pull fabric down (center). Smooth fabric (right).

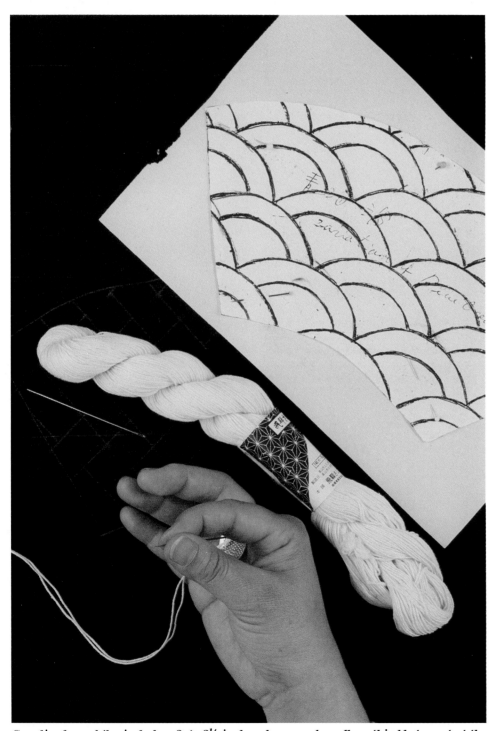

Supplies for sashiko include a 2- to 2½-in.-long large-eyed needle, a thimble to protect the base of the middle finger on the sewing hand (worn as shown), 100% cotton sashiko or candlewicking thread, tracing paper, a predrafted pattern, and fabric. During stitching, the sewing hand grasps the needle between thumb and forefinger, which are stretched as far as possible. The eye of the needle rests against the thimble.

specially designed sleeveless vests when hauling lumber on small sleds. Grid-based *sashiko* was placed on the shoulder or side of the vest, where the hauling rope was slung. Like regular *sashiko, hitomezashi* is now used for artistic decoration rather than practical reinforcement. Its elegant beauty reminds me of European lace.

Sashiko also developed into forms that are similar to needlepoint, called *kogin* and *hishizashi*, but I'll be talking only about the running stitch and grid-based *sashiko*.

The basic running stitch—The stitch used for *sashiko* is easy to learn. It is done with a push-pull rhythm of needle and cloth, aided by a Japanese thimble. You grasp the needle between your thumb and forefinger, with your fingers stretched out as far as possible and the eye of the needle always resting against the plate of the thimble (photo at left). Your thumbs work on the right side of the fabric, while your hands and forefingers work on the fabric's underside (photo, p. 115). The art of achieving beautiful *sashiko* is to keep all stitches even and straight.

To practice the running stitch, you need a 2- to 2½-in.-long large-eyed needle, *sashiko* or candlewicking thread, fabric, and a *sashiko* thimble (photo at left) to wear on the base of the middle finger of your right hand (all directions are for right-handed people). If you can't find a *sashiko* thimble, stick adhesive tape to the base of your middle finger to protect your palm. I prefer to keep *sashiko* simple, and the soft matte-finish untreated *sashiko* thread suits it well (see "Supplies," p. 118).

Cut the thread 50 to 53 in. long, thread the needle and double the thread. Poke the needle into the fabric and put the eye of the needle against the thimble (see above photos for stitching process). Hold the needle and fabric between your thumb and index finger. Place your left hand about 4 in. ahead of your right hand. Pull the fabric slightly to provide some tension. This is important for straight, even stitches.

For the first stitch, push the needle into the fabric with your thumb. At the same time, pull the fabric into the tip of the needle and toward yourself with your left hand. Then lift your right index finger and inch it toward the point of the needle. For the

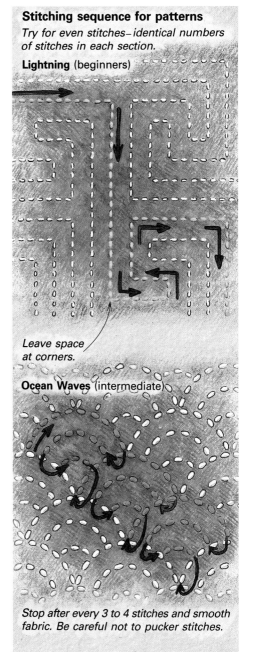

Stitching sequence for patterns

Try for even stitches–identical numbers of stitches in each section.

Lightning (beginners)

Leave space at corners.

Ocean Waves (intermediate)

Stop after every 3 to 4 stitches and smooth fabric. Be careful not to pucker stitches.

Seven Treasures of Buddha (advanced)

Draw a small circle in white pencil in center of each intersection and do not enter circle with stitches.

Illustrations by Christopher Clapp

Stitches in the table runner Hiroko Ogawa holds are, from top to bottom: Cypress Fence, Seven Treasures of Buddha, Hemp Leaves Variation, Blue Ocean Waves, Lightning, and a Blue Ocean Waves Variation. Hiroko's dress contains, from top to bottom: Sayagata (a traditional pattern to ward off evil), Basketwork, Armor of the Mystic Warrior, Bishamon, Blue Ocean Waves, and Hemp Leaves. Sierra Madre, invented by Hiroko, is behind the table runner.

second stitch, push the needle up through the fabric with your right index finger, and pull the fabric into the tip of the needle and away from yourself with your left hand. Inch your right thumb toward the tip of the needle. Repeat the seesawing motion with your hands, inching your right index finger and thumb alternately along the stitching line at the point of the needle until the needle reaches the left hand and the fabric is bunched on the needle. Then hold the tip of the needle with your left thumb and index finger and pull the fabric smooth over the needle and thread. Don't scrape the thread with your fingernails; this makes the thread fuzzy. Your stitches should be neither too tight nor too loose, and they should look like evenly spaced short-grain rice kernels, with the stitches on the right side of the fabric slightly longer than those on the wrong side. Keep practicing, and adjust your stitches to a gauge of 4 to 5 stitches per inch. You can use more stitches per inch, but keep your gauge consistent.

Stitching sequence—To start a project, I trace a pattern onto the fabric with pattern tracing paper and a ballpoint pen. I stitch the border before going to the inner design. I use photocopies of patterns I've already drafted and prepare a copy that covers the entire area I plan to stitch. This pre-vents inaccuracies in pattern placement that might appear if I had to move a smaller photocopy around. I judge the scale of the pattern I should use by considering how it will look in my project. There's no set scale; I use the scale that appeals to me.

The goal in stitching a pattern is to keep thread waste and knots to a minimum and to stitch the longest possible lines before jumping to a new line. Look for long, continuous lines, whether undulating or straight. At intersecting lines the rule is: "Start sewing after the line and stop before the line." This means you must put some space between stitches at intersecting lines, junctions, and corners. Don't cross stitches or attach them to each other unless crossed stitches are part of the pattern. Each traditional *sashiko* pattern has its own effective stitching order, but I usually experiment to try to determine an efficient sequence. Lightning is a good pattern for beginners (for patterns, see drawings and photo, p. 117) because it consists of straight sections of continuous lines. The tricky part is to stitch just up to, and after, the corner, leaving a space at the corner itself. Ocean Waves is of medium difficulty because it is hard to adjust the tension of the curving lines of stitches. The Seven Treasures of Buddha is for advanced stitchers because the flowers in the center of each motif require very precise stitches. To make sure the spaces in the flower centers are all the same, I draw a tiny circle at the intersection of the circular motifs and stop my stitches outside the circles. Again, keeping the stitches even and smooth is difficult.

Grid-based sashiko—*Hitomezashi* combines straight running stitches and interlaced stitches plus double and single strands of thread. The interlaced threads don't go through the fabric unless you're tying a knot. I use thinner thread, and, with a sharp white pencil and ruler, I draw a grid pattern on my material before I begin. This may sound like a lot of white lines, but the white brushes off as you work the pattern.

The Tortoise Shell (drawing and photo below) is a good beginning grid pattern. First I stitch horizontal rows of running stitches with single strands of thread. Then I weave vertical lines of single-strand thread through the edges of the horizontal stitches on the right side, going to the wrong side only to tie off the strands. (I knot most of the woven strands at the ends of a column.) The effect is something like the plates of a tortoise's shell. □

Hiroko Ogawa designs clothes and other items embellished with sashiko *and teaches* sashiko *on the West Coast.*

Books

Benjamin, Bonnie. *Sashiko: The Quilting of Japan from Traditional to Today.* Glendale, CA: Needlearts International, 1986.
An introduction to sashiko *for quilters. (Benjamin doesn't employ the stitching technique that is traditionally used in Japan.) Discusses pattern drafting.*

Ota, Kimi. *Sashiko Quilting,* 1981. Distributed by author: 10300 61st Ave. So., Seattle, WA 98178.
An introduction to sashiko. *Includes several tracing patterns and projects.*

Supplies

Kasuri Dyeworks
1959 Shattuck Ave.
Berkeley, CA 94704
(415) 841-4509
Sashiko thread, indigo fabrics, books, unpunched plastic pattern templates (sashiko stencils).

Needlearts International
Box 6447, Dept. T
Glendale, CA 91205
(213) 227-1535
Thread, prepunched plastic pattern templates, books (wholesale and retail).

Hiroko Ogawa
1661 Neil Armstrong St., #243
Montebello, CA 90640
(213) 726-8632
Thread, thimbles, paper patterns, needles, handwoven fabrics.

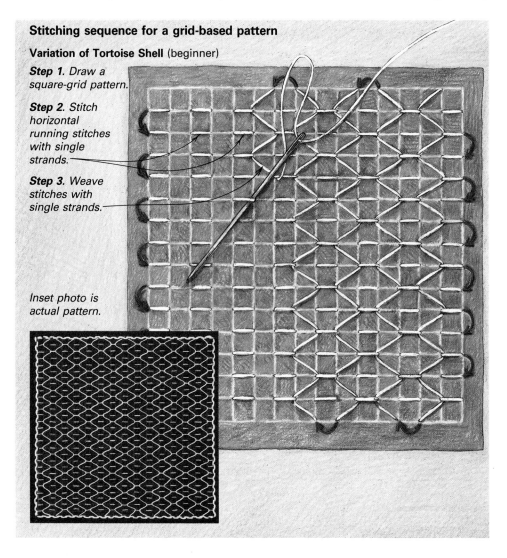

Stitching sequence for a grid-based pattern

Variation of Tortoise Shell (beginner)

Step 1. Draw a square-grid pattern.

Step 2. Stitch horizontal running stitches with single strands.

Step 3. Weave stitches with single strands.

Inset photo is actual pattern.

Needle Lace

"Stitches in the air" are the simplest and freest form of lacemaking

by Eunice Kaiser

If you can thread a needle and sew a crooked seam, you've already mastered the first step in making beautiful lace. You'll soon be able to dazzle friends and family with an intricate-looking heirloom of the future, while secretly laughing because you know how easily that effect can be achieved.

Needle lace is just what the name implies—a simple lace made with needle and thread, consisting of buttonhole stitches grouped in various ways to create designs. There are no threads or stitches to be counted and no big expenses for equipment or supplies. The piece is easily carried and is ideal to work on at odd moments.

My method consists of drawing the outline of the motif on a cloth construction pad, then couching down two or more strands of thread along the outline. These threads become the framework, or skeleton, of the piece. I work filling stitches onto these construction threads until I've filled in the desired areas. I then remove the couching stitches, and the lace becomes free of its cloth backing. It becomes *punto in aria,* "stitches in the air."

Setting up a design—The cloth for the construction pad should be a closely woven cotton. A piece from a used percale bed sheet is ideal. You may draw the motif directly on the cloth or transfer it from a paper pattern, tracing lightly with dressmaker's carbon or a heat-transfer pencil. If a motif works well, you may want to use the pad again. Darken the lines with waterproof ink or liquid embroidery while you're constructing the pad. This will enable you to launder the pad.

An alternate method is to lay a piece of thin, transparent cotton fabric directly over the drawing of the motif and trace the lines with the waterproof ink or liquid embroidery. (Nonwoven fabric or a slick woven synthetic is unsuitable.)

After putting the motif on the cloth, cut out the shape, allowing about a 1½-in. margin around it. If you choose the thin material, fuse a piece of Pellon to the back for stability. Cut two more pieces of percale the same size and shape as the first. Stack the three pieces with the drawn motif on

top, making sure they lie flat and smooth. Turn under the raw edges, and stitch the layers together around the outside edge.

When using the percale as the top layer, you can use Pellon in lieu of the middle layer of percale or as an additional layer to give more firmness. The pad should be firm enough to maintain the intended distance between the stitches without buckling, yet soft enough to allow you to fold under areas you're not working on.

There should be strong color contrasts among the construction pad, the couching thread, and the lace or filling thread. This makes the work easier; it also facilitates removal of the couching once the piece is completed. My favorites are a light-blue pad, bright-red sewing thread for the couching, and white lace thread.

You have a wide choice of lace threads. Time spent experimenting with different fibers and combinations of threads and colors is time well spent. For both the construction outlines and the filling stitches I prefer 30/3 linen. It has a hard twist and enough body to lie well, yet it is flexible. I

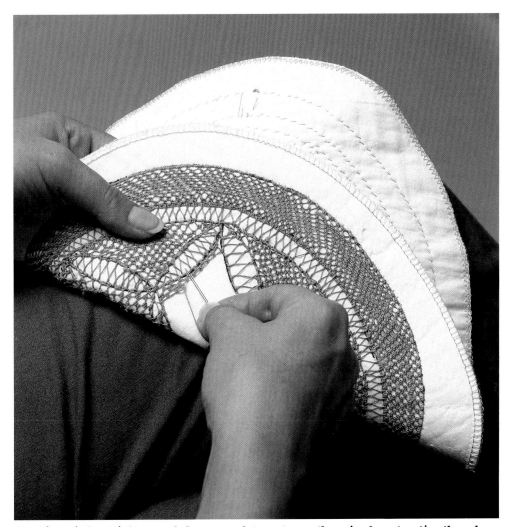

Couching stitches (pink) are only long enough to cross over the pair of construction threads on the surface of the pad. On the underside of the construction pad, the stitches slant and are about ³⁄₁₆ in. long. The pad, two layers of percale with Pellon between them, is firm enough to lie flat, yet flexible enough to be folded when you're working.

also like DMC's 20/2 Cebelia crochet thread. If you enjoy working with finer thread, so much the better. However, I suggest that you do your first piece with thread heavy enough to produce stitches that can be seen easily.

Laying the construction threads—Now you are ready to make the lace. Thread a sewing needle, and knot the end of the thread. Lay two strands of construction thread along the outline, staggering the ends (see drawing at top left). To outline the motif, narrow braids, tape, or commercially made lace or ribbon may be used instead of the pair of construction threads. (See the article on pages 16-20). Couch them down with a whipstitch, sewing through all thicknesses of the construction pad. Try to have as few breaks in the outline threads as possible. If you have to make a break, join the ends by staggering them about an inch, as shown in the drawing at top, near right.

The whipstitches should be slanting, about ³⁄₁₆ in. long on the underside of the pad, and just long enough on the surface to cross the laid threads (see photo, page 119). Pull them snugly against the outline threads. It is important that the couching stitches be evenly spaced, because that will make the filling work easier and more attractive. A few backstitches made into the underside of the construction pad will secure the end of the couching thread. Instead of cutting off the construction thread close to the last couching stitch, leave a 36-in. to 48-in. length to be used for filling stitches. This eliminates two additional ends to be worked in.

Filling stitches—When all the couching is complete, the sewing needle and thread are replaced by a tapestry needle carrying the filling thread. From this point on, make sure the stitches go under the construction thread only and not—I repeat—not into the cloth. Leading with the eye of the needle rather than the point facilitates this.

When we were children, Mother disapproved of our using an extremely long thread to avoid rethreading the needle. Her discipline resulted in my sister's dreaming she sat in a sewing circle where Satan was using such a long thread that he had to jump out the window each time he pulled the needle through. I don't recommend that long a thread, but I do use one thread that's considerably longer than I'd use for sewing a garment. The tapestry needle is easily threaded, but too many thread ends can make an unwanted bulge in the outline. The drawing at top right shows one solution to the long-thread problem.

The filling buttonhole stitches, which are worked the same as blanket stitches, can be grouped in various ways. The basic stitch may be combined with other stitches, embellished, or worked very tightly or in varying degrees of looseness, depending on the effect desired in a given area; but it is al-

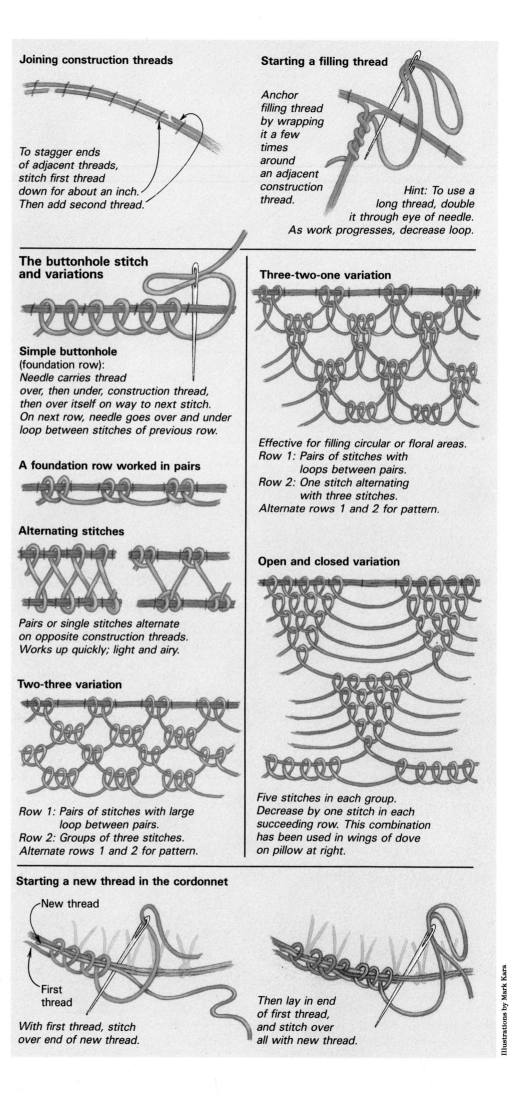

Joining construction threads

To stagger ends of adjacent threads, stitch first thread down for about an inch. Then add second thread.

Starting a filling thread

Anchor filling thread by wrapping it a few times around an adjacent construction thread.

Hint: To use a long thread, double it through eye of needle. As work progresses, decrease loop.

The buttonhole stitch and variations

Simple buttonhole (foundation row): Needle carries thread over, then under, construction thread, then over itself on way to next stitch. On next row, needle goes over and under loop between stitches of previous row.

A foundation row worked in pairs

Alternating stitches

Pairs or single stitches alternate on opposite construction threads. Works up quickly; light and airy.

Two-three variation

Row 1: Pairs of stitches with large loop between pairs.
Row 2: Groups of three stitches.
Alternate rows 1 and 2 for pattern.

Three-two-one variation

Effective for filling circular or floral areas.
Row 1: Pairs of stitches with loops between pairs.
Row 2: One stitch alternating with three stitches.
Alternate rows 1 and 2 for pattern.

Open and closed variation

Five stitches in each group. Decrease by one stitch in each succeeding row. This combination has been used in wings of dove on pillow at right.

Starting a new thread in the cordonnet

New thread

First thread

With first thread, stitch over end of new thread.

Then lay in end of first thread, and stitch over all with new thread.

Needle lace can be used for decorative items or apparel. The pillow uses hairpin-lace construction threads as an intricate part of the design. Note the five-stitch-group pattern in the dove's wings. The beauty of the simple 18-in. doily is in the contrast of the stitch patterns. They are worked, from the center, in this order: five-stitch groups (drawing, left) in the stylized flower, pairs of stitches worked on opposite construction threads, spiders or wheels (drawing, right), four rows of the five-stitch groups, and a border of pairs on opposite construction threads.

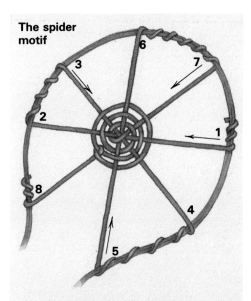

The spider motif

Another useful stitch is the spider motif (shown in photo at left). It is worked into the intersection of seven threads. Weave under and over the seven threads (legs of spider), going around circle three times. Make small stitch back into resulting circle; then carry thread to new point, making eighth leg and completing motif.

ways made the same way. (There are many other needle-lace stitches in Thérèse de Dillmont's *The Complete Encyclopedia of Needlework*—see "Further reading" at right.)

Shading and contrast of light and dark areas, which bring out the shape of a motif, are determined not so much by the stitch grouping as by how loosely and how far apart the stitches are worked. This amounts to applying more or less thread in an area, in much the same way that an artist uses more or less pigment on an oil painting. It is literally painting with threads. Frequently, one stitch pattern can be easily exchanged for another in a given space, but the same rules of contrast apply. To ensure that the lace lies flat, stitches at the edges of a piece should be compact. If they are made too loosely, the edges often stretch and produce a ruffled effect.

Before beginning the filling stitches, mark the areas of the pattern you plan to work very closely. Since these areas tend to stabilize the piece, fill them in first.

To anchor the filling thread at the start, wrap it two or three times around an adjacent construction thread. Never make a knot. (End a thread the same way.)

Make the foundation row by putting a pair of buttonhole stitches between every two couching stitches (see drawing at left). Pairs are invaluable as a filler. They can be worked very close together or with large loops between pairs. When worked loosely, the light and airy effect forms a good background to emphasize the motif. In densely filled areas, single stitches may be used. However, unless they are small and very close together, they will become uneven when the following row is worked into them.

Sections can be worked back and forth or around and around, depending on the shape and pattern. Hold the last row of stitches in each section in place by carrying the thread under the construction thread between that section and the next section to be stitched. The circular motion that makes the buttonhole stitch also twists the thread. To reduce the twist, twirl the needle between your thumb and forefinger as you pull the thread through, or hold the work in midair and let the needle dangle.

To avoid running out of thread in the middle of a row, estimate how much thread you'll need. This will vary with different stitch combinations, but a general rule is two and a half times the distance across the row. If you must join threads halfway across, split the ends of the old and new lengths, twist together half of each strand, and then wrap them with very fine thread.

Finishing—When all areas are filled in, finish the piece by retracing the outline of the motif with two additional strands of thread. Couch them down and buttonhole-stitch over the additional threads to tie them together with the construction threads and any other lace threads that have been laid on the construction threads. This is called the cordonnet.

These stitches should be very close so the other threads are covered and smoothed over. When you're working the cordonnet, cover the start of a new thread with the end of the old one: Lay the new strand of thread over the threads added for the cordonnet and continue working over all with the thread left in the needle (see bottom drawing, facing page). When there are only

a few inches of thread in the needle, unthread the needle and lay the remaining short end over the cordonnet threads. Thread the needle with the new length of thread and run the needle through the last few stitches. Continue with the stitching.

After you've completed the cordonnet, whipstitch a few times into the edge of the work, and cut off. You may lightly spray the piece with starch and press it from the underside of the construction pad. Never move the iron back and forth over the lace.

Remove the couching threads, clipping them on the back of the pad so you can pull them out. Lift the lace, and lay it over a dark background. Now admire!

Eunice Kaiser, of Odessa, TX, is a fiber artist who specializes in lacemaking, weaving, and knitting.

Further reading

Bath, Virginia Churchill. *Lace.* New York: Penguin Books, 1979.

Close, Eunice. *Lace Making.* London: William Clowes and Sons, 1975.

De Dillmont, Thérèse. *The Complete Encyclopedia of Needlework.* Philadelphia: Running Press, 1972.
Contains a wealth of information, including lace stitches; $7.95.

Kaiser, Eunice Gifford. *Enjoy Making Teneriffe and Other Lace,* 1981. Kaiser Crafts, 604 Placer, Odessa, TX 79763. $8.95, $1.50 P/H; $.45 tax in Texas.

Voysey, Cynthia. Needlelace in Photographs. London: B.T. Batsford, 1987. Distributed by Robin and Russ Handweavers, McMinnville, OR; $26.00

Contemporary Needle Lacers

Early needle lace from the 16th century, derived from cutwork and drawnwork, was mostly geometric in design. But during the late Renaissance in Europe, when it was discovered that the construction threads could be as free as any pencil line, needle lace began to blossom into florals and all sorts of naturalistic and imaginative images.

Pounced parchment served as a sturdy foundation for the often-used patterns. As the photos on these pages show, contemporary lacemakers are taking the technique still further. Some are using three-dimensional frameworks as the foundation or are combining needle lace with other techniques, such as macramé, tatting, weaving, and machine embroidery.

The motifs in Jean Goldberg's "Australian Wildflower Shoe" come from the natural colors and shapes of local flowers. The upper, sole, and heel were stitched as separate pieces and mounted on a thin acrylic sheet. Motifs of silk thread and glass beads are grounded on a mesh made with nylon monofilament. Length, 8 in. (Photo by Goldberg)

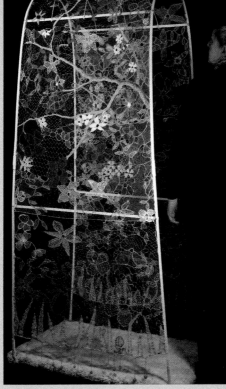

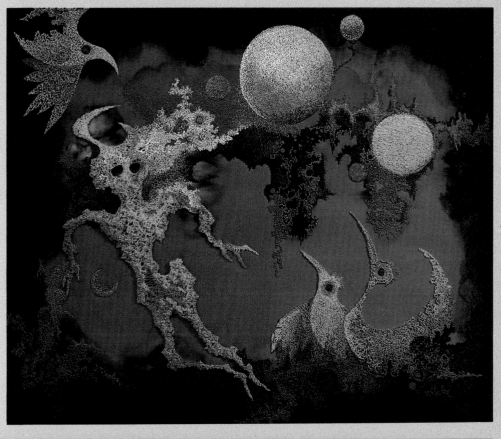

Wilcke Smith, of Albuquerque, NM, approaches needle lace in an informal and textural way, combining it with other techniques. For "Realm of the Ancient Moon," she dyed a silk ground fabric and worked over that with a hand needle and sewing machine. The birds are machine-loop-stitched, the moons and background textures are machine- and hand-stitched, and the figure is random, interlaced detached-buttonhole stitch. For this piece, she worked with Veloura, Ostara, rayon gimp, wool, and Danish cotton. (Photo by Smith)

Goldberg, of Victoria, Australia, walks into her "Dreaming Place in Needle Lace," made of linen, cotton, silk, and acrylic materials ranging from fine threads to knitting yarns. The lace panels are mounted on a painted aluminum frame. 75 in. x 25 in. x 36 in.

Goldberg worked "Wheels" over cut-up newspaper ads in very fine linen and joined the motifs with decorated bars, proving that sources for images can be found almost anywhere. 14 in. x 18 in. (Photo by Goldberg)

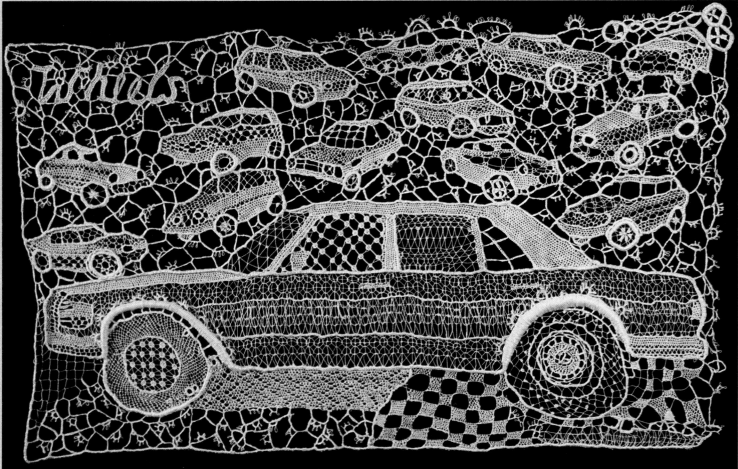

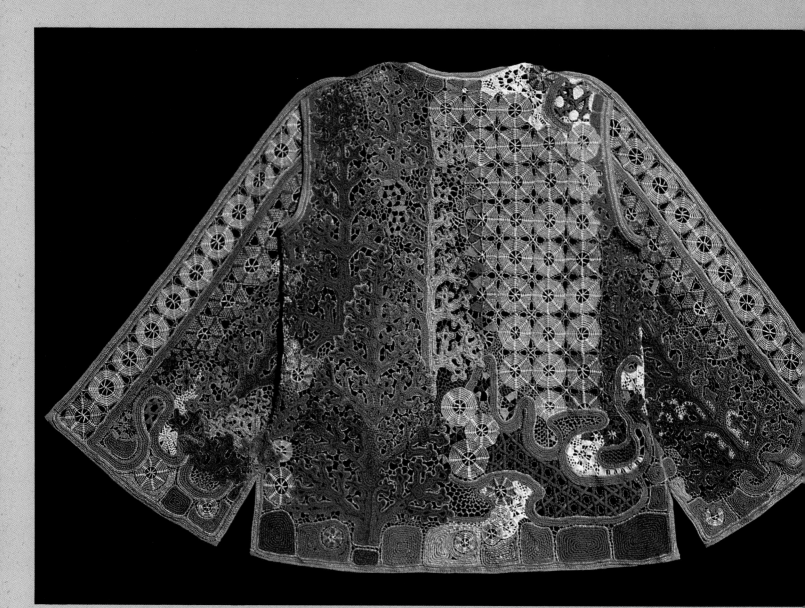

Virginia Churchill Bath, author of Lace (see "Further reading," page 121) and other needlework books, makes needle-lace constructions, using wire rings, wood, and Plexiglas as frameworks. "Long Construction" (far right) combines needle lace with raised embroidery, in linen, silk, cotton, synthetics, and suede with mica, wood, and metal. Her "Red Tree 2" jacket, above (detail, facing page, top left), in linen, wool, silk, cotton, and suede, uses geometric fillings on a ground of tight buttonholed bars, or bridges. (Photos by Bath)

Bucky King raises thoroughbred horses in Sheridan, WY, and makes lace "for love and freedom of the soul." She handspun the beige Brussels linen for "Lace Flower," right, which has detached petals and a raised center. (Photo by King)

For her "Edwardian Lace Hat," left, Christina Larkin, of Cloverdale, CA, used cotton yarn, which works up quickly. She combined Irish-crocheted flowers and edgings with the needle lace. The separate pieces for the hat's brim, top, and sides began with chain-stitch crochet-covered wire, couched to a double-layer paper construction pad. When the wired pieces are joined with a fagoting stitch, the soft cotton hat holds its shape. (Photo by Larkin) □

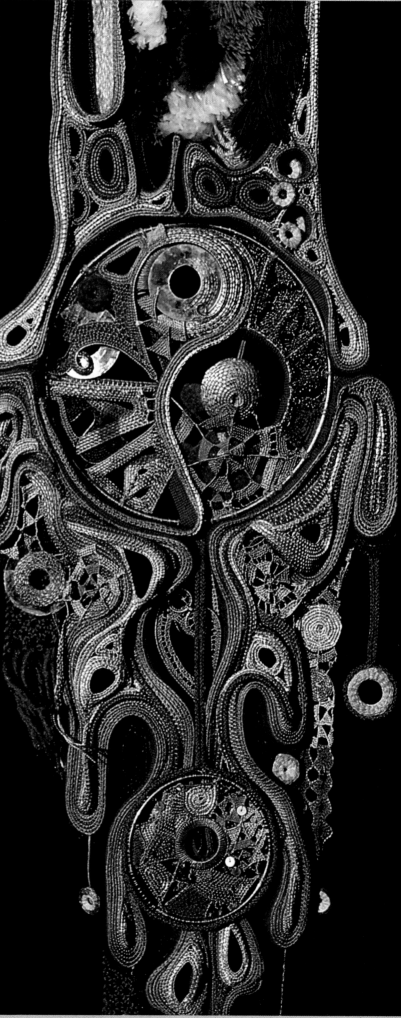

Index

If you enjoyed this book, you're going to love our magazine.

A year's subscription to *THREADS* brings you the kind of hands-on information you found in this book, and much more. In issue after issue - six times a year - you'll find articles on sewing, needlecrafts and textile arts. Artists and professionals will share their best techniques and trade secrets with you. With detailed illustrations and full-color photographs that bring each project to life, *THREADS* will inspire you to create your best work ever!

To subscribe, just fill out one of the attached subscription cards or call us at 1-203-426-8171. And as always, your satisfaction is guaranteed, or we'll give you your money back.

Use this card to subscribe to *THREADS* or to request information about other Taunton Press magazines, books and videos.

☐ 1 year (6 issues) for just $24 - over 15% off the newsstand price. Outside the U.S. $28/year (U.S. funds, please. Canadian residents add 7% GST)

☐ 2 years (12 issues) for just $40 - almost 30% off the newsstand price. Outside the U.S. $49/year (U.S. funds, please. Canadian residents add 7% GST)

Name

Address

City

State _____ Zip

☐ My payment is enclosed.   ☐ Please bill me.

☐ Please send me information about other Taunton Press magazines, books and videos.

I'm interested in:

1 ☐ sewing   5 ☐ knitting
2 ☐ embroidery   6 ☐ quilting
3 ☐ woodworking   7 ☐ homebuilding
4 ☐ gardening   8 ☐ other _____

BTH